Reading Life

Reading Life

Chris Arthur

Negative Capability
PRESS

Cover by Megan Cary
Interior Design by Jordan Knox

Library of Congress Control Number: 2017908290

ISBN: 978-0-9986777-1-2

Negative Capability Press
62 Ridgelawn Drive East
Mobile, Alabama 36608
(251) 591-2922

www.negativecapabilitypress.org

We all read ourselves and the world around us in order to glimpse what and where we are. We read to understand, or to begin to understand. We cannot do but read. Reading, almost as much as breathing, is our essential function.

Alberto Manguel, *A History of Reading*

Contents

Introduction

The Shimna – whose name in Irish means "river of the bulrushes" – rises in the Mourne mountains near Lough Shannagh and meets the sea at Newcastle, County Down, a town whose setting must be one of the most beautiful in Europe. It's where, in the words of Percy French's famous song, "the Mountains of Mourne sweep down to the sea." They really do, and Newcastle, with its main street and esplanade built only a stone's throw from the waves, enjoys the majestic backdrop of the mountains rising steeply and spectacularly behind it. For part of its way, the Shimna flows through Tollymore (from *Tulaigh mhór*, "the big hillock"), a forest park whose densely wooded acres on the lower slopes of the Mournes offer a delightful choice of walks. My favorite involves crossing the river by a set of stepping stones. If the river is in spate, the stones can become impassable. In a dry midsummer, when the water level is sufficiently low, the stepping stones and their foundations protrude like a recumbent section of battlements affixed to the river-bed. You can walk up and down their steps quite dryly almost all the way across. With only a trickle of flow, the river reduced to a few puddled threads of shallow, sluggish movement, it's more like walking on some ruined castle's crenellated wall than crossing a stretch of water. The most challenging conditions are when the spaces between the steps are entirely submerged, just managing to contain the snaking currents coursing through them, and the steps themselves – a dozen diamond-shaped granite blocks greened with moss – seem like a little linear archipelago, the islands separated by the Shimna's powerful flow. They offer a line of steps – at once enticing and intimidating – only millimeters above the river's level. Going across under these conditions is as close to walking on water as any of us is likely to experience. It requires concentration. The river's great moving sweep right at your feet is mesmerizing. It can undermine even a strong sense of balance. I've seen some walkers take a few unsteady steps across, falter, almost topple and then retreat, preferring to continue on the bank-side path and cross at the bridge further upstream, rather than risk falling in or being stranded halfway over by a sense of water-induced vertigo.

*   *   *

1

At one point on the walk by the Shimna, not long after crossing the stepping stones, you come to a high bank that affords a good view of some of the river's largest pools. These must be seven or eight feet deep at least, but the water is so clear you can make out the precise shape of every stone at the bottom. The water has a definite greenish tinge to it. I'm not sure if this is caused by some kind of mineral dissolved in it, or if it's the color of the stones on the river bed that gives the water this particular tint. Or maybe it's a property of the overhanging trees, their verdant shade making the water take on the appearance of a weak, leafy brew. Whatever the cause of this coloration, I've often watched salmon swimming in these green-deep pools, their sleek forms moving effortlessly in their element – ghostly torpedoes hinting at the presence of another world close to, yet different from, our own.

Watching the salmon always reminds me of the traditional tale of Finn Mac-Cool and the Salmon of Knowledge. Finn (to use the common Anglicization of *Fuin Mac Cumhal* or *Fionn Mac Cumhaill*) is one of the great heroes of Irish mythology. Tradition has it that he was destined to become leader of the band of warriors known as the Fianna. To join this elite group – let alone become its leader – demanded more than merely military prowess. Finn knew he would have to be well-versed in traditional poetry and learning too (would that such literary accomplishments were always a prerequisite for those who take up arms). Accordingly, so the legend goes, the young Finn apprenticed himself to Finnegas the Bard, a renowned poet who had been living on the banks of the river Boyne for seven years, perfecting his art and trying to catch the Salmon of Knowledge. An ancient prophecy foretold that whoever ate this fabled fish would gain all the wisdom of the world. The salmon lived in a deep pool in the river overhung by oak trees. I imagined it having the same green translucence as the Shimna's pools at Tollymore.

One day, after all his years of effort, Finnegas finally catches the elusive Salmon of Knowledge. He instructs his acolyte to prepare it, warning Finn that under no circumstances must he eat any of it himself. The story tells how Finn faithfully obeys his master, but that some hot fat from the cooking fish spits onto his thumb. Without thinking, he puts his thumb in his mouth and sucks it to relieve the pain – and in that moment becomes enlightened. Bringing the fish to Finnegas, the poet immediately notices the change in his young disciple. Questioning him, he discovers what has happened and instructs Finn to eat the rest of the salmon, whose knowledge, so we are told, came from having eaten the nuts of nine hazel trees that grew beside a magic undersea well.

In *Theories of Everything*, astronomer John Barrow suggests that myths "do not arise from data or as solutions to practical problems." Instead, "they emerge as antidotes" for humankind's feelings of "smallness and insignificance." Given our position in the world, and the fact that so much is beyond our understanding or control, it's not surprising that we feel the need for consoling antidotes that hint at fathomable meanings. Stories offer some kind of psychological compensation for not being in control, for feeling overwhelmed by the scale and complexity of things and their often baffling lack of sense. The story of Finn and the Salmon of Knowledge offers a kind of narrative balm for the fact that our understanding can only ever be partial. What I particularly like about it is the way the story celebrates the rich fecundity of fragments. A single fish that is the embodiment of all knowledge, hazelnuts that contain the secret of everything – these are wonderful symbols for the depths of meaning contained in the ordinary, seemingly simple things around us. From a tiny splinter of being – a splash of hot fat – Finn gains insight into totality.

*   *   *

One summer afternoon after I'd crossed the stepping stones and was watching the salmon swimming with their mysterious heavy gracefulness in the Shimna's green-deep pools, a dog appeared on the opposite bank. He too spotted the salmon and proceeded to try to catch them, jumping in with ungainly splashes – pounces of tremendous energy, but complete ineptitude. They posed no danger to the fish; depth and refraction kept them safe. The transparency of the water and the dark, alluring shapes moving below, seemingly so close, kept the dog entranced. He jumped in repeatedly, pausing on the bank only for long enough to let the ripples settle so that the swimming shapes could be seen clearly again. Their tantalizing presence caused him to bark and growl excitedly, to wag his tail uncontrollably, as the puzzlingly elusive forms beckoned to instincts that could not be resisted.

*   *   *

I'd not thought of Tollymore, the stepping stones, or the salmon-chasing dog for years. But faced with trying to explain the nature of this book, they came back to me again. I don't know how I knew to summon them from whatever stratum of the mind holds the ore of metaphor, nor did I do so consciously, but I'm glad they returned.

At first, the stepping stones were what I welcomed most. They seemed to offer a fitting symbol for what *Reading Life* attempts. I liked the idea of seeing it as building a series of crossing points across life's rivers, laying down footholds close to – right in – the water of experience so that we can feel its surge and flow, savor the rich flavors that it carries. The way each stepping stone is self-contained, yet contributes to the line of steps of which it's a part, seemed to fit my style of writing more than, say, a bridge would, with its one continuous structure, more elaborate building materials, less simple construction technique, and the promise of more distanced – albeit safer – crossings.

But it wasn't long before the comparisons I smelted out of this piece of metaphorical ore buckled and failed. There are too many dissimilarities between actual stepping stones and those in *Reading Life* to allow the parallel to stand unchallenged. With the Shimna stones, you can see across to where you want to go; both banks of the river are in plain sight. The steps offer a direct way across, a straight line that runs from one side to the other. The stones themselves are regularly spaced and on a uniformly solid foundation. None of them tip or wobble. You can see all of them at once in a single glance, imagine your passage across before setting out. Their flat tops are made with the size and shape of a foot in mind. They're fixed, immovable, designed to take a weight. The stepping stones I've assembled here, by contrast, offer no such reassuring certainties. They're rarely linear and walking on them often feels like attempting to cross the Shimna when the river is in massive spate, the current tugging powerfully at your ankles. Not only are the stones submerged by the surging flow of whatever river they're attempting to offer a way across, but they've also been dislodged from any pattern of secure alignment, making it necessary to feel forward precariously, testing for steady footing. There are no guarantees that there will be another stone, or that what's laid out will bring you to dry land.

I've not given up on the stepping stone comparison completely, thus its presence here. But, in the end, out of all the metaphorical ore my memories of Tollymore offered, it was the dog and the salmon that seemed to mirror most closely the way *Reading Life* proceeds. I've come to think of my writing as attempting to catch some of the unexpected salmon I see moving in life's pools. They're not the Shimna's sleek, torpedo-bodied fish, but instead have all manner of unlikely guises – a child's feet, a whale's tooth, a wartime pistol, three old walking sticks, books by Flann O'Brien, Michel de Montaigne, Seamus Heaney and other writers. Such things may not have been fed by magic hazelnuts growing by an undersea well, but each of the fragments that have caught my eye seems laden with a cargo that's worth teasing out, however commonplace they may at first appear. Like the Shimna salmon, they hint at the presence of another realm of meaning close to, yet different from, our workaday preoccupations.

The fact that I was born in Belfast and grew up in Northern Ireland, at a particularly turbulent time in that small country's history, means that many of my salmon bear distinctive Ulster markings – sometimes scars. The fact that I left Ireland in my twenties and that, in any case, my reading had already taken me to distant destinations, means that my salmon also swim far beyond any Irish waters. And unlike the dog that simply hurled itself into the Shimna's green-deep pools, I can fish with all the sophisticated tackle words afford. If, like the dog, depth and refraction mean I miss my targets, I can only keep on trying. If, to a reader's eye, some of my salmon of knowledge seem more like sprats of inconsequence, I can only say that as we gaze into the waters around us we each must pursue whatever shapes strike us as worth catching.

*   *   *

The title of the book emphasizes its major concern – *reading*. This is sometimes meant in the literal sense of reading books, sometimes in the broader, metaphorical sense of reading the objects and events around us. I've arranged the essays so as to alternate between these two senses. Common to all of them is a search for the meanings that lie behind or beyond the superficial readings of ordinary discourse. "Reading Life" – the book's title essay – brings together the two fundamental threads of reading books and reading the world around us.

I know, of course, that I'm fishing for things I'll never catch. But the hope remains that a splash of water from the pools in which I cast my line will contain a few droplets that once brushed a salmon's side, and that these may find their way into my mouth and the mouths of my readers. Tasting them won't bring about some sudden, Finn-like moment of epiphany, a tsunami of realization in which everything falls into place. All they offer is a closer, deeper reading of a few fragments of experience. But such reading will, I hope, serve the function Alberto Manguel points to in the epigraph I've chosen for the book – namely that it will help us to catch some glimpses of what and where we are.

Footnotes
(Reading my daughter's feet)

The way in which her bare feet respond and how, in turn, my hands react to the silent prompts delivered by her toes, is almost like a silent language. Its wordless sentences eloquently express affection – love. But they also spell out thoughts and feelings that I find deeply disconcerting. It's as if, in their soft tattoo of reciprocal movements, the subtly exchanged pressures of touch, our hands and feet unwittingly semaphore a password, form some secret sign, tap out a combination that opens an unsuspected vault hidden right at the heart of their little intimacies. In it sits something wonderful and terrible – and of such gargantuan scale it seems incredible that it can be contained within something so ordinary, so matter of fact, as our hands and feet.

* * *

My daughter is still young enough at ten not to feel self-conscious about sitting on my knee. I'll miss it when she crosses whatever Rubicon it is that makes children feel they're too old to indulge in such physical closeness with a parent. If she's barefoot – as is frequently the case – her feet act as magnets for my hands; they beckon to them irresistibly.

When she settles on my lap I knead her feet, gently pull her toes, stroke her soles firmly enough not to tickle, squeeze the thick skin on her heels. She doesn't mind – I think enjoys – this affectionate caressing of her feet. It's something I've done since she was tiny, when a foot was no longer than my thumb. An evening will often find us thus, sitting contentedly together, her feet warm in my hands.

* * *

"Sitting contentedly together......"

That's such a partial truth it courts dishonesty. Granted, a measure of contentment is there; it's part of what I feel on these knee-sitting, foot-caressing moments that I know won't last much longer. But any contentment is fragile. It's threatened – often eclipsed – by the thing that sits in the secret vault of the familiar, exposed by the inadvertent unlocking of our foot-play.

Sometimes, aghast at what I've glimpsed hiding there, I sink into a kind of reverie, haunted by disturbing images. At such moments, her curiosity sparked by what must be my change of mien, my daughter invariably asks me what I'm thinking. I always give the same reply: "Nothing."

"Nothing" is, of course, a lie.

I feel increasingly guilty when I tell it.

This is my attempt to tell the truth.

*   *   *

"Meditation on a foot" was how I used to think of it. The phrase seemed to offer an easy way to refer to the disconcerting state of mind that overtakes me as I sit with my daughter, her bare feet in my hands. But it isn't a good way to describe what happens. Like "sitting contentedly" it contains only a trace of truth; in the main it is misleading. "Meditation" has a philosophical or religious ring to it. It suggests a mind that's disciplined, untroubled, one that obediently follows well-trodden steps – all of them safely sanctioned by tradition – in order to reach a point of inner calm and insight. Meditation is something controlled, deliberate, and focused. To me, it conjures up the picture of a robed figure, graceful and serene, sitting cross-legged, straight-backed, saturated with the kind of composure that betokens unshakeable tranquility. What happens in my mind is altogether less benign, more frantic, sometimes close to panic; it has a kind of savage exuberance, a wildness that I don't know how to tame.

*   *   *

The feet I'm holding – so alive in the voltage of vitality they carry – seem able every now and then to kick-start a particular train of thought. Its momentum increases rapidly so that soon it plunges off the rails of easy labeling and becomes a kind of rogue meditation, something that, far from focusing and calming, distracts and disturbs the mind with a dizzying blizzard of impressions. I'm not sure what makes this happen, or how to stop it. All I know is that when I'm holding my daughter's feet I often see them not as they are at that precise moment. Rather, they take on the guise of something almost fluid as I picture them changing form at different stages in their history.

*   *   *

To begin with, picturing how they appear as they move across their temporal trajectory is relatively straightforward.

Instead of seeing them just as two warm, ten-year-old girl's feet held relaxed and responsive in my hands, I imagine them at their beginning and end. How they must have been at the moment of conception; how – most likely – they'll become old feet, the skin dry and papery, the nails thickened, the skin stained with a tracery of broken veins. Then, between these two poles, a flood of images starts to pour through my mind's eye. I imagine the microscopic processes of orchestration that shepherd an embryo's undifferentiated cells into the body parts they'll form, and that conduct the story of their growth and aging. Like reciting a kind of manic rosary, or walking between Stations of the Cross that have proliferated uncontrollably, my imagination runs through a cluster of key "firsts": the emergence of recognizable foot shapes in the womb; the feet at birth, captivating in the beauty of their miniature twinned perfection; the first time I touched her toes; the first steps she took unaided; the delight that was evident the first time she paddled in the sea; her first steps in a new country; wearing new shoes on her first day at school; solemnly shod in black at the first funeral she went to. My imagination tries to encompass all the steps that have led to this moment, sitting on my knee, her bare feet so vigorously firm-soft in my hands. It's as if their soles have engraved upon them a swirling filigree of hidden Braille and that running my fingers over their intricate, invisible curlicues I can read the milestones that mark out her ten-year walk to here.

Then, beside this known back-story, to much of which I've been a witness, images start to form of what's likely to happen next – where her feet will go beyond this present moment, held safe in my grip. A slew of possibilities flashes past: the places she may walk to; the countries she may visit; the people she may lay her steps beside – strangers, friends, and lovers; what will happen to her as she steps into her future.

*   *   *

Sometimes I ask her directly, "Where do you think these feet will take you?"

It's an odd way to inquire about what she plans to do with her life. I'm keen to find out where she wants to go, what she wants to do, where she sees herself in five or ten years from now. I know that wherever her steps may lead, it will be her heart and mind that decides the direction; it's not as if her feet will take her anywhere of their own accord. But when she's sitting on my knee and I'm holding her bare feet in my hands, thinking about all the steps they'll take, all the places they'll go, all the places they've been, it's easy to give them a priority I know they don't really warrant, simply because of the active role they play in bringing her to all her destinations.

At ten, she's not much interested in speculating about the future. She's more focused on the present, the immediacies of family, friends, school, food and fashion. But she always answers – or deflects – my question. Her manner is usually tolerantly dismissive; polite but not entirely serious. She tells me that her feet will take her to China, or Peru, or to somewhere sunny, or to chocolate, or the moon, or "Away from your silly questions."

*   *   *

Thinking about where her feet will really take her, I reflect on the state of the world and the nature of humanity; the terrible things that we do to one another. I look into the dark corners of my heart and see flickering there traces of the very things I fear may assail her. However geographically distant they may be, so many of the horrors reported on the news have their roots in nothing more remote or alien than human nature. I know her proximity to peril.

And so, although I'm not blind to the beautiful and benign sides of life, and wish them for her in abundance, I worry the same worry that has always troubled parents: the fear that our children's feet will be placed on paths that bring them hurt. I worry that my daughter will tread too trustingly on ground that's treacherous, that she'll walk too close to those who mean her harm.

*   *   *

When I'm holding her feet, I often think of the opening lines of Louis Mac-Neice's great poem, "Prayer Before Birth:"

> I am not yet born; O hear me.
> Let not the bloodsucking bat or the rat or the stoat or the
> club-footed ghoul come near me.

Although it's written from the viewpoint of an unborn child, what it expresses is equally the apprehension felt by parents for children already in the world. The worry about encountering "the man who is beast or who thinks he is God" is precisely one of the concerns that surfaces when my daughter is sitting barefoot on my knee and I'm wondering where her feet will take her, who she'll encounter as she steps her way through life. Like so many parents, I've felt the helpless, impotent urge to bestow a blessing; to enwrap my offspring with the kind of protective benediction that gives MacNeice's poem its arresting solemnity.

Sometimes, truth be told, I make a kind of silent incantation as I'm sitting with my daughter. I squeeze her feet and say inwardly:

Let no harm befall her.
May she be protected on life's way.
Let no one of evil intent come near.

Of course this is no more than wishful thinking. Magic doesn't work. I know I can't affix some kind of apotropaic device to ward off evil. There's no such thing as a charm to keep her safe. But the comfort rationality offers is so meager compared to the dangers that surround her that it makes me grasp at straws and spells. Being raised in a supportive home, having parents who love her, being well educated, gaining the confidence to walk through life with assurance, learning to stand on her own two feet – this is what will bestow the best protection she can have. But I want something rawer, more primitive, something that rages with an intensity good sense doesn't summon. I want something to howl and snarl like a wolf at her side, ready to tear out the throat of an assailant. I would enlist all of the monsters in MacNeice's poem, distill them into a single terrible essence and mold it into a protective totem, an invisible guardian to pace beside her.

*   *   *

Sitting holding her feet, my mind wanders into realms far removed from what must seem to an onlooker to be just a quiet moment of uncomplicated father-daughter affection.

"What are you thinking about, Dad?"

"Nothing."

In fact I'm thinking of wolves and demons, of club-footed ghouls and totem creatures, of the evils that may overtake her. I'm thinking about the story of her feet from the moment of their conception until now, the places they have walked, the paths they will follow. I'm thinking of the feet that will walk towards her, be welcomed by her, help kindle within her the tiny feet of whatever babies she may bear. I'm thinking of the children she may dandle on her knee, perhaps play with their feet and remember the way I used to play with hers. I'm thinking of her feet standing at my graveside and then walking away from it into a future in which I am absent, a future I can only hope will be happy. I'm thinking about her feet growing old and frail and one day dying. I'm thinking about the power and the powerlessness of love, about how little time we have together.

*   *   *

Even focused on no more distant horizons than my daughter's single life, her one individual existence from embryo to corpse, I find my foot-musings disconcerting. But they become much more so when the focus widens to create a perspective so encompassing that all of us become like dust specks, or sand grains, or whatever well-worn metaphor is chosen to highlight personal insignificance. I'm not sure what causes this change of gear, but when it happens it's as if her foot unravels into threads as fine as cobwebs. The filaments run like nerves through time's fabric, vanishing into spans of such duration it's hard to pick out any ending or beginning.

Instead of starting with her own coming into being, the imagination reaches back through the timeline that led to that moment of conception, picturing the ancestors that stretch back, two by two, far beyond me and my wife, our parents, their parents, until it becomes a blur of predecessors paired in the ghostly umbilical that's stowed within the ark of every person's history. Each ark's manifest records a cargo showing that the individual vessel depends for its existence on those who stand before it – the anchor chain of inheritance stretching back so far in time it's hard to put it into any readily graspable measure. Our mundane calibrations of days and months and years are soon exploded by the fact that it's taken aeons to shape us. Our bloodline plummets through time's strata; it reaches back to single-celled organisms and their slow ascent to humanness.

*   *   *

Then, without pause, as if a spinning top just changed direction, anticlockwise conjured instantly to clockwise, the current of my speculation changes. My imagination now follows the filaments of my daughter's unthreaded feet into the far future, picturing those who will come after her to populate the years that stretch out into time's unmapped amplitude. When these feet I'm holding have taken their final step, when their children's children and their offspring are all dead a thousand years, when no memory of any of us remains in any mind, when the days we occupied have become ancient history, what feet will tread upon the same ground that we've stepped on? When, finally, the Sun goes nova and destroys all life on Earth, will there still somewhere be human feet continuing the long walk that our species is embarked on?

Sometimes, my daughter sitting on my knee, I feel crushed by the swarm of lives before and after ours, the crowd of others so dense that it squeezes us to almost nothing. Sometimes I'm awed by the grandeur of the saga that we're part of – our sentient presence, evolved over millennia, on this four-and-a-half-billion-year-old planet circling a burning star, around which space extends for incredible distances, threaded with an uncounted multiplicity of other heavenly bodies.

*   *   *

"What are you thinking about, Dad?"

"Nothing."

"Nothing" has some small claim to truth, but I don't mean by it anything as innocuous as the "nothing much" implied. I'm thinking about how nothing will be left of us, how we'll leave no trace, how such precious moments as these are fated to oblivion. And I find myself thinking of my daughter's feet not as anything familiar, not as something set in the unique fixity of this one cherished person, but rather as pieces of life-ore – shaped and molded countless times before they set into the singular specificity of her body. I'm thinking of the 800,000 year-old footprints recently discovered in Happisburgh, Norfolk. And, since the prints of both adults and children were found there, I'm wondering if, among those who left these intimate yet anonymous traces, there might have been a father who held his daughter's feet and wondered where they'd take her. Africa holds the earliest fossilized footprints yet discovered that display our modern foot's anatomy. They are some 1.5 million years old. Yet more ancient tracks have been found, also in Africa. There's a trail of prints that's 3.7 million years old, left by *Australopithecus afarensis* as these creatures walked across volcanic ash in Laetoli, Tanzania. I think of all the steps we hominids have taken, all the steps that are to come, the individual story each foot tells and the greater story it is part of – for the tread of the species imprints all of us with its mark, as we all contribute our own infinitesimal individual impression to the footprint that it leaves. Will the life-ore from which my feet, my daughter's feet – everyone's feet – are forged still issue in any footprint we would recognize as human a million years from now?

* * *

I'm not a foot fetishist. But at an aesthetic, symbolic, and perhaps spiritual level too, I've always found bare feet curiously moving. They have an air of ungainly innocence that hands almost never possess; they seem to carry with them a sense both of our vulnerability and toughness. Sometimes when I hold my daughter's feet I can almost feel again their tiny newborn form. And I can imagine them cold and still, the feet on an old woman's body, her coffin carried by children whose embryonic feet budded within her, as hers did within her mother, as mine did within mine in the repeated repertoire of humanness we follow.

Despite the particularity of her feet, the fact that they're grounded in who she is, in who I am, despite the intensely focused specificity of this singular moment sitting on my knee, and all the equally particular moments that had to happen to give rise to it, her feet also have a sense of being in flux. This sense of flux stems from the knowledge that beside all our steps there are the paths we might have taken. Our stories are woven out of countless contingencies and choices. Rather than being immovably fixed in the precise grid of twists and turns that constitute our history, there's a sense that – with just a feather-light touch of difference – what happens to us, the experiences we embrace, the events that befall us, could have been quite otherwise. Beating in the warm, familiar substantiality of my daughter's feet as they are at this moment in all their specificity, I can also feel the strong pulse of potential, alternative, the many routes she might take closely shadowing the ones she has and will. Knowing how various are the paths that we can follow, how much we're at the mercy of the accidental, how closely catastrophe and contentment run beside each other, makes me fearful for my daughter. I hold her feet in wonder and with worry, thinking about what patterns they'll tread, in what directions they'll take her, to what destinations they'll lead, what other feet will lay their weight upon the ground beside her.

*   *   *

An observation of Paul Auster's struck me so much when I first heard it that I committed the words to memory. They're spoken by Auggie Wren, one of the characters in the 1995 film *Smoke*, for which Auster wrote the screenplay:

> People say you have to travel to see the world. Sometimes I think that if you just stay in one place and keep your eyes open, you are going to see just about all that you can handle.

Auggie (played by Harvey Keitel) owns a small tobacconist's shop in Brooklyn, New York. The film focuses on a diverse group of his customers. The shop acts as a kind of narrative hub. It's touched by numerous storylines, which intermingle like threads of smoke. One of the ways in which Auggie "keeps his eyes open" is by taking a photograph of the same street-view every day. He's been doing this for fourteen years. Studying the images makes him attentive to unsuspected seams of interest running through what, at first glance, appears tediously mundane and repetitive.

The idea that you don't have to travel far to see incredible things often comes to mind when I'm holding my daughter's feet. Although it's fun to visit foreign places, you don't have to walk any great distance to see wonders. All you need do is look down at your own feet and ponder on their nature – where they've come from, where they're going, the long walk that they're such a tiny part of. There are wonders – and terrors – wired into what seems entirely pedestrian. I would never have guessed before it happened that in the familiar circumstance of affectionately caressing my daughter's feet there could be so much unnerving strangeness. Sitting cheek-by-jowl with the little particularities of family life we know so well there are dwarfing anonymities of time and space and number. As we play "this little piggy went to market" on our children's toes, seven billion other humans are alive. Each of us is part of a lineage whose beginning and end we cannot see. Generation succeeds generation on a planet that's just one minuscule part of a universe thought to be some fourteen billion years old.

*   *   *

Auster's words often take on a particularly powerful resonance when I'm seeing my daughter off to school in the morning. She puts on her socks and shoes in the porch. I open the front door. We say our goodbyes and she walks down the drive, one foot following the other, stepping into her future.

What could be more everyday, familiar, unremarkable?

Yet it often leaves me with an overwhelming sense of seeing just about all that I can handle.

Her walking away not only calls to mind the trail of individual footprints her life is making, and the species story that they're part of. This quotidian leave-taking, like every departure, also stands proxy for something on an altogether different scale. As I stand at the door and watch her till she's out of sight, I know that time holds a moment when we'll say goodbye forever; when we'll move out of one another's sight and not come back. One moment will be the last time we exchange a smile; one touch will be the last one felt. This small parting as she goes to school – understated, ordinary – presages something so much vaster. It's as if it acts as a kind of icon – a reminder of, and rehearsal for, the larger partings we must somehow bear.

*   *   *

Sleeping at the heart of the ordinary – caressing feet, leaving for school – lying alongside the most familiar horizons, there's a perspective whose lens is ground not by the day-to-day dust of routine, but by something ancient and elemental. A voltage high enough to shock surges its way through the ordinary. The charged wire of our finitude is worked into even the most commonplace moments – however much we contrive to forget it. A foot holds in its familiar form the bloodline of the species; an unremarkable goodbye acts out in miniature the momentous farewell implicit in our transience. It's hard to take proper cognizance of the fact that all the familiar territories we tread, for almost all of time – apart from this minutest of slivers that hosts our fleeting, breathing being – are characterized by our absence. My rogue meditation on feet touches the electricity of what it means to be alive – or so it feels – and the shock is jarring.

*   *   *

My hands on her feet, my mind rapt in a swirl of disconcerting ideas, my daughter asks me her usual question: "What are you thinking, Dad?"

To answer demands an impossibility – laying out in neat lines on the page an inventory of the mind's shifting cargoes. Yet even our simplest, most slow-moving thoughts unfold at speeds that mock the lumbering pace of words and cover distances that soon exhaust the tread of sentences. Ideas, imaginings, feelings, fears – all the elaborate intricacies that weave consciousness together – how can language hope to keep pace with the speed of their luminescence?

There are twenty-six bones in a human foot. How much that's written in their alphabet can we catch in the twenty-six letters that are the bones of language? The great Japanese haiku poet Matsuo Basho once said: "Let not a hair's breadth separate your mind from what you write." Words can't provide a perfect transcription of what we're thinking, let alone what's in the heart. I've tried to close to as narrow a space as I'm able the distance between what's written on these pages and what fills my mind with love and anguish as I hold my daughter's feet. But I know there's far more than a hair's breadth between the experience and my attempt to record it. The gap is wide enough for much of what I think and feel to escape through, leaving only a few remnants caught in these footnotes. They're like tattered pennants, regimental colors that help steel the spirit, marshal concentration; battle standards cut to ribbons in the struggle to understand the sheer strangeness of our existence and the imponderables that face us.

Breath
(Reading an entry from the Goncourt brothers' Journal)

A little girl's breath can't leave a splinter. And yet that's precisely what it feels like. Even though she's long dead, her breath has got under my skin and left something sharp embedded there. It nags like a splinter – calling for attention, but at the same time wanting to be ignored; touching it is at once compulsive and painful.

I suppose because splinters occupy the same sharp, wounding contours as thorns do, the little girl's breath-splinter calls to mind a famous Zen saying:

> Self is a thorn in the flesh. Zen is another thorn to dig it out with. When self is out, throw both thorns away.

It may seem inappropriate to mention in the same breath a sordid historical vignette and a great spiritual tradition. But I think it's more than just the congruence of thorn and splinter that makes me couple girl and Zen together in this way. The invisible thorn she's breathed into my flesh suggests the need for Zen-like determination to root it out. Its intimate wounding feels as difficult to exorcise as the illusory sense of self that Buddhism decries.

How did I come to feel the breath of this little girl – breath taken in Paris almost a century before I was born? How did it reach out across the miles and years to touch me and leave this splinter prickling my memory and imagination? Her breath was stored in words, of course, those unlikely, near-magical containers into which we load all manner of cargoes in order to transport them between mind and mind. Their voyages make light of time and distance.

*   *   *

Every morning, on the same day of the year as they were written, I read that date's compilation of excerpts in *The Assassin's Cloak*, Irene and Alan Taylor's marvelous anthology of what they dub "the world's greatest diarists." For May 5th there are extracts from the diaries of the brothers Goncourt, C.S. Lewis,

Lawrence Durrell, H.L. Mencken, Evelyn Waugh, and Woodrow Wyatt. This cluster of reflections emphasizes a point made repeatedly in the course of the book, namely how varied a tonnage is carried by the verbal vessels language lets us construct to navigate our way across the uncertain waters that lie between person and person.

On May 5th 2015, what catches my eye is a passage from the Goncourt brothers' journal. It's dated May 5th 1863:

> Aubryet [man of letters Xavier Aubryet] told us the other day that a little girl in the street offered him her sister, a child of fourteen. Her job was to breathe on the windows of the carriage so that the police could not see inside.

Why did this glimpse of child prostitution in nineteenth century France strike me so forcefully that it felt – still feels – as if it left a splinter? In part, this is no doubt due simply to the vividness with which the Goncourt brothers' words conjure an ugly carnal cameo. I can see the halted carriage with its breath-misted windows. It moves slightly on its wheels, though the brake has been applied, and the reins and bridles jingle, rocked by the movements of the unseen occupant as he pleasures himself on the girl, her little sister not just witness to whatever gross acts are happening, but made into an accomplice in their undetected performance.

*   *   *

But the Goncourts' words, with their ready procurement of disturbing images, are not in themselves enough to account for the impact I felt when I read them. Two other factors combined to create the conditions needed for a kind of fissile reaction to happen, such that what was written on May 5th 1863 became a time-bomb whose ticking stopped on May 5th 2015.

The first catalyst for this explosive reaction is simply the fact that I have two daughters. With five years between them it means that when the older one was fourteen her younger sister would have been nine, about the right age in nineteenth century Paris to importune strangers and pimp her own flesh and blood, offering to thwart any legal intervention by misting the carriage windows with her breath.

I know nothing about these two desperate waifs beyond the glimpse that Aubryet gives – I don't know their names, what they looked like, where they lived, how they spoke. They bear with them all the anonymity of the vulnerable, the exploited, the dispossessed. Faced with such shadowy figures, the mind reaches for what's familiar to give them substance. Inevitably, I think of my daughters at comparable ages. This makes me thankful they've not been raised in conditions of such abject need or brutal exploitation, but outraged and saddened that any children, anywhere, should be forced to prostitute themselves.

*   *   *

The second catalyst stems from a coincidence of dates. On May 5th 2015 – when I read the extract from the Goncourt brothers' journal, written exactly one hundred and fifty-two years earlier – news reports in Britain were dominated by a story that resonated unpleasantly with what had happened in 1863. It focused not on Paris, but Rotherham and Sheffield, and not on two little girls, but an estimated 1400. It emerged that police and council officials in these two English cities had, for a long while, taken no action – despite having received warnings that organized gangs were grooming and abusing little girls. The story hit the headlines in the immediate aftermath of the convictions of some gang members. It was clear that their activities had been going on unchecked for years.

Such systematic child abuse – like the instances that have rocked the Catholic Church – may seem a long way from a girl breathing on carriage windows to veil from public view what's being done to her sister. But even though the scale has been horribly inflated, the dynamic that's at work is essentially the same – hiding from view a preying on the vulnerable.

*   *   *

Having two daughters, combined with the coincidence of hearing about child abuse in Rotherham and Sheffield on the same day as I read the extract from the Goncourt brothers' journal, honed to a particularly sharp point the picture of a little girl breathing on glass. But in addition to these factors there's also something about the nature of breath that imports a special quality to things, making the splinter penetrate even more deeply. We all row our way across whatever time we're given via the gentle oar-strokes of our breathing. The push and pull of our inhalation and exhalation is as constant an accompaniment to our lives as our heartbeat. So close to our fundamental selves is breathing that breath often stands proxy for life itself, serving as a symbol of our soul or essential spirit.

It is with breath that we form every word we utter, shaping the vocables into which we load whatever meanings we wish to trade with others – from the tenderest endearments to the lewdest offering of a sister. To use our breath deliberately to besmirch things, to obscure from view, to prevent the truth from being seen, seems like a particularly intimate betrayal; for a little girl to be forced into doing it is surely a heinous desecration of her innocence.

But could something not be salvaged from this horrible situation? Perhaps the child was acting in her sister's interests, trying to draw a shield across her humiliation; attempting, however ineffectually, to offer some protection, rather than merely providing clients with immunity through the invisibility she created. But such a reading, however truly it might catch the girl's real motives, offers little comfort. It has about it a sense of clutching at non-existent straws. It's hard to see how we could redeem into anything positive the fact that she was put in a situation where she felt she had to act the way she did.

*   *   *

Just as net curtains draped across house windows may act to make passersby more curious about what's going on inside, so too with breath-misted carriage windows. They may have precisely the outcome they were intended to deflect, drawing people's eyes and making them wonder about what's happening behind such a hastily improvised screen.

On reading the Goncourt brothers' journal entry for May 5th 1863, I certainly found that the breath-misted windows tugged at my imagination far more strongly than would any lurid scene laid out nakedly to view. My imagination takes me not to some prurient catalogue of what these little girls may have been forced to witness or to do, but rather to a breath-centered wondering about their lives.

Where did they first draw breath? Who was their mother? Who was their father? Were they unwanted, begun by accident in a carriage with misted windows, or was their genesis rooted in a gentle act of love? Were they bullied and abused at home, or cherished and looked after? Was it the unexpected death of a parent, some impossible debt, the loss of a father's livelihood, a mother's illness or alcoholism – some catastrophe – that led to their wandering the streets of Paris, selling themselves? Or was such a fate decided from the very first moment of their being in the world, made inevitable by the circumstances they were unlucky enough to be born into? Where did they sleep at night? Did they get enough to eat, or did they go to bed hungry? Was there anyone to comfort them when they had nightmares? What was their favorite food, their best memory; what was their worst? Was there anywhere they felt safe?

From that moment of encounter with Aubryet, recorded by the Goncourts, how did their lives turn out? How long was it between then and whenever they took their final breaths? Which one died first; where were their bodies laid to rest – did anyone mourn them; did they have children of their own? And, if they did, were they the result of unwanted couplings with customers, or of liaisons chosen and desired? Did they work carriage-after-carriage, encounter lust and violence, betrayal, trickery, disease, and hurt? Or did some stroke of luck intervene to bring into their blighted lives some kindness and good fortune – so that the littler one never had to hah her breath again on carriage windows and listen to heavy-breathing strangers close-quartered with her sister?

A century and a half away, I hope for a happy ending to the story that I caught a glimpse of in the Goncourt brothers' words. But I know how unlikely such an outcome is. The chances are high that these nameless Parisian girls will have endured disappointment, brutality, injustice never set to right, servitude, exploitation, sexual slavery, rather than anything I would wish for them. They feature, almost certainly, in history's great compendium of miserable stories.

* * *

The title of Irene and Alan Taylor's anthology of diary extracts, *The Assassin's Cloak*, is taken from a comment in William Soutar's *Diaries of a Dying Man*. Soutar, a Scottish poet left bedridden from a spinal disease he contracted during the First World War, suggests that "a diary is an assassin's cloak which we wear when we stab a comrade in the back with a pen." The nine volumes of the *Journals de Goncourt* of course contain attacks of this kind. But the brothers' entry for May 5th 1863 seems at once less focused and more deadly. Rather than an assassin with a particular victim in their sights, these two sentences about Aubryet's encounter with the girls has the potential to trip every reader up, sending them headlong into the pit-trap of history that's still happening. Though we may soon enough clamber out and continue on our way, I doubt if I'm alone in feeling that what happened on May 5th 1863 leaves a splinter. Its insistent prick points to the way in which – as individuals, as a society, as a culture – we've misted with the breath of ill-considered words and silences so many panes that should have been left clear. These are the real thorns in our flesh. How can we dig them out and – once out – learn how to throw them far away?

Fuchsia

(Reading a patch of fallen blossom)

I

Blood?

The pool of unexpected red/the pull of unexpected red – whichever way you look at it, this is what caught my eye. Its bright splash was so vivid on the grey asphalt of the street that for a moment it made the whole scene around it look washed out, ghostly, dimmed to sepia tones by this sudden gash of color. It was as arresting as glimpsing a naked body would be amidst a crowd of people who are fully clothed.

Naturally, my first thought was of blood.

Accident? Injury? Nosebleed? Attack?

Braking almost to a stop and looking round, I was relieved to see no sign of any victim. Then I noticed the branches overhanging the wall and the moment resolved itself into the lineaments of a different interpretation. Not blood, for all the impression of a wet slick of gore, but freshly fallen fuchsia flowers accumulated in a bright drift, at once like a kind of lurid snowfall or a patch of glowing embers. The strength of the color demanded only extremes in the comparisons it called up, no matter that there was discord between them.

I cycle past this temporarily reddened spot several times each week. It's on a route I follow regularly when I go out on my bike first thing for exercise before work. But it's only recently I've noticed the fuchsia. Somewhere in my mind, no doubt, the green of its branches overhanging the wall must have registered, but they didn't do so consciously. It was only when numerous fallen flowers pooled under it that I realized the bush was there. The house in whose garden the fuchsia grows is on a stretch of road approaching a narrow junction where buses swing wide into the path of oncoming traffic as they negotiate the turn. Cyclists have to take especial care. I like to think my tardy recognition of the fuchsia's presence was because of this – the need to focus my attention elsewhere – rather than some more general failure to observe. But the truth is, we routinely overlook a great deal of what's around us.

II

Take a single fuchsia flower. What's instantly apparent is its flamboyant color and graceful, pendulous shape. The outer crimson sepals splay open to reveal a glimpse of the purple petals beneath them. If you lift the skirt of the sepals and examine the inner flower more closely, you'll see that the petals are tightly furled, overlapping each other in a pert roll. They form a tubular, sheathing core, the outer skin of which is creased with the lines of numerous soft folds. Penetrating this open heart or (depending on the perspective you take) sprouting from it, is an array of delicate cabling – the clustered filaments of stamens and pistil. These are gently swollen at the ends, bulbous-headed, as if there's a little bouquet of butterfly antennae drooping from each flower. They look as if they're stretching out, yearning for the nectar of connection.

In terms of their color and form – what immediately meets the eye – fuchsia flowers possess an aura of unambiguous natural beauty. But they're also imbued with a complex medley of undertones – they seem secretive, enticing, almost carnal. They have the air of something verging on a forbidden delight, luscious yet poisonous looking (though in fact they're edible). But there's nothing in the appearance of the flowers, lovely and suggestive though they are, to point to what lies behind them. Like so many things, they conceal an enormous tonnage of time and connection. I love this sort of hidden cargo, the way in which so much can be contained in so little. It's as if the world enjoys playing a kind of peek-a-boo, where gargantuan things hide behind improbable disguises – like fuchsia blossom – and then jump out, startling us with their unexpected dimensions.

I cycled past the pool of fallen bloom perhaps fifteen or twenty times during the brief period that the bush shed its flowers. Prompted by them, I began to muse my way along a fuchsia contour. As I did so, I was soon ambushed by unexpected linkages and led into a dense latticework of memories and reflections. It was as if some gigantic presence slumbering beneath the flowers woke up. For a moment, it cast aside its crimson camouflage and showed me glimpses of its real nature.

III

It didn't happen instantly.

This wasn't a one-time-only occurrence that unfolded all at once, triggered by a single view that simply threw a switch, bringing an immediate glow of illumination. Rather, each morning I cycled past, for the short while the blooms splashed the asphalt red, it was like another gentle tap gradually hammering the fuchsia-nail deeper and a little deeper into mind.

One thing was instantaneous, though, happening at my first sighting of the fallen blossom: the reawakening of memories of Lizzie (I've changed her name of course). I guess the fuchsia nail didn't have far to go before it hit that nerve. Lizzie and I haven't been together for years, so the seam of memories that holds her should be safely buried beneath the weight of time that has elapsed. But such crude quantitative measures, though they may pace out mere duration accurately enough, are not well suited for catching the drift and flow of feelings. For that, a subtler calibration is necessary.

Remembering Lizzie meant that on each subsequent occasion when I cycled past the patch of fallen fuchsia blossom, some portion of my mind wasn't there in those present coordinates of time and place – St Andrews, Scotland, September 2013 – instead, I was miles and years away – in Donegal, on Ireland's northwest coast, and I was in my twenties again. It was around this core memory that my thinking about fuchsia crystallized. Naturally, part of this process involved doing some reading and research about the flower. This in turn prompted further musing whenever I cycled past and the red blossom on the ground caught my eye and tapped on the fuchsia-nail again.

IV

Occasionally, I find it hard to know if I'm remembering something as it was, or remembering a photograph that was taken of it. Particularly with people's faces, I'm often unsure if what I bring to mind is the real face with its actual features, or the face as it's held in photographs, or a hybrid construct made out of real and photographed elements mixed indiscriminately together. This is especially the case when someone's dead, or if I no longer see them regularly. With the pictures I have in mind of my parents, for example, both long deceased, I wonder how much they owe to the photos I still look at from time to time and how much stems from their actual features as these were laid down on my senses, unposed, over a period of so many years.

Although Lizzie and I only visited Donegal once together, soon after we started going out, and though we can't have stayed more than a week at most, I strongly associate her now with Donegal and fuchsia hedges. The bulk of our two years together was spent living in Edinburgh, where we rented an icy attic flat overlooking the Dean Gardens. But I took a series of photographs of Lizzie in Donegal, including half-a-dozen on the day we walked around Horn Head, a bleak headland that plunges its cliffs into the sea near Dunfanaghy. The village's name comes from the Irish *Dun Fionnachaidh*, meaning "fort of the white field." There are some indeterminate ruins on the headland, little more than a stony residue that's hard to decipher into whatever structure left them – it could as well have been a farmhouse as a fort – but the "white field" must surely refer to the pale bobbing heads of bog cotton that still stipple the dark earth hereabouts like lots of little snowy lanterns.

Perhaps if I'd photographed Lizzie in Edinburgh's Dean Gardens, where we often walked, it would be images of that place that would rule my recall, rendering the fallen fuchsia blossom powerless to tap its way so quickly into this particular stratum of the psyche. It's interesting how much more potent moments in a life can be – in terms of our remembrance of them – when they're underscored by photographs. For me, fuchsia blossom will always be close-shackled with Lizzie. I doubt if that chain would have been forged so strongly, or at all, if I hadn't had my camera with me on the day we walked around Horn Head.

We were in Donegal in part just for a holiday. For me, it's the most beautiful part of Ireland and well worth visiting for that reason alone. But Dunfanaghy is also where my paternal grandmother came from – the family's farm is just outside the village. Though it had passed to new owners by the time we were there, I could remember visiting as a child. Lizzie was as interested in my background as I was in hers. So in part we'd chosen to come to Donegal for the same reasons that we'd visited the village in the Scottish Highlands where her grandfather had been born. As we thought about a future together, weighed up possibilities of cohabitation, marriage, children, it seemed natural to look back a little way along our respective bloodlines, mapping how the flow and surge of what we felt could be traced back through those stations of attraction that families represent.

V

One photo in particular has lodged in mind and I suspect accounts in large measure for the way in which those fallen fuchsia flowers I cycled past in St Andrews prompted my recollection. The photo shows Lizzie sitting on a boulder outside a ruined cottage that's surrounded – almost smothered – by fuchsia in full bloom. She's smiling, her hair is tousled and the buttons of her green and white checked shirt are fastened all awry. The sky is unsettled. There are patches of blue, but dark clouds are massed above the cottage. In their muted light the rich color of the blooms is accentuated. It was a day of sunshine and showers. Unsurprisingly, we got soaked shortly after we left the cottage to resume our walk on the narrow road – in places little more than a track – that winds its precipitous way around Horn Head, giving walkers such spectacular views of the Donegal countryside and of Tory Island, whose jagged outline looms darkly on the horizon a few miles out to sea.

The fuchsia grew rampantly all around the cottage in towering, untrimmed hedges that must once have marked the boundaries of the property but that now almost engulfed it. Great bursts of fuchsia were even growing in the cottage's interior, branches laden with blossom splayed across the space of what had been bedroom and kitchen. The empty windows were filled with a dense glaze of foliage, some of which cascaded over the sills to shed pools of blossom on the ground outside. The cottage was roofless, with no trace remaining of any thatch or rafters. The fuchsia's tallest branches almost reached chimney height. The whole cottage had become a kind of stone cloche, a growing frame or scaffolding that helped the fuchsia flourish. Horn Head juts its massive bulk out into the ocean and forms a natural breakwater that shelters Dunfanaghy from the storms that regularly sweep in across the Atlantic. On a tinier scale, the ruined cottage provided a sheltering bulwark for the fuchsia. Within the haven it created, the plant had thrived.

Since it was only a mile or so from my grandmother's farm, I wondered if she – or any of her siblings – had ever walked past the cottage. It is surely almost certain that they did. Likewise, in such a small community as this, she must surely have known the people who once lived here. It gave a kind of frisson of connection to think of her heart beating in the same place that Lizzie's and mine were beating; to think of her eyes taking pleasure from the fuchsia flowers of this same hedge – though in her day it would doubtless have been neatly trimmed.

I'm not sure if it was the fuchsia blooms' suggestive red, or just the fact of our being together where she had been before us, but something created the feeling of raw consanguinity – as if an invisible artery had entwined around us, melting our separateness with the warmth of lifeblood pulsing through it.

VI

The name "fuchsia" comes from the German physician and botanist Leonhart Fuchs (1501-1566), professor of medicine at Tübingen. Fuchs never saw a specimen of the genus that was to take his name. It only did do more than a century after his death, when the plant's so-called "discoverer," Charles Plumier, named it in his honor. Plumier (1646-1704), a French monk and botanist to Louis XIV, made several expeditions to the West Indies at the end of the seventeenth century. On one of them, to the island of Hispaniola (present-day Haiti and the Dominican Republic), he found the plant that's now called *Fuchsia triphylla*. Plumier had such a high regard for Fuchs's work, particularly on the medicinal use of herbs, that he named this "new" genus as a tribute to his highly regarded botanical forbear.

Fuchsias – which belong to the same family (*Onogracceae*) as willowherbs and evening primroses – today flourish far beyond their natural range. In addition to the one hundred or more species known in the wild, there are now also numerous cultivars. Originally, the plants grew mostly in south and central America with a few species also found in the south Pacific. Though they can grow quite tall – witness the branches stretching almost up to chimney height in the ruined cottage on Horn Head – most fuchsias are shrubs or bushes rather than trees. The one exception to this rule is a New Zealand species (*Fuchsia excorticata*) which can reach a height of almost fifty feet.

Fuchsia first appeared in Britain in the eighteenth century. The details of its introduction admit of different tellings. One version has a Captain Firth returning from his voyages in 1788 with a specimen of what was most probably *Fuchsia magellanica*. He presented it to the Royal Botanic Gardens at Kew, from which foothold, via various green-fingered growers, it soon became widely available. Another version has an unnamed sailor returning home from South America with an unusual plant. He grew it in a pot in the window of his London lodgings, where it was spotted by a passing nurseryman, Mr James Lee. Lee was so excited by this unknown flower that he negotiated a price on the spot, quickly closed the deal and went on to make a considerable profit from the fuchsias he propagated from this original progenitor. Captain Firth and the unnamed sailor are not always easy to distinguish and may, in fact, refer to a single individual. Sometimes, instead of the plant being presented to Kew, or grown in a lodging house's window, we're told that it was given by the sailor (or by Firth) to his wife as a seafaring husband's homecoming gift after his long absence in distant climes. It's she who is subsequently persuaded – after initial reluctance – to sell it to James Lee. In other versions of the story, the enterprising Mr Lee acquires the plant direct from Kew. Alternatively, some credit Charles Plumier himself with introducing the plant to Britain, claiming that he took some fuchsia seeds there soon after his botanical explorations in the West Indies.

One thing is certain. We know from published horticultural catalogues that fuchsia was first sold commercially by the Vineyard Nursery. Built on the six acre site of a former vineyard in the London suburb of Hammersmith, the nursery had been established by James Lee around 1745 in partnership with fellow Scot, Lewis Kennedy. They specialized in exotic plants and supplied many of Britain's finest gardens. The firm also advised the Empress Josephine and supplied specimens for her gardens at Château de Malmaison. In fact Pierre Joseph Redoubté, the artist whose paintings of flowers at Malmaison were to become so famous, was one of a roster of celebrity visitors to Lee and Kennedy's nursery. The quality of Redoubté's work soon earned him the epithet "the Raphael of flowers."

Lee himself became a well known figure in his own lifetime, though his fame was short-lived. If he's remembered at all today it's only by a handful of gardening historians and via a kind of vague, secondhand remembrance brokered by the obscure genus of tropical plants – *Leea* – that Linnaeus named after him. His renown was due in part to his association with fuchsias and other exotic flowers – the Vineyard Nursery was, for example, the first to grow plants from seeds collected by Joseph Banks in Australia. Banks was the naturalist on board *Endeavour*, when Captain James Cook "discovered" the east coast of Australia ("discovered" in the same sense that Plumier discovered fuchsia). But Lee was probably best known for bringing to the attention of an English-speaking audience Linnaeus's ideas about botanical classification based on plants' sexual characteristics. Lee's *Introduction to Botany*, first published in 1760, rapidly went through several editions and attracted a wide readership. It's essentially a translation rather than an independent work. As Lee puts it in a Preface addressed to Linnaeus (with whom he corresponded): "The *Introduction to Botany* owes its first principles to you, being collected from your works, particularly the *Philosophia Botanica;* nothing in it can be called mine, but its being clothed in an English dress."

However it got to Britain, fuchsia didn't take long to become established. Within seventy years of the first plant arriving, if we accept the date of 1788 as accurate, specimens of *Fuchsia magellanica* were being reported growing in the wild. Interestingly, *The New Atlas of the British and Irish Flora* (2002) specifically picks out "abandoned cottages" as one of the principal places fuchsia flourishes. Certainly in Donegal, where there's an abundance of such cottages, it's common to see them rife with fuchsia. In fact, fuchsia hedges – particularly overgrown ones – are such a typical Donegal sight that it's strange to think of the plant's South American origin and comparatively recent introduction into Europe. Ruined cottages engulfed by fuchsia now seem as quintessentially of Donegal as peat bogs, donkeys, and thatched cottages. They're one of a handful of markers that are so characteristic of the place they've become almost stereotypical.

VII

Lizzie and I had to push through a bush filling the cottage's doorway to get inside. Then we were engulfed by a sense of secret interiority, as if we'd closed the door on the world behind us. Though we'd only crossed a fuchsia-obstructed threshold to get in, it felt more as if we'd fallen down a shaft and found ourselves in a hidden cavern, shielded from everything outside it. What clear ground was left inside the cottage was littered with a cushioning of red blossoms, spiced with glints of purple. This exotic carpeting, together with the bloom still on the bushes, transformed the light within those rough stone walls. It fell softly on us, bestowing on our rubied skin what seemed almost a kind of luminescence. Recalling it now, I'm reminded of some comments of Alexander Theroux's in *The Primary Colors*. He says that red "is a color with a strange gigantic life, an enigma encompassing everything from sunsets to the roseate tint of our innards." Though he can see a masculine side to it, Theroux suggests that there are "deep and abiding feminine implications" in what he calls "virtually every measure and morph of red." It is, he says, "the color of excitement, hypertension and cardiovascular changes, of nervous and glandular activity, of vital force, of sex."

The ruined cottage filled with fuchsia made a secret bower perfect for new lovers still spellbound with each other. Lying there, we wondered about the original occupants of the house we'd borrowed for our tryst. How long had they lived here, trying to farm this inhospitable place, before the barrenness of the peaty land – inimical to pretty much everything except bog cotton, heather, and fuchsia – defeated them? Who had planted out the fuchsia hedge now growing all around us in such wild profusion? Our blood pulsing in our veins, our flesh reddened by the light of fuchsia flowers, in the grip of life's vigorous flow through our bodies, we thought of whoever had once called this cottage home and we wished them well. The play of feelings in our hearts, the flushed roseate warmth that blossomed in us, created a sense of fellowship although we were alone. It felt as if we were tapping into human archetypes, playing out our part in an ancient drama that had been enacted countless times before and yet was entirely novel. And we hoped – in that companionable afterglow of contentment that lovers would readily extend in benison to others – that whoever had lived here had felt like us; that the toil of their existence had been tempered with the electricity and comfort of caress.

VIII

It seems odd to credit Charles Plumier with the "discovery" of fuchsia and, however worthy he may have been, to graft Leonhart Fuchs's name so inseparably onto the plant in question. Such namings are a common occurrence in Plumier's great work, *Nova Plantarum Americanum Genera* (Paris, 1703). Now common-sounding species such as bromeliad, lobelia and magnolia were then exciting novelties to a European perspective. Like fuchsia, all were named in commemoration of individuals Plumier wished to honor (Olaf Bromel, Matthias de L'Obel, Peter Magnol). Although he never called a plant after himself, Plumier too came to be honored in this way when a genus – *Plumeria* (Frangipani) – was subsequently named after him. But the fact is that all of these plants long predate humanity. Fuchsia has flourished namelessly for forty million years or more, a timescale that makes any human claims of discovery ring minutely hollow. Our namings seem like a kind of flimsy scrimshaw etched on the thin rind of the present, beneath them there's an aeon's deep unfolding of the phenomena in question.

Ireland is a long way distant from fuchsia's native haunts. Jack Lamb, of the British Fuchsia Society, describes the plant's distribution as ranging "from Venezuela and Colombia to the southern tip of Tierra del Fuego, the south east coastal mountains of Brazil, Haiti, the Dominican Republic, the mountains of Mexico, Central America, New Zealand and Tahiti." This register of exotic-sounding places is far removed from the barren bog-land of Donegal's Horn Head. The variety that – improbably – has come to flourish there brings us to another naming. According to *The New Atlas of the British and Irish Flora*: "Nearly all the fuchsia hedges in Ireland are the cultivar *Riccartonii*."

"*Riccartonii*" has a ring to it that seems to suit the provenance of fuchsia. But in this case the apparent foreignness of the word is deceptive. If Lizzie and I had left our icy attic flat in Edinburgh and headed west, a bus ride of some 40 minutes would have taken us to the area from which this name is derived – Riccarton. The first written reference to a place so named dates from 1296, when one Marjory of "Richardestoune" was listed among the thousands of Scottish landowners obliged to take an oath of loyalty to the English king. Who the "Ricarde" or "Riccard" was after whom the land was named is uncertain. But we do know that another Marjory (this time more often spelt "Marjorie") was associated with the place. Robert the Bruce gave the land as a dowry in 1315 when his daughter Marjorie married Walter Stewart. This ill-fated Marjorie spent much of her short life imprisoned by the English (though she at least escaped being kept in an iron cage hung from the walls of the Tower of London, open to public view, which had been the king's original intention for her). Her release came when she was traded for some English nobles taken captive at the battle of Bannockburn. Not long after her marriage, she was thrown by her horse when heavily pregnant and went into labor. The child survived (delivered by Caesarean) but his nineteen-year-old mother perished.

Riccarton was subsequently occupied by the Wardlaw family, and then by the Craigs (who became the Gibson-Craigs). The castle in the grounds was extended in 1621 and again in 1827, the original fortress being progressively transformed into a mansion. During World War II, Riccarton was used first as an army base and then a resettlement camp for ex-POWs. Thereafter, the house fell into increasing neglect and disrepair, eventually becoming structurally unsound. It was demolished in 1956. Thirteen years later the estate was gifted to Heriot Watt University and remains the University's Edinburgh campus.

The name "Riccarton" is laid on these acres like the touch of a hand upon a stone. It warms it into temporary familiarity, a story peopled with individuals and events that happen on a scale that we can grasp, but it has as little claim to permanence as "fuchsia." Our namings occupy surfaces, peripheries, rather than penetrating to the deep structures of things or bearing witness to the temporal oceans surging beneath them.

The Gibson-Craigs were keen horticulturalists and invested considerable time and money in creating a beautiful estate at Riccarton, planting it out with numerous exotic species. One of their gardeners, James Young, developed a cultivar variety from *Fuchsia magellanica* – *Fuchsia riccartonii* – naming it after the estate on which he worked. The plant can still be seen today in those parts of the campus at Riccarton that have survived as garden. Young's new variety was created sometime in the 1800s. But when it was taken to Ireland, by whom, and how it came to flourish so abundantly in cottage hedgerows there is not known in any detail, though it seems likely that a key role was played by John Templeton (1766-1825), a man described by Robert Lloyd Praeger as "the most eminent naturalist Ireland has produced." Certainly it was Templeton who first succeeded in growing fuchsia in the open air in Ireland.

However the plant's colonization of Ireland was effected, I find it curiously satisfying that there's a kind of fuchsia nerve that can be traced between Donegal and Edinburgh. Such threads of connection are, I know, coincidental, if not illusory. Likewise – beyond the provisionality of language – all our names ("fuchsia," "Lizzie," "Riccarton," "Horn Head," "Edinburgh," "Ireland") are only transient labels of convenience, minted in the currency of our thirst for manageable meanings. Scratch below the simplifications they offer and before long our words come back bankrupt as the slumbering giants beneath them awaken, rupturing our neat cells of verbal containment.

IX

In his essay "How Flowers Changed the World" (in *The Star Thrower*), Loren Eiseley says:

> Without the gift of flowers and the infinite diversity of their fruits, man and bird, if they continued to exist at all, would be today unrecognizable, Archaeopteryx, the lizard-bird, might still be snapping at beetles on a sequoia limb; man might still be a nocturnal insectivore gnawing a roach in the dark. The weight of a petal has changed the world and made it ours.

Eiseley's poetic depiction provides a glimpse of alternative destinies; the way in which, if key circumstances are altered, whole chains of consequence become unfettered – their links broken as new pathways of unfolding are forged and locked into place. Take away "the weight of a petal," to use his striking image, and the way in which our species' bloodline played out across time's acreage might have followed a different pattern entirely. The evolutionary impact of flowers, their influence on our human story, has been profound indeed. They have affected what Eiseley calls "the enormous interlinked complexity of life" in such fundamental, wide-ranging, and multiple ways that it's hard to grasp in specific detail the extent of their significance; such a momentous scale of occurrence and outcome does not yield readily to our notation.

Even at the level of the microcosm – the way in which individual lives are patterned – it's far from easy to map how one thing leads to another and how it in turn locks a whole network of unfoldings into place; or how a life might have been different if the weight of a petal had been added to, or taken away from, the complex, branching genealogies from which our day-to-day experiences are born. If our past was given different ancestors at any point along its way to those who have shepherded things along the tracks we recognize, if at any moment some circumstance was altered, who knows what routes we might have followed? I know how little it would have taken for the fallen fuchsia blossom to have meant nothing to me, or for it to have carried a completely different cargo of association from the one that happens to have been loaded onto it. Everyone passing by that red daub on the street will have read it in their own way; extracted from it their own particular associations. Like all the things around us, fuchsia splinters on the anvil of individuality and shatters into a multiplicity of perspectives. It sometimes seems as if complex filigrees of swirling lines are etched into even the simplest, smoothest-seeming surfaces. These capillary networks, carrying the blood of possibility and variation, run like lines across the palm of every moment, tracing out the trajectories we follow. Delving into the deep-time of its origins and evolution, or looking at the complex processes and structures that a microscopic examination soon reveals, it's clear that fuchsia flowers, for all their beautiful simplicity, are pock-marked and cratered with complexity. Even at the superficial level of fuchsia's history over the last two and a half centuries – a minute fraction of the course it's run – the flowers are smudged with the whorls and spirals of our fingerprints. The interventions of Plumier, Lee and countless unnamed others have constructed frameworks of possibility within which fuchsia has unfolded in a swathe of new types and locations. If Plumier had never sailed across the Atlantic, if Lee had never seen a fuchsia flower, how different the plant's story might have been.

How the fluidities of possibility, of what might be, settle into the solid-state fixities of what has happened can often surprise us. If, in our Horn Head cottage, the breeze trembling through the flower-laden bushes had whispered that Lizzie and I would separate, lose touch, live hundreds of miles apart, settle eventually in different countries, have children with then unmet partners, I'd not have believed that this was the history our present would gradually settle into. Nor would I have thought it possible that there would come a time when, sparked by the stimulus of fallen fuchsia blossom, I'd think of her again, years later, and not be sure if it was the face I'd kissed that I was remembering, or only the image of it captured by a lens.

X

After the initial jolt, when the fallen fuchsia blossom first drew my eye, subsequent glimpses as I cycled past were, for the most part, set at a lower voltage. After a fortnight or so the pool of red started to have a dried out look. There were fewer flowers on the bush and both they and those that fell lacked the opulent freshness that had made the first ones so suggestive of the glint of blood. Soon all trace of such svelte succulence was gone and the few remaining flowers were tattered, desiccated, dull. The last time I cycled past, the asphalt of the street was unmarked by any trace of red and the fuchsia had returned to being the anonymous green bush overhanging a wall that I'd failed to notice for so long. It will be a year before its splash of color ambushes me again.

Most of the fracture lines that happened as the fuchsia nail was tapped into my attention were predictable enough: my memories of Lizzie and that ruined cottage on Horn Head; my wanting to find out about the plant's naming and how it had come to Ireland; the sense of wry satisfaction at discovering – via *Riccartonii* – a fuchsia thread running between Donegal and Edinburgh. But one fracture line was entirely unexpected. As I noted the fuchsia's impact, tried to map and convey its electricity in words, I found myself thinking repeatedly of suspension bridges.

What have these massive structures of iron and cable to do with fuchsia? To begin with, all I could think of to account for what seemed like a bizarre linking of two utterly dissimilar things was that I was prompted to forge this pairing because of the way the fallen blossom pointed to a gulf separating two moments in my life: the fuchsia bush on my St Andrews cycle route, and that flower-filled cottage on Horn Head from so far away and long ago it seemed almost like another life. To maintain some sense of continuous identity, a sense of self, requires repeated crossing between past and present. Since they afford such convenience in spanning what's divided, suspension bridges are perhaps not so strange to think of when one is trying to link life now and then. For all their littleness and beauty, those fallen fuchsia flowers acted in a way like bridges, allowing me to weave back and forth between considerable spans of miles and years. But however plausible I may try to make this sound, I think a more unnerving and less rational connection also played a part in my fuchsia-prompted thoughts of bridges.

If I wanted to visit Riccarton now, the quickest route to Edinburgh would be across the Forth Road Bridge. Opened in 1964 it's an impressive structure, made doubly so by being sited close to the Forth Rail Bridge, whose great cantilevered spans are one of the glories of nineteenth century engineering. The two bridges together make a dramatic sight. But every year, around twenty people jump to their death from the high platform the road bridge's walkways afford. Such acts of desperation stand at the opposite pole from any attempt to weave elements of a life together, to bridge, join, and connect. Instead, this is to cut, stop, sever, isolate and end. I think my knowledge of the regularity of jumpers was as instrumental in my putting bridges and fuchsias together as any sense of linking past and present. I hope I'm never visited by the despair that has driven close to a thousand people now to launch themselves into oblivion from the bridge. But, for all the connections language lets us make, for all the bridges we can talk and write into being to weave our lives together, to make sense of what's around us, to suture now and then into sufficient continuity to allow us to forge a way ahead, words can sometimes ring hollow with a terrible impotence. When they do, the safe passage that they promise looks flimsy if not fraudulent; it seems as reasonable to contemplate jumping from whatever platform they construct as to believe in the fictions of the crossings that they offer.

XI

Beside one of Leonardo da Vinci's marvelous anatomical drawings – which show such a peerless blend of accurate intricacy and beauty – there's a comment written in the artist's hand that I think has far wider application than to the subject of his study. Leonardo's comment, and the drawing of the human heart it accompanies, date from around 1513, two hundred and seventy five years before fuchsia was introduced to Britain. His comment takes the form of a question: "How could you describe this heart in words without filling a whole book?"

Like so many of the little hearts that beat around us, the fuchsia's is likewise resistant to description. It could spark volumes in the effort to record its rhythm, explain its nature, take the pulse of its presence here upon this earth. Just as Plumier's name for it is merely a superficial label – an invention foisted on the plant for our convenience – so all the words we bring into play have a flimsy provisionality about them that cannot in the end catch the fuchsia's real gravity of being. I've tried to trace around it here a little way, draw a contour map to show the rise and fall of some of its gradients of existence and connection, how it touches me, how it has touched others; where it flourishes; a little of its history. But though my verbal map may give some rough indications of direction, I have a profound sense of being lost and of any cartography I can offer being underlain at no great depth by chasms that I cannot cross or fathom.

Beyond the metronome beat of names and facts and dates and memories, blizzards of time and connection are released as soon as we start to pick out individual threads from the knot we label "fuchsia." Take one crimson bloom and place it on your palm, weigh the cool substance of its presence there, its almost absence of weight, the fact that you could blow it away just like a feather. Delicate and insubstantial though it seems, that frail bloom is linked to a species-umbilical that runs back for generation after generation. It's rooted somewhere long before *Homo sapiens*' emergence. Hidden behind every blossom are aeons of flowering, networks of cause and effect, occurrence and outcome that led to particular plants growing in particular places and to their flowering, seeding, rooting, dying. There are temporal tendrils invisibly affixed to every blossom, inexorable as anchor chains, connecting each one to a lifeline whose voltage sparks across the years in their millions upon millions. Somewhere in its lineage were the factors that carved and colored the flowers to precisely the right form and hue to draw humming birds to them (they are the plant's principal indigenous pollinators). Somewhere in the tangle of these tendrils was the moment of interconnection with whoever brought the plant to Ireland, whoever planted a hedge around that cottage at Horn Head; whoever planted the bush in St Andrews. Prisoners of War at Riccarton waiting to be repatriated will have seen fuchsia flowers as they walked about what's now a campus, glad the War is over but apprehensive about their futures. Students today, come late August or September, will still find drifts of fallen blossom on the same ground which, centuries before fuchsia was so named, Robert the Bruce gifted as a dowry to his ill-fated daughter. Millennia before us, fuchsia blossom will have registered on the eyes of long-vanished humming birds in forests innocent of any human presence. As our planet wheels through space laden with its astonishing cargoes, fuchsia threads – and everything they touch – are just one detail in time's tapestry. So much lies dormant behind what we see around us. Invisible immensities create a baffling acoustic in which our voices echo with resonant uncertainty.

We lay our net of names upon the world. Bred to our purpose, words sit on the backs of massive, mysterious phenomena. Amidst the babble of our talk, it's easy to imagine they're not there, or that we've tamed them, made them walk to heel – that with our verbal spurs and leads and reins we can break to the demands of meaning all the diverse elements of our experience. But what is "fuchsia" really beneath the name, beneath the varied associations that get snagged on it as individuals negotiate their way through whatever transient niche of time and place they occupy? What reasons can finally account for the delicate interstices and folds within each flower's pendulously lovely heart? Their existence is as enigmatic as is ours. We weave countless bridges with our talk, all railed with the apparent sense of sentences. But sometimes, haunting even the most careful wording I can craft, I see a figure standing at the very brink of what I've written, poised determinedly to jump.

"When a dog barks late at night and then retires again to bed..."
(Reading Flann O'Brien)

If the inhabitants of a certain Victorian townhouse in Lampeter, west Wales, ever strip the wallpaper in one of the upstairs rooms, they'll be surprised to find what's hidden underneath it. The bare plaster of the walls is covered with an array of word-clusters written in thick black pencil. Prominent among them is this one:

> When a dog barks late at night and then retires again to bed, he punctuates and gives majesty to the serial enigma of the dark, laying it more evenly and heavily upon the fabric of the mind.

I wrote this sentence, together with the other fragments of poetry and prose that adorn the walls, when I redecorated the house shortly after moving into it in 1989. Knowing that the words would soon be covered over with new paper made writing them on the walls – something I'd normally not dream of doing – seem not only acceptable but called for.

Thinking about it now, years later, long after selling the house and leaving Wales, this writing on the walls doesn't strike me as anything trivial. Rather than being a light-hearted, spur-of-the-moment impulse, or some temporary lapse into minor vandalism, these word-bursts of literary graffiti were more like the inscribing of a signature onto the very substance of the house. They acted as a constellation of hidden signs, secret tattoos that marked the place as mine. My wall-written words had the air of ritual about them, rather than mere whimsy. They were like talismans or charms, something that might be whispered into the ear of a newly born child; a kind of sacramental incantation.

Everything on the walls was written from memory; I was transcribing from what was in my mind, not copying out of books. Each text-fragment was taken from a piece of writing that had made sufficient impact for me to want to memorize some key part of it. What we know by heart like this, according to George Steiner, "becomes an agency in our consciousness, a pacemaker in the growth and vital complication of our identity." He argues (in *Real Presences*) that "what is committed to memory and susceptible to recall constitutes the ballast of the self." The epigraphs I wrote on those bare plaster walls were precisely this kind of ballast. Since, en masse, they provided revealing clues about the "vital complication" of my identity, it's no wonder I preferred them to be covered over. In a sense they functioned as a kind of secret name, known only to its bearer.

II

"When a dog barks late at night and then retires again to bed..." is from Flann O'Brien's novel, *At Swim-Two-Birds*. For me, this sentence has the kind of haunting lyricism more usually associated with poetry. I can't remember ever consciously learning it, but it's been in my mind word-perfect for years. I guess I must have committed it to memory at my first reading of the book. So far as I can determine, this happened in 1974, when I was nineteen.

Reading *At Swim-Two-Birds* again today, forty years later, has been a curious experience. It feels more like peeling off skin than wallpaper, paring things back to the bare bones of what was laid down in the deep strata of my reader's psyche all those years ago. Covering over my first impressions of the book with the very different textures woven by my current reading, doesn't feel like the obliteration of what went before – *At Swim-Two-Birds* is too deeply ingrained for that to happen – but it has made me recalibrate the way I see it, and recognize more clearly than I did before the impossibility of recapturing in more than ghostly outline the feelings that accompanied my first encounter with what's been described as O'Brien's "novel within a novel within a novel."[1]

Of course I shouldn't be surprised to find a mismatch between two readings separated by so many years. It would be as naïve to imagine that literary landscapes could be revisited after long absence and be found unchanged as it would be to suppose that a favorite place from childhood would be just the same when we return to it as adults. However much the words on the page or the contours of the land remain fixed in their positions, the fact is that we change. Heraclitus made the point that you can't step in the same river twice. Books, I suspect, for all their apparent fixity, have a similarly mercurial quality. Their words don't

---

[1] This description is given on the dust-jacket of the Hart-Davis MacGibbon edition, first published in 1960.

change of course – "When a dog barks late at night and then retires again to bed...", like the rest of *At Swim-Two-Birds*, remains exactly as O'Brien composed it seventy-five years ago. But the way these unchanging words fall upon the fabric of the mind at nineteen and at fifty-nine isn't the same at all. In four decades that fabric has received many rents and bruises, much weathering. I like to think it has matured and that, however much I may lament the loss of a nineteen-year-old's energy, my mind today is marked by all manner of intricately nuanced shadings and inflexions that weren't there in 1974.

Given how the "growth and vital complication" of identity develops, it's inevitable that *At Swim-Two-Birds* should strike me differently today. Books are static entities, the author's words like insects caught in the amber of the page. But reading is a live transaction between psyche and text which acts to melt the amber, lets its prisoners fly free. What patterns their flight will trace out as they weave and pirouette through a reader's mind is impossible to predict, beyond the certainty that no two readings will ever be the same.

III

How we find our way to books can be utterly straightforward – the set text at school, the recommendation of a friend, a gift, reading prompted by a persua-sive review, choosing something from the volumes that just happen to be sitting on the bookshelves of wherever we live; part of the furniture of home. But often I'm at a loss to map in any detail the routes that have taken me to particular titles. Looking back, many of the books I now regard as foundational in terms of the place they occupy in my personal reading canon seem to have been discovered more or less by accident – though the accidents in question were often ones I courted by spending time in bookshops.

At Swim-Two-Birds certainly wasn't a set text at school or university, nor do I recall any personal recommendation from a friend, or high praise in a review. And it wasn't remotely the kind of volume that my parents would have wanted on their shelves. It was, I'm almost sure, a piece of literary flotsam picked up on one of the many occasions when I was beachcombing in bookshops in my late teens. There were no bookshops then in my hometown of Lisburn, County Antrim, so I regularly made the short train journey to Belfast to spend a few hours wandering around that troubled city, exploring what its bookshops had to offer.

I'm not sure why *At Swim-Two-Birds* caught my eye. Why, on that long-vanished day, did I decide that it, rather than some other volume, was worth buying and reading? Even if I had perfect recall of that moment forty years ago, I doubt if I could answer such questions convincingly. The alchemy of impulse yields few of its secrets to our thirst for reasons. At one level, buying a book is a simple undertaking. But behind it lies a complicated maze that's rooted in the mystery of each individual's personality, with its unique catalogue of likes and dislikes, inclinations and hesitations. The complex interaction of mood and moment, history and the present, attraction and availability, the subtle, shifting coincidence of thought and feeling, the interplay of interest and circumstance – this shifting network of interconnected factors only needs to change its alignments fractionally for the outcome in terms of selecting and reading particular books to be entirely different.

Looking at the copy of *At Swim-Two-Birds* that I (almost certainly) bought in a Belfast bookshop in the early 1970s, and have just read again, I can see nothing in the physical attributes of the book itself that would explain why I was first drawn to it. It's the Penguin Modern Classics paperback edition, first published in 1967, with reprints in 1968 and 1971. The cover illustration features "The Bus by the River," a painting by Jack B. Yeats (brother of the poet). There's no back cover blurb extolling the author's virtues in the manner of contemporary publishing's catechisms of puffery. Front and back covers are almost entirely taken up by Yeats's painting, which I don't find particularly appealing. The only text that appears is, on the front, "Penguin Modern Classics" (with the Penguin logo), "Flann O'Brien" and "At Swim-Two-Birds"; and, on the back, in small print at the side of Yeats's canvas, a list of prices whose paltriness emphasizes how much has changed since 1971.

Inside the front cover there's a brief blurb about the book. We're told – surely unnecessarily – that 1939, the date of its first appearance, "was hardly the time for exuberant literary experiments." With its reissue in 1960 came the recognition that *At Swim-Two-Birds* is "a classic of its time and of ours." Two celebrity endorsements are included to add weight to this assertion. According to Dylan Thomas it's "just the book to give your sister, if she's a loud, dirty, boozy girl." For James Joyce, Flann O'Brien is "a real writer, with the true comic spirit" and *At Swim-Two-Birds* is "a really funny book." All that's said about the book itself is

When a dog barks late at night and then retires again to bed...

this dilute account of it:

> The story introduces us to Finn MacCool, legendary giant; Sweeny, accursed bird-king of Dal Araidhe; the Pooka McPhellimey, a member of the devil class; and a fast-drinking cast of students, faeries, cowpunchers and clerics.

There's also a short biographical note on Flann O'Brien, explaining that this is the pseudonym of Brian O'Nolan and giving outline details of his life and publications. We're told he was "a life-long friend of James Joyce, whose influence can be traced in the experimental blend of satire, fantasy and farce in *At Swim-Two-Birds*."

IV

There's nothing obvious about the book to explain why it exerted enough appeal to make me want to buy it. Was it the allure of something experimental? Or perhaps what clinched it was Joyce's name, a totemic token of high culture, its presence acting as a guarantor of literary sophistication. I liked Dylan Thomas's poetry – to the extent that several of his verses got written on the bare plaster walls of my house in Wales – but I can't imagine that his vulgar-sounding recommendation would have impressed me. Or maybe I picked the book up and was intrigued by its opening paragraph:

> Having placed in my mouth sufficient bread for three minutes' chewing, I withdrew my powers of sensual perception and retired into the privacy of my mind, my eyes and face assuming a vacant and preoccupied expression. I reflected on the subject of my spare-time literary activities. One beginning and one ending for a book was a thing I did not agree with. A good book may have three openings entirely dissimilar and inter-related only in the prescience of the author, or for that matter one hundred times as many endings.

Of course it's also possible that far from being persuaded by the quality of the prose, its experimental nature, or its endorsement by two great writers, I bought the book for entirely non-literary reasons. Perhaps there was a pretty girl serving in the shop and I thought that buying this arcane, Joyce-blessed item would impress her with my intellectual prowess. Or it could be that mention of Finn MacCool – "legendary hero of Old Ireland" – sparked an affectionate connection with home by reminding me of the pottery tankard that stood on a tallboy in one of our bedrooms, a souvenir from the Giant's Causeway. There was a picture of Finn on one side, with details of his heroic exploits on the other. When you picked it up, the tankard turned musical box and played Percy French's famous melody "Where the Mountains of Mourne Sweep Down to the Sea."

When I came to reread it, I wondered if native loyalty to locale might have been a factor in my being drawn to Flann O'Brien; that I bought *At Swim-Two-Birds* out of a kind of literary patriotism, wanting to support a writer from Northern Ireland. But looking at the Penguin Modern Classics edition there's nothing in the biographical note to suggest that O'Brien was, like me, an Ulsterman. The emphasis there is on Dublin, where he spent his adult life. It must have been some time after my first reading of the book that I discovered he was born in Strabane, a town in County Tyrone that we drove through every summer on our way to seaside holidays in Donegal. Not only was I innocent of Flann O'Brien's provenance on that first reading, I had no visual image of him either – the Penguin Modern Classics edition doesn't include an author photo. In fact I knew next to nothing about him. Today, by contrast, I approach *At Swim-Two-Birds* having read several biographical studies, some of which include photographs and portraits of Brian O'Nolan. How much does knowledge of an author's life, an awareness of his struggles and disappointments as a writer, a picture of his face, affect a reading of his work?

One result of rereading *At Swim-Two-Birds* and thinking about the way my nineteen-year-old self first discovered the book – and how easily he might never have done so – has been to make me wonder more generally about how the reading profiles that come to characterize us are formed. This in turn has sparked more fundamental questions: Why do we read? What are we looking for in books? What do we take away from them? I think reading plays a significant role in determining the features of that inner physiognomy that seems so intimately to reflect us, but it's hard to make any point-by-point correlation between the people we become and the books we read along the way. Even so, I believe that if *At Swim-Two-Birds* was deleted from my syllabus of reading, I would be somehow changed and lessened.

V

Whatever first drew me to it, *At Swim-Two-Birds* rapidly became a favorite book. I was entranced by O'Brien's exuberantly complex comedy, thought his writing style combined unforced elegance with a sophisticated, tongue-in-cheek mockery that seemed at once philosophical, lyrical, and amusingly fantastical. I warmed to a book that had three separate beginnings and that intruded into the text an occasional "synopsis of what has gone before for the benefit of new readers." The cleverness of interweaving the different narrative threads impressed me, and I was won over by the way O'Brien allowed fictional characters a life of their own, apparently independent of their authors. His mixing of the mundane and the mythological made for moments of hilarity, and the relaxed fluency of his diction drew me into the intricate absurdities he was constructing. It appealed to me to have the traditional form of a novel repeatedly interrupted with asides and notes that drew attention to what the author was doing, with the reader being stopped in his tracks on a regular basis by italicized subheadings flagging up the names of figures of speech being used, the nature of silences encountered, and the description of characters. Today, the book is described as a "metafictional text" or an "anti-novel." To me, an amateur, independent reader, innocent of the terminology of literary criticism, it simply seemed amusing, original, beautifully written and thought-provoking.

Essentially, *At Swim-Two-Birds* is a comedy of characters created by authors who are themselves the inventions of other writers. There are ten "biographical reminiscences" scattered through the book. These sections are written in the first person and detail the interactions of an unnamed individual – the "I" who is reminiscing – with his Uncle, his friend Brinsley, and others. This "I" is himself a writer. The manuscript on which he's working features one Dermot Trellis, who in turn is also a writer. Some of Trellis's characters start to write works of their own – and they also bring Trellis to trial for the suffering he has caused his protagonist, John Furriskey. Trellis's seduction of one of his female characters, and the subsequent birth of Orlick Trellis, his son, adds to the complication. This mix-up of writers and characters is given a further bizarre twist by the inclusion of figures from Irish mythology – Finn MacCool, the bird-king Sweeny, a devil and a fairy – together with some Dublin cowboys from the pulp fiction of a local writer of westerns.

The book's strange title comes from one of the places traditionally visited by Sweeny during his purgatorial odyssey around Ireland. The medieval Irish work

Buile Suibhbe tells of how he was cursed and made to wander the country as a bird in punishment for his attack on Saint Ronan. *Snámh-dá-en*, or Swim-Two-Birds, is described as being "by the side of the (river) Shannon." The place has only the most minor relevance in O'Brien's novel, being mentioned just once in passing and playing little role in the events that unfold. In fact, as I later discovered, O'Brien himself proposed changing the book's title, but his publishers preferred the original to his suggestion of *Sweeny in the Trees*.[2]

VI

It's hard to measure the influence reading has on a life, let alone calculate the effect of any single book. Some titles carry so little in the waters of their text that the words just wash over us and vanish, leaving no discernible trace. Others are more like boulder-loaded waves, a turmoil of water and sediment pounding on our shores. They feel as if they leave us marked by the storm of their passage. But do we really understand what happens when a book touches us (or when it fails to)? Can reading rewire the psyche, leave an impression that's indelible, or is it no more than something of the moment, its impact evaporating as soon as we disengage the reading eye? At least with *At Swim-Two-Birds* there are several tangible markers that hint at the depth of impact the book had on me, even if it's impossible to take soundings that might measure this precisely, fathom it in quantifiable units.

To begin with, I made extensive notes on it – just for my own interest rather than for any set academic purpose. The notes, dated "Belfast, April 30th 1974,"

---

[2] On O'Brien's suggested alternative title, see Eva Wäppling, *Four Irish Legendary Figures in At-Swim-Two-Birds: a Study of Flann O'Brien's use of Finn, Suibhne, the Pooka and the Good Fairy*, Acta Universitatis Upsaliensis, Uppsala: 1984, p.17. Wäppling also notes (p.19) that O'Brien originally wrote *At Swim Two Birds* thus, without hyphens, but that his publisher, Longmans, preferred them to be put in. Seamus Heaney's *Sweeney Astray* (Faber, London: 1984) provides a modern translation of *Buile Suibhne*, the medieval text that describes Sweeney's tribulations. The poem traditionally spoken by Sweeney when he reaches Swim-Two-Birds appears on pp.18-20 in Heaney's rendering. Note that O'Brien's and Heaney's spellings of Sweeny/Sweeney take different views on the presence of an e before the y.

were handwritten, in blue fountain pen, in a hard-backed notebook that I've kept safe all these years. I guess I wrote them very soon after finishing the book, which is why I put my age at nineteen for that first reading. The notes mostly consist of direct quotes copied out – sections of the text that particularly appealed to me (like "When a dog barks late at night..."). But there are also several pages about the structure of the book. I was clearly impressed by the multi-layered narrative, its interlocking threads featuring the characters of different writers, all ultimately invented by Brian O'Nolan. I've also noted some points of comparison between *At Swim-Two-Birds* and other books I was reading around the same time. Pirandello's *Six Characters in Search of an Author* is mentioned in this context, as is Kurt Vonnegut's *Slaughterhouse Five*. I can understand the parallel with Pirandello, but it's harder for me now to grasp what thread of connection I evidently saw between O'Brien and Vonnegut – unless it's simply their common recourse to the fantastical. Reading my notes from 1974 today feels a bit like finding a message in a bottle, something my younger self cast into the waves forty years ago, with no idea which distant island in the self's archipelago of ageing his handwritten pages would find their way to.

Another sign of how much *At Swim-Two-Birds* meant to me was the way it prompted me to buy and read all of O'Brien's books, including those written under his other pseudonym, Myles na Gopaleen. And when I could afford to, I systematically replaced my initial paperback editions with hardbacks. As a student in Edinburgh I continued the bookshop beachcombing that I'd started in Belfast, only now I was particularly drawn to the secondhand and antiquarian shops and, as well as being open to the finds of serendipity, one of my goals became finding a first edition of Flann O'Brien's novel. These are particularly rare because Longmans' premises were hit by a German bomb in the autumn of 1944 and among the stock destroyed were copies of *At Swim-Two-Birds*.[3] Alas, I never found a first edition. The hardback copy of the book I have is only a

---

[3] In his "Cruiskeen Lawn" column in the *Irish Times* – written under his Myles na Gopaleen pseudonym, O'Brien quipped that Adolf Hitler loathed *At Swim-Two-Birds* so much "that he started World War II in order to torpedo it" but that "in a grim irony not without charm, the book survived the war while Hitler did not." See Ann Clissmann, *Flann O'Brien: A Critical Introduction to his Writings*, Gill & Macmillan, Dublin: 1975, pp.78-79.

fourth impression of the Hart-Davis MacGibbon 1960 edition. This copy is signed "Chris Arthur, Oxford 1976." I have only the vaguest memories now of this visit to Oxford, but I do remember that finding the hardback on the shelves in Blackwell's bookshop was like meeting an old friend unexpectedly in a foreign city. I couldn't resist buying it. Like the Penguin Modern Classics edition, this Oxford-purchased one has marginal pencil marks scattered through it, evidence of the fact that I must have read the book at least twice before this current re-reading.

That *At Swim-Two-Birds* and its author soon became important touchstones in my life can also be seen in the way in which, in addition to the primary texts, I started to buy some of what was written *about* O'Brien. Back in the 1970s this didn't amount to much – what George Steiner describes as "the locust mechanics" of the secondary hadn't got properly into gear. I can still remember my mother's horrified disapproval in 1975 at my spending the then astronomical sum of £9.50 on the first full-length assessment of O'Brien's writing – Anne Clissmann's *Flann O'Brien: a Critical Introduction to his Writing*. This extravagance was soon followed by purchases of Peter Costello and Peter Van De Kamp's *Flann O'Brien: An Illustrated Biography*, Anthony Cronin's *No Laughing Matter: The Life and Times of Flann O'Brien*, and Timothy O'Keefe's edited collection, *Myles: Portraits of Brian O'Nolan*.

VII

My interest in O'Brien was still running strong in 1985. I can say this with certainty because in that year I delivered the Gifford Research Fellowship lectures at the University of St Andrews and began the lectures – and the book that derived from them – by quoting the scene from *At Swim-Two-Birds* where Dermot Trellis gives birth to a fully grown man. An extract from the local press reports that "the new arrival, stated to be doing 'very nicely' is about 5 feet 8 inches in height, dark and clean shaven." This is John Furriskey, the protagonist in Trellis's story – Trellis being the invention of the "I" of the "biographical reminiscences," himself the creation of Flann O'Brien, who is in turn the creation, or alter ego, of Brian O'Nolan. I also drew my audience's attention to Trellis's trial, at which he is cross-examined by some of his own characters about the nature of Furriskey's arrival in the world.

When a dog barks late at night and then retires again to bed...

'In what manner was he born?' the court asks.

'He awoke,' replies Trellis, 'as if from sleep.'

'What were his sensations?'

'Bewilderment, perplexity. He was consumed by doubts as to his own identity.'

In an effort to dispel these doubts, Furriskey is seen, shortly after his impromptu entrance into the world, "searching his room for a looking glass or for a surface that would enable him to ascertain the character of his countenance."

The court is particularly outraged at Trellis's seeming indifference to the severe mental anguish he has occasioned by creating a character who is left so uncertain about who he is and what he ought to do.

'Why,' they ask him, 'did you not perform so obvious an errand of mercy as to explain his identity and duties to him?'

To this, Trellis has no answer.

With a nod to Furriskey searching for a looking glass, my lectures and subsequent book were entitled *In the Hall of Mirrors*. I began them with extracts from *At Swim-Two-Birds* because I thought the impromptu birth of Furriskey would catch an audience's attention in the same way that it had caught mine. But it also seemed to me that Furriskey's doubts about his own identity and purpose – and his discontentment with the nature given to him by his creator – resonated with fundamental features of our existence, as did his seeking out some reflective surface by which he might see things more clearly. Like his dog barking late at night, O'Brien's prose – for all its fantastical elaborations – lays the human condition more evenly and heavily upon the fabric of the mind, emphasizing its essential characteristics.

As well as hooking an audience's attention and providing a kind of existential paradigm, *At Swim-Two-Birds* provided me with a precedent-cum-prelude for giving birth to someone of my own invention. *In the Hall of Mirrors* focuses on "Cipher," a fictional character who is intent on exploring the various reflections of humanity shown in the mirrors of the world's religions. Of course Cipher wasn't just a philosophical fiction designed to aid an exploration of religious pluralism. He was, in part, autobiographical, a reflection of the fact that in 1985 I was myself struggling to make sense of the world's diverse faiths and philosophies, trying to establish whether any of them offered a view of existence that would shed light on questions of identity and purpose. But I've often wondered since if I'd have thought of using a character like Cipher if it hadn't been for the influence of *At Swim-Two-Birds*.

When I moved to the University of Wales in 1989 to take up a lectureship in Religious Studies, O'Brien's star remained bright in the firmament of my thinking. I still have a folder of notes and jottings and photocopied articles about his writing that I started to put together around that time, and added to intermittently for years. My intention was to write something about the religio-philosophical themes in O'Brien's work. That I never did perhaps reflects a waning of interest, or perhaps it was just a reflection of how the demands of a new job leave little time to pursue such things. Or maybe, an outsider to the world of academic English literature and its specialist discourse, I was daunted by the sheer amount of material that had by then accrued about O'Brien. It seemed as much an entombment of the original as an elucidation of it, still less a celebration. When I look today at the proliferating swarm of O'Brien-related articles, books, theses and conference proceedings it brings a comment of George Steiner's to mind. He talks about "a mandarin madness of secondary discourse" that "infects thought and sensibility." As a lover of O'Brien's work, perhaps it's not surprising that I was reluctant to add to this thickening carapace of commentary that threatened to constrict the very thing that gave rise to it.

VIII

Rereading what I've long regarded as one of my favorite books turned out to be less of a pleasure than I'd anticipated. I found myself impatient with its often slow pace, its longwindedness, its lack of any conventional chapter breaks. Some of what originally appeared as integral and amusing embellishment now seemed closer to tedious digression. What, in 1974, according to my own handwritten notes, was "extremely funny" rarely made me smile. Some of the humour just seemed juvenile. The complete absence of any credible female perspective, something not noticed in 1974, now grated as an obvious deficiency. The intricately worked literary design that had so impressed me when I was nineteen now looked, in parts, lumbering and laboured. Now and then I was, frankly, bored with what seemed little more than silly shenanigans. If my impression first time round had been like this, I might soon have grown weary with *At Swim-Two-Birds* and abandoned it half read.

And yet – I know it will sound strange – the fact that I can see its flaws more clearly now has, if anything, increased my affection for the book. In the same way as, when we grow up, we can see our parents' frailties but love them none the less, so it seems to be with *At Swim-Two-Birds*. It played a not insignificant part in my growing up. Feeling sometimes disappointed with it now is akin to seeing lines and wrinkles on a parent's face, or noticing their forgetfulness. Far from being the discovery of culpable faults, such realizations seem more a recognition of essential nature – and of the unreasonableness of expecting perfection.

It's worth remembering how much readings are influenced by the milieu in which they happen. Reading something in the course of a passionate affair, on a long sea voyage, whilst recuperating in hospital, or whilst serving time in prison, will not result in identical impressions of a book. Reading in a library, in an airport, sitting outside naked in the sun are very different experiences – likewise reading at different times in an individual's life. Reading *At Swim-Two-Birds* at nineteen and at fifty-nine involves radically different circumstances being brought into play, for all the underlying commonality stemming from the fact that it's the same person reading.

It would be extraordinarily unrealistic to expect the book to make the same impression now as it did back then. And yet, a part of me wanted precisely that – longed for *At Swim-Two-Birds* to lay upon the fabric of the mind the same spell that it cast when I was nineteen. Had it – impossibly – done so, I hope I would have had the sense to be disappointed with myself. For if my reading now had yielded exactly the same outcome as it did then, it would surely suggest a worrying stagnation. It would be completely unreasonable to expect what had an impact when I was fresh out of school, single, living as a student in Edinburgh, or with my parents in Northern Ireland at the height of the Troubles, inexperienced in terms of reading, relationships, employment or travel, to have the same impact all over again today when I'm nearing retirement age, married with a family, settled far away from Belfast's sectarian poisons, my parents long dead, and with a history of employment, reading, relationships, and living in different places behind me.

IX

Rereading *At Swim-Two-Birds* has been a bit like revisiting a well known place held in affectionate remembrance but, as you walk around it, knowing that you won't be there again. This sparks a mixture of sadness and a feeling that it's time to move on; the knowledge that you no longer really belong here. Journeying through O'Brien's familiar wordscapes increasingly took on an elegiac quality. My rereading was underlain by the growing certainty that I wouldn't be here again – so that, as well as allowing a re-acquaintance with an old friend, this reading also acted as a bidding of goodbye. Any inclination to judge *At Swim-Two-Birds* as wanting was tempered by the forgiving acceptance of nostalgia (made more affectionate by this sense of leavetaking), and by the recognition of the impact the book once had on me. For the fact remains that my first encounter with it laid down an important part of the jigsaw of my reading life, the pieces of which are sutured to my real life in complex patterns of interaction. In any case, however differently I might view it now, for me to sit in judgment on my younger self's experience and evaluation would be as absurd as Trellis's characters taking him to task for various shortcomings. Things happen in their time and, as *At Swim-Two-Birds'* epigraph puts it (with a line from Euripedes), "All things go out and give place one to another."

I rarely reread books. It's a mark of the esteem in which I've long held O'Brien's comic masterpiece that I've read it at least twice before embarking on this current rereading. If I find it wanting now, that's only to be expected. As folk wisdom has it: you only have one chance to make a first impression. *At Swim-Two-Birds* made its first impression in 1974; it would be as unreasonable to expect it to repeat that impression forty years later as it would be not to acknowledge the depth of impact that it had back then. I also take heart from the fact that O'Brien himself in later life damned the book for which he's now most famous. In a letter to Tim O'Keefe dated October 15th 1965 he said:

> I am so sick of this *At Swim-Two-Birds* juvenile scrivenry that I just can't take it seriously on any level and absolutely loathe the mere mention.

In the same letter he says that if he gets "sufficiently drunk over Christmas" he might read "that damned book," but he acknowledges that, for all the flaws he now perceives, "those birds must have some unsuspect stuffing in them."[4] O'Brien was only twenty-eight when *At Swim-Two-Birds* was published. These comments about it were made when he was fifty-five. I can't help seeing a parallel between my reading at nineteen and at fifty-nine. I can't help agreeing about the "unsuspect stuffing."

Even if I'm lucky and have another two or even three decades of reading life ahead of me, I doubt if I'll go back to *At Swim-Two-Birds*. The time seems too short to lavish yet more hours on this one volume. Yet thinking that I'm unlikely to traverse these wordscapes again makes me feel a kind of homesickness for the book already, so perhaps – who knows? – I will be minded to revisit it. As well as making me think about my own experience of the book, rereading it has also made me curious about other readers. In the forty years between this reading of *At Swim-Two-Birds* and my first one, how many people around the world have let their eyes be led through the artful maze of O'Brien's prose? Who are they, this unmet tribe of fellow readers? What impact has the book had on them? What difference has it made to their lives?

I wonder, too, about readings yet to come – and how far into the future *At Swim-Two-Birds* will stretch its beckoning word-paths. Will people still read it in 2514? In particular, I wonder about what readings await my own copies of O'Brien's books. Who will read them after my death? What will they make of my marginal pencil marks? Is this where they too would place an emphasis, or would different parts of the text strike them as noteworthy? My rereading has tripped some switches I expected and some that I did not. Naturally, it has gone hand in hand with memory – rereading and what I remember from previous readings interacting with each other, alongside the baleful note of what I'd completely forgotten. More surprising has been the way in which going over the familiar ground of *At Swim-Two-Birds* has acted at once to emphasize my finitude and solitariness – the lonely reader and his inevitable end – at the same time as pointing to other readings and the community, albeit spectral, of other readers; the way the book draws to its strange, alluring light a crowd of moth-readers who, however unbeknownst to each other, flutter around a common flame and partake of the same wordy communion. Walking along the word-paths that

---

[4] I'm quoting from extracts of O'Brien's letter given in Wäppling, op.cit., p.20.

O'Brien has laid down, I know my reader's tread is as invisible today as it was when I was nineteen. Yet, for all that we leave no residue of ourselves in the reading territories we traverse, I've sometimes thought that on the cusp of a particular sentence, amidst the foliage of certain word combinations, I've glimpsed a shadow, some ghostly remnant of the person I used to be, so perhaps traces of others are lingering invisibly here too, their fugitive presences haunting the sentences that house them.

Perhaps in another forty years, in the unlikely circumstance of my being here to do it, I should schedule a final reading of *At Swim-Two-Birds*. Whatever I might make of the book at ninety-nine, I'm sure it would be different to my readings at nineteen and at fifty-nine. That thought makes me wonder about who the oldest reader is of *At Swim-Two-Birds*, who the youngest, and how much their readings overlap and differ. And, on a more sombre note, I wonder what will be the last book I ever read, the last printed page the eyes take in, the final words, before they shut forever.

X

As we go through the world, what do we carry with us? I don't mean our material possessions, the actual things that are the lumber of our lives. Rather, if we strip away the wallpaper of all our tangible accoutrements, what's written on the bare plaster of – for want of a better word – our souls? In our essential aloneness and nakedness what resources can we call upon to sustain us as we face what William Meredith calls life's "sensual astonishments?" These happen with "the whole galaxy gaping there" beside us and "the centuries whining like gnats," emphasizing at every turn the contingency and brevity of life;[5] the fact that – to use O'Brien's epigraph again – "All things go out and give place one to another."

I can give no clear or convincing answer here, since I place no trust in those dogmatic certainties with which some people seek to shore up their lives, making them proof against the terrors and delights of existence. It's more a case of

---

[5] These phrases are from Meredith's poem, "Accidents of Birth." I'd inscribe this in its entirety on any bare plaster surfaces I decided to write on now.

falling back on the mosaic of who I am, and knowing that many of the tiles in it have been shaped and colored by what I've read – even if I can't specify exactly how, book by book, this shaping influence has happened. All I can say is that some aspects of some books – and *At Swim-Two-Birds* is one of them – feel as if they've got under my skin to the plaster of the psyche-soul and became a part of me.

If I was redecorating my house today and stripped the wallpaper off, I know I would be minded to write another constellation of word-clusters on the walls. My repertoire of fragments known by heart has expanded since I lived in Wales. The literary fingerprints I'd leave would show a different spoor of words, a denser veining of reading paths followed and landmarks that have struck me as I paced them. But I know that any tattooing of the fibre of my current house that I might do today, although it would have a different store of possibilities to draw on, would still prominently feature "When a dog barks late at night and then retires again to bed...." Why should that be, particularly now, when the book has slipped a notch in my estimation? In part because this nugget of prose still retains its own intrinsic lyrical appeal; in part because – no matter how much I think of it in isolation – it's embedded in *At Swim-Two-Birds* and comes trailing filaments steeped in a flavor I once savored and seasoned with all sorts of memories.

When I summon this piece of wordy ballast from the psyche and say it to myself, I'm reminded of fingering an appealing shell or pebble found on a beach and put for safekeeping in a pocket, a keepsake of the world, heavy with the weight of associations it's imbued with, associations that recall the landscape, weather, moment of its finding. Not only does this little word-cluster come smudged with traces of the riotous imaginative world of O'Brien's book, but clinging to it like barnacles or streamers of stubborn seaweed are aspects of my own life that have become entangled with the book. Saying it brings back to mind the long-haired nineteen-year-old wandering around Belfast's bookshops, the "earnest inquirer after truth"[6] using O'Brien's words to begin a lecture series,

---

[6] The Gifford Research Fellowship is governed by the terms of Lord Gifford's will (1885). These stipulate that appointees "shall be subject to no test of any kind," except that they be "true thinkers, sincere lovers of and earnest inquirers after truth."

the fifty-nine-year-old writer attempting to bring into focus the way *At Swim-Two-Birds* has acted – still acts – on the "growth and vital complication" of his identity. However unlikely a lifebelt it may seem, "When a dog barks late at night and then retires again to bed…" gives me a sense of buoyancy in life's waters. I hope I will carry it with me until the fabric of my mind perishes and I am claimed, as we all are claimed, by the serial enigma of the dark that surrounds us.

Priests
(Reading fishing and desecration)

I

The first priest I ever met was cold, thickset, and murderous – something that, inevitably, colored all my subsequent encounters. It was as if this initial meeting coded into the very fiber of the word a skein of connotations that, although they have no legitimate place there, did much to determine how I understood "priest" for years. So far as I was concerned, beside its ordinary meaning there was a dark penumbra of associations, all to do with violence and death.

Raised as an Ulster Protestant, in a tribe deeply suspicious of its Catholic neighbors, in our tongue "priest" had no familiar point of reference; we had plain ministers. A priest was a high functionary of Northern Ireland's minority faith, and therefore, in our eyes, suspect. Catholicism was, for us, a kind of fifth column within the body politic. Its members followed a different set of allegiances to ours – looking to Dublin and Southern Ireland, not London, Britain and the Crown. We viewed "papists" more as traitors than fellow Christians.

In the view of Roman Catholicism we harbored – as ill-informed as it was deep-seated – priests were thought to wield enormous influence over their flocks. This meant that they were blamed for turning a blind eye, giving the nod of tacit approval, whenever any black sheep went astray. Priests were also seen as celebrants of rituals we deemed morally dubious at best. As the stranglehold of the Troubles tightened in the 1970s, and parts of Belfast began to resemble war zones, it wasn't uncommon to hear priests accused of complicity in terrorism. In offering absolution – via confession – for crimes we thought too heinous ever to forgive, they were regarded as aiding and abetting the violence that was disfiguring the Province, however much they publicly condemned it.

Yet, for all their supposed authority, and no doubt adding to their air of wielding power behind the scenes, priests were remote, alien figures so rarely spotted as to seem a kind of invisible presence. I don't ever remember seeing one in Lisburn, the predominantly Protestant town near Belfast where I grew up – though the priest's house, right beside the chapel, was always pointed out in hushed tones and with furtive glances any time we walked past it. The gruesomely realistic crucifixion scene, depicted in life-size statuary just outside the chapel door, meant that the sense of violence and death I already associated with priests was strengthened on those rare occasions when we ventured into this part of town.

The sinister mystique we bestowed on priests was given further emphasis on our annual summer holiday in Donegal – that most beautiful part of the country, situated in the far northwest of Catholic-dominated Eire. At the hotel we stayed in, a small group of priests often congregated in the bar to drink whiskey and chat together animatedly. They were a loud, convivial presence, their black suits an incongruous garb for the liveliness they invariably displayed. In our virtually teetotal household, whiskey drinking would have been questionable behavior for anyone. But for *priests* – who, however alien, were still supposedly men of God – it was seen as tantamount to sin. What they were doing was a flagrant, yet delicious, flouting of our straitlaced standards. We could no more imagine our minister drinking whiskey in a hotel bar than we could imagine him patronizing a brothel. Finding priests openly embracing hard liquor was at once shocking and confirming. By indulging so openly in what we disapproved of they reinforced both their difference from us – their outsider status – and the general air of dubiety we were so ready to believe surrounded them.

The first priest I got to know properly was when I was a student in Edinburgh, living miles away from Northern Ireland's antagonistic assumptions and deep-rooted prejudices. Thankfully, this intelligent, cultured, humorous and tolerant man was a powerful antidote to my earlier misapprehensions. Even so, first impressions have a durability that makes them hard to shift. His benign counterexample notwithstanding, I suspect that, subconsciously, even now, as soon as "priest" is mentioned, that original set of negative connotations still casts a shadow somewhere in my mind. This is a specific instance of a general truth it's best not to lose sight of: words can continue to carry illicit cargoes long after we've ceased to be complicit in their smuggling. Like an unfair verdict overturned, yet whose taint is never quite erased, "priest" still whispers "guilty" to me even though I know that this conviction is unsound.

II

It's always hard to tell what molds us into the people we become, but I view as a particularly formative part of my childhood the time I spent with my father when he was fishing. The stretch of water that he visited most regularly – where my first fateful encounter with a priest took place – wasn't one of the beautiful lakes or rivers of which Ireland is full. Instead, it was a small, unobtrusive reservoir that occupied a nook of farmland close to where we lived. It would seem ordinary enough to any stranger passing by, indeed it would be easily overlooked as an unremarkable feature of the landscape. But for me it was somewhere explored minutely and loved intensely. I got to know those few rough acres with such closeness that it transformed the place into somewhere so finely textured I could read the secrets of its knap and weave with a fluency that left me feeling illiterate elsewhere.

In this childhood paradise I knew where to look for sticklebacks and shoals of minnows. I knew exactly where to squat without throwing a shadow, so that I could watch these little fishes glide and dart in the shallows where the clear water of a feeder stream gently pooled into the reservoir. The occasional glints of scarlet on the male sticklebacks' bellies – their breeding livery – were like tiny embers warming the water. I knew where the large trout – an eight-pounder at least – circled the deep water around a rusty iron gantry that jutted out from the dam wall. The fish's dark form, a startlingly large and solid shape in the formless liquid of its medium, made it seem as if the water had been taken by surprise and inadvertently allowed its secret psyche to be glimpsed. But no matter how often I directed my father to cast his line into the territory of this circling giant, it never took the bait.

I knew at what points it was safe to wade, and where the mud was treacherous. By frequently walking round – and wading in – the perimeter drainage ditches, the little feeder streams, and overflow channels, I'd learnt the way in which the sluice and ooze of water followed a series of weather-related patterns. I knew by heart the patchwork calendar of wildflowers that grew in such varied profusion amidst the tussock grass and rushes and in between the large, square-cut stones with which the main water channels were clad. I could take you to the best spot from where the distant Mourne Mountains could be viewed, or to the reedy bay where herons often stood, motionless in their poised grey stillness, strange water-sentinels alert to any movement.

I knew that stationing yourself on an appealing promontory that jutted out into a deepwater channel would soon leave you chilled to the bone because of the way the wind flowed and surged around this spot, and that moving only a few steps left or right made a perceptible difference to the temperature. I knew to within a finger's length where small-copper butterflies liked to sun-bask on the steep bank that ran the length of the dam wall. The bank backed the reservoir's stone-lined receptacle with a grass-covered rampart, reminiscent of ancient earthworks, as if the water pooled behind it had conjured for its own protection a line of heavy fortification. I knew the best spots to find meadow browns, ringlets, marsh fritillaries, orange tips, and the other butterflies that, for a few months every season, brightened the days with their presence. I can still see in my mind's eye the moorhens and coots and great-crested grebes, the tufted duck and goldeneye and occasional pair of swans, and where each species favored for their nests.

III

My father's angling club didn't have a junior section, so I couldn't join. But fly-fishing never made much appeal to me, so being thus disbarred by age was not a disqualification that I minded. I was content to spend the hours my father was fishing exploring the reservoir and its surrounding territory, savoring its flavors, reading the fine print of its flora and fauna, learning the minute alphabets of the landscape. If my father wanted to fish the middle waters of the reservoir, I'd row him out and act as oarsman – once I was old enough to manage the heavy wooden boat. But he mostly preferred to fish from the bank, or to wade in almost as far as his thigh waders would allow, giving me the freedom to roam. Sometimes, on a still day, if he'd waded out to fish and I was on the other side of the reservoir looking across at him, it was as if there was half a man balanced on the water, his torso casting delicately judged loops across the mirror-surface, his body cleanly bisected by the shiny disc of water on which his chest seemed balanced, legs invisible below the silvered surface.

We almost never referred to "Boomer's reservoir," or "Boomer's dam," by name. This was how it was signposted and marked on maps, but to us it was simply "the dam," or "Dad's reservoir." Built towards the end of the nineteenth century, it became for a time Lisburn's main water supply. As the town grew into a sprawling city, the reservoir was retired into auxiliary use, drawn on only to supplement supplies in dry summers. In 2012 it was declared surplus to requirements and included on a list of 28 reservoirs that Northern Ireland's governing executive put up for sale. The last time I was there was, for me, a heartbreaking experience. I know it's impossible to go back to childhood haunts and find them unchanged. What's seen through a child's vision can never be reclaimed in adulthood. I don't think I was attempting the absurdity of trying to recapture the idyllic place it used to be for me. I was simply saddened to find a once tranquil, unspoiled spot in a state of desecration. What had been a stretch of clean water in pleasant countryside had become circled by a maze of new roads and houses. Litter in and around the water repeatedly caught the eye. Nature's rich texture had been stripped, reduced, denuded – hedges gone, fields built over, trees cut down, streams culverted or fouled. A straggle of dandelions and a few scavenging crows seemed all that had survived. They made a kind of miserable residue that merely underlined how much had been lost; the rime of life's tide that had once filled this place with its abundance.

Boomer's dam was named after Renny Boomer, who had owned the farm on whose land the reservoir was built. The Boomer family, some of whom still live in the area, are descended from French Huguenot refugees – Protestants who fled religious persecution in France in the seventeenth century. Many Huguenot families, the Boomers among them, settled in Lisburn, bringing with them their expertise in linen, which soon became the town's chief trade. "Boomer" was originally "Boullmer". It became "Boomer" – as René became "Renny" – as the local tongue smoothed these strange-sounding names into homely versions that fitted more comfortably into the contours of familiar diction.

Even as children we knew the unfamiliar word "Huguenot," but were innocent of the historical detail surrounding the appearance of those so-named in our midst. All we were taught – or all that we remembered – was that these foreign Protestants were somehow living proof of persecution and, of course, of Catholic treachery. To me, the Huguenots were further evidence of the murderousness of priests.

IV

In their Introduction to *The Magic Wheel* (1985), an anthology of fishing in literature, David Profumo and Graham Swift suggest that the experience of angling involves "a confrontation with another world." They see fishing as essentially "a meeting with, a peering into, another universe." This concern with something other, even alien, an encounter with a realm beyond our ordinary, waking, dry-land reality, is accompanied, they say, by an inner journey. Profumo and Swift describe it as "a Narcissus-like in-peering, inescapably yearning, entranced, nostalgic."

The boy who used to wander around Boomer's reservoir would have dismissed such notions as high-blown theorizing, remote from anything to do with him. But looking back, I think it offers more illumination than exaggeration to say the time I spent there involved excursions into some kind of other world; a parallel universe contiguous to, yet different from, our own. And though I'd query its likeness to anything as self-centered as Narcissus, I think such excursions did work upon the psyche a kind of meditative spell, causing it to still and pool in quiet contemplation.

My father's fishing certainly fits the blueprint Profumo and Swift sketch out. Yes, at one level, it was all quotidian enough: fishing was a hobby indulged in without flourish at an unremarkable spot conveniently located close to where we lived. Like me, Dad would have shrugged off talk of peering into another universe as so much flowery overstatement. Yet, in the way he and the other anglers worked the water; in the manner they prepared, dressed, interacted with each other; in their wielding of equipment and their handling of fish; in what was written in the club's record book (a thick, hard-backed ledger with a waterproof cover that was treated almost like a Bible), there was a definite strain of something more than commonplace. "Sacred" and "profane" may not quite fit – they suggest too clear-cut a distinction between two realms that are intimately entangled – but they flag up better than any other straightforward verbal pairing I can think of the way in which much of what took place at Boomer's reservoir involved a journeying between two states of being; two attitudes of mind and heart. Though of course the term would have made us bridle, a great deal of what we did there was, in essence, priestly. It involved a kind of ritualized performance of unspoken sacraments, an unacknowledged shamanism that mediated between two worlds.

V

Profumo and Swift assert that:

> It is not surprising that fish should embody our ideas of the mysterious and the magical, of regions not wholly within our power or ken.

Certainly there was something magical about catching a brown trout (*Salmo fario*) – a species with which Boomer's reservoir was amply stocked. They are beautiful fish. Indeed, in his *Observer's Book of Freshwater Fishes* (a well-thumbed volume in my boyhood library), Lawrence Wells claims that "if there can be said to be such a thing as a 'perfect fish' then that fish is the trout." There's remarkable variation in size, color and markings between different trout, but I've never seen one that's anything less than arresting in its beauty. When you catch one and finally see it close-up, instead of via those tantalizing glimpses of the fish in water, it's almost as if these sleek torpedoes of trimly muscled fish-flesh swim on into the eye, lodge there like a dart in the brain, and explode in a burst of chromatic spectacle, taking deeper, underlining, making more astonishing, what's hinted at when they first break the surface of the water. I can readily identify with the sentiments Izaak Walton records in *The Compleat Angler* (1653). On catching a trout he says: "the very shape and the enamelled colour of him hath been such as have joyed me to look on him." Yes, trout certainly "joyed me" to look upon, but a verbal account can catch only a trace of their lovely livery of enameled color. The barrel of the body is freckled with irregular clusters of circular markings – blacks, reds, browns, pinks and greens – a different constellation for each fish. To draw one from the water is to capture a kind of numinous splinter, glinting with white and silver, a tangible token plucked from another world.

Was it this sense of mediation between worlds – the angler drawing out on the invisible thread of his line hard evidence of something rainbow-beautiful below – that made us reach for "priest," centuries ago, when we were perfecting the tackle of our language, looking for words that fitted what we did? Or was it a priest's presence at a deathbed that accounted for our following of this particular etymological pathway – since death was meted out as soon as a fish was netted? I'm not sure of the exact steps leading to the derivation, but it seems to me entirely apt – catching the sacramental aspect of what's involved – that "priest" should be the name given to the club with which fishermen dispatch their quarry.

VI

My father's priest, the first one I ever met, was cold, thickset and murderous. Its lethal weight meant it always sank to the bottom of his canvas fishing bag. To get it, all you had to do was to reach in deeply, pushing aside fly-tin, souwester, spare socks, cigarettes, matches, gloves and other bits of tackle, until your fingers closed around its cold, snub-nosed bulk. It fitted snugly in the hand, adding to it a deadly weight. Big-headed, tapering slightly for a better grip, it was a polished wooden cosh whose dull sheen had about it a hint of sinister purpose. Yet, for all the ugliness of what it did, this bulbous wooden artifact also acted as a kind of miniature lightning conductor; its impact earthed the voltage that shimmers between this realm and its twin.

I often passed my father the priest once he'd netted a fish and brought it in. Sometimes, when I was older, under close supervision, I was initiated into wielding it myself. Not surprisingly, many regard fly-fishing as a cruel sport – the deliberate hooking of a living creature and dragging it in for slaughter via a line attached to the barbed spike on which the fish's bite has impaled it. What's involved sounds like some sort of obscene medieval torture. Was my father blind to the pain he was inflicting? Or did he just not care? Given the nature of fishing, it may seem implausible to claim he was a kind man, yet I don't believe there was any cruelty in him – or at least no more than runs in any of our veins.

In *Do Fish Feel Pain?* (2010), Victoria Braithwaite points out that: "we wouldn't accept killing chickens by throwing them into a tank of water and waiting for them to drown." Since that is so, "why don't we object to fish suffocating on trawler decks?" Braithwaite, Professor of Fisheries and Biology at Penn State University, sees "no logical reason why we should not extend to fish the same welfare considerations that we currently extend to birds and mammals." Her view is based on the well-supported conviction that there are as good grounds for supposing fish feel pain as there are for supposing birds and mammals do. The evidence she details makes disturbing reading. I wonder what my father would have made of her findings. Fishing was something he'd done since boyhood. It was simply part of his world. He wasn't oblivious to the suffering of fish, but whatever pangs of empathy or conscience he might have felt had long ago been subsumed beneath angling's traditional practices, its routines and rituals. I suspect he thought as little of the fish he caught as he did of farm animals when he was eating meat (and of course we ate the trout – they were a tasty seasonal addition to our household's menu). Yet he held in contemptuous disapproval those few anglers who withheld the coup de grâce, instead just landing their catch and letting it suffocate in air, thrashing on the ground until death brought eventual stillness. But I could tell he disliked using the priest, even though he did so with a practiced executioner's efficiency. I can still hear, echoing pitch-perfect in my memory, the exact sound made by the hard slap of wood on a fish's head, and the instant, lolling change that claimed the fish as its life was extirpated and it became, in that moment, just a corpse.

VII

According to David Profumo and Graham Swift:

> More than anything it is the glinting, tantalizing horizontal surface of the water, dividing so absolutely one realm from another, which gives angling its mystery, its magic, its endless speculation.

The sense of water as a veil, its surface separating the visible, everyday world from another realm, is not just a feature of fishing. It's (presumably) precisely this same sense that fed the ancient Celtic tradition of making votive offerings by throwing precious objects through the portal water offers, sending gifts to the unseen otherworld below.

Lough Gur in County Munster is perhaps the most famous site in Ireland where Bronze and Iron Age peoples submerged valuable artifacts in what we now interpret as attempted communication with their gods, attempts to reach out from this world into another. Metal axes, spearheads, swords and daggers have been retrieved from Lough Gur's waters. On a darker note, bodies were sometimes sunk in lakes and bogs as seasonal sacrifices to make the land fertile, offering bridegrooms to the brooding earth. Seamus Heaney has made rich symbolic use of such practices in "The Tollund Man" and "The Grauballe Man" – poems that point up disturbing similarities between such brutal betrothals and sectarian killings in modern Ulster.

The deliberate casting of objects into water is by no means confined to Ireland. When, for example, a pond near a mountain shrine in northern Japan was drained at the beginning of last century, in order to build a bridge for pilgrims, engineers found hundreds of bronze mirrors embedded in the mud. One of these, dating from around 1000 AD, eventually found its way to the British Museum. Neil MacGregor, the Museum's Director, comments: "People have been throwing valuable things into water for thousands of years." Archaeologists have retrieved things so disposed of from all over the world, as the Museum's collections amply attest.

The Japanese bronze mirror, a work of exquisite craftsmanship, was made in

Kyoto some ten centuries ago. It belonged to a member of an aristocratic family. According to MacGregor:

> At some point its owner decided to dispatch it, in the care of a priest, on a long journey to the northern shrine, and there it was thrown into the sacred pond – still holding within it the likeness of its owner and carrying a message to the other world. What neither owner nor priest could have guessed was that it would one day be a message to us.

VIII

My father required no priest as intermediary to help transport to Boomer's reservoir the precious object he consigned to its waters. It wasn't an offering to any deity, but whenever I think about it now I can't help seeing it as belonging to this same repertoire of human behavior; it's close kin to the throwing in of axe heads, swords and daggers. What he did had more of an air of ritual about it than any merely routine disposal.

I didn't witness the moment, so can only speculate about exactly how it happened. Did he throw it in, I wonder, or just slip it over the side of the boat? Was it done in daylight or, more furtively, after dark? (Night-fishing was something my father loved – he would have agreed with Walton's view that the best trout are likely to be caught then.) Did his secret offering make a splash as it hit the water, perhaps causing another angler to think a fish had jumped? Was it wrapped and weighted, or just tossed naked into the water, its own heaviness ensuring that it sank?

I can find answers to none of these questions now, long after my father's death. I've run different scenarios through my mind, but it's hard to determine which of these variations on a theme most closely matches what actually transpired. The boy who explored Boomer's reservoir was innocent of what his father had put into it – and I'm glad of that. I'd have been interested, of course, though shocked as well. It seems a proper withholding of knowledge that I wasn't told until I was an adult.

Dad never said much about the gun, only that it was a Beretta. He'd brought it back from the war, together with a box of ammunition. Long before I found out about it, I remember him telling me that one of his duties as an officer was preventing the troops under his command from bringing home potentially lethal ordnance as wartime souvenirs. Alongside the commonly favored bayonets, helmets, and enemy cap-badges, of which no notice was taken, some returning soldiers tried to secure as keepsakes live mortar rounds, grenades, artillery shells, and machineguns complete with belts of bullets. But he didn't tell me then – he didn't tell me for years – that he had himself succumbed to this same beach-combing urge. He must have put a high value on the gun to have brought it with him all the way from North Africa back to Ireland. Nor was his homecoming direct. He spent months recuperating from injuries, partly on board hospital ships, partly in hospitals in South Africa and England. I picture the gun's heavy, hidden lethality, an incongruous presence in a ward's bedside locker, as he lay being tended by doctors and nurses.

Why he wanted the gun I'm not sure. Had it saved his life? Did he feel safer with it? Was it just a wartime memento to which he'd become attached? Dad was reticent about it, saying little more than that he thought "it might come in handy someday." His father had been chased through the streets of Londonderry by IRA gunmen in the 1920s, only narrowly escaping with his life, so maybe Dad's sense of homecoming from the War wasn't to a peaceful country but to still contested territory where violence might flare again – as of course it did in 1969, though by then the Beretta had long settled in the mud at the bottom of Boomer's dam. Getting rid of it was one of the sacrifices of marriage. My mother insisted that it went. She hated having a gun in the house. For a short while after their wedding, it was kept in an old tin deed-box in a wardrobe in their bedroom – a mechanism of death within easy reach of where they must have lain together and made love. Finally, after repeated urgings, she got her way and Dad took the gun and bullets to the reservoir and let the water claim them. Did either of them come to regret it, I wonder? Perhaps, as Ulster plummeted into its years of civil strife, as bombings, shootings, and burnings-out increased in frequency, as intimidation became commonplace, they would have felt less vulnerable if they'd had a gun to hand, a secret weapon of last resort. Or maybe having such a weapon in the house would merely have increased the likelihood of violence overtaking them.

IX

From the way in which he spoke about it, my guess is that my father regarded the gun as a kind of talisman, something that symbolized one phase of his life. Throwing it into the reservoir constituted the crossing of a threshold, a final stepping away from the war-world, the young man's world of adventure, travel, danger, proximity to death, to an embracing of the settled world of marriage, job, and family responsibilities. However he viewed it, when I picture the scene now it becomes conflated in my mind with those ancient Japanese bronze mirrors thrown into the pond by pilgrims. Just as they were cast into the water bearing with them the reflections of their owners, so I picture the Beretta's opaque metal casing carrying invisibly on it the imprint of all those who had held it. How often had the gun been fired before it fell silent, stoppered by the water and the mud of Boomer's dam? Had this small black pistol ever killed anyone? Had my father used it to lethal effect against an enemy? Photographs of him from the war show him wearing a holstered revolver on his belt – standard issue for British army officers – but he told me once that he preferred the Beretta's size and smoothness of operation; it was lighter, faster, easier to use.

Beretta is one of the world's oldest gunsmiths. Established in the sixteenth century, there are records from as early as 1526 of the Arsenal of Venice ordering harquebus barrels from one Bartolomeo Beretta. To us, the harquebus is a primitive gun indeed. But as Saul Frampton points out in his intriguingly entitled study of Michel de Montaigne – *When I am Playing With My Cat How Do I Know She Is Not Playing With Me?* (2011) – it was "the AK47 of its age." Reflecting on the riding accident that nearly cost him his life, Montaigne notes that "The first thought that came to me was that I had gotten a harquebus shot to the head" (in fact another rider, on a heavier horse, had collided with him at speed). It could well have been Beretta pistols that Montaigne was talking about in the 1570s when he wrote in another essay (*Of War Horses*):

> But as for the pistol......except for the shock to the ear, with which by now everyone has become familiar, I think it is a weapon of very little effect, and hope that some day we shall abandon use of it.

How differently the history of armaments turned out! Montaigne's "weapon of very little effect" must have slain thousands – millions? – in the centuries since he wrote his assessment of it. On the smaller canvas of Ulster's troubles, such guns were certainly responsible for many deaths.

Thinking about Dad's Beretta sinking down through the water at Boomer's reservoir, its weight slowly pressing it further into the sediment on which it settled, I sometimes wonder about how many other pieces of illicit weaponry it would have joined there. Boomer's reservoir is no Lough Gur, but given its proximity to Belfast and our tendency to cast things into water, I'd be surprised if there wasn't a small arsenal of secret, submerged offerings peppering the mud. Perhaps in centuries to come they'll be retrieved and seem as antique to whatever generation finds them as a harquebus or sword seem to us. Whatever message these leavings carry to the future, they'll bear a likeness of us as surely as that bronze mirror carried a reflection of its owner's face.

X

Guns and wooden clubs, like spearheads and daggers, point to obvious territories of hurt. The image reflected in the mirror of our weaponry speaks unambiguously of the violence we do. But the last priest I encountered, who put me in mind of the first one I ever met, inflicted hurt via less obvious means. What reminded me of Boomer's reservoir after all these years, what made me stop and write these reflections about it, was a news story about a priest who lived in one of the houses that now ring the dam, claiming the land that used to be my Eden. I can't remember his name, or the details of his offences, nor do I wish to research such matters. All that's necessary to say is that he was found guilty of systematic child abuse over a period of many years – a manifestation of the poison that has so disfigured the body of institutional religion.

It was hard enough for me to learn to put things into a different perspective after what was laid down by my first acquaintance with a priest. For years the cold, thickset, murderous quality of my father's cast a shadow over the way I thought of priests in general. Yet these are trivial associations compared to those that must be branded into the word for anyone who has suffered abuse at the hands of a priest. Trying to find ways in which the pain of such victims may be tended is, of course, the paramount concern. But this kind of abuse also carries with it a linguistic violation. When something so completely divorces a word from its original sense, it may not be possible to retrieve it, to rehabilitate it for ordinary use. In such a situation, where words become corrupted, broken, it's worth remembering that they can have manifold senses and that not all of them are compromised. Priests come in more variety of forms than we might think. If one fails us, others can step forward to serve our need for mediation between self and other, sacred and profane, the mundane and the miraculous. Though they may seem unlikely hierophants, fishing, memories of a boyhood haunt, a wooden club, and a rusty gun long holstered in wet mud, have helped me gaze into life's waters and see the glitter there of things beyond the commonplace.

Thinking about the way in which words' associations shift and change, how their meanings are more flexible, more open to individual coloration than a dictionary's monochrome definitions can convey, it strikes me that writing has some similarities with casting precious objects into water. I guess language has become my reservoir now; with it I can try to restore that lost Eden of my childhood, throwing into its waters my chosen words, each one bearing with it some reflection of what I feel and think. Sentences, in their ripple and splash, can glint as enticingly as the enameled colors of a trout. And just as water has a "tantalizing horizontal surface" that divides "one realm from another," so language forms a kind of interface between one mind and another, one heart and another, allowing us to drop gifts into other consciousnesses and receive reciprocal bounty from them. Words can help us see into and share other people's worlds, and share ours with them in our turn. They let what we might even term our souls enjoy communion, allowing us to warm our isolation at the fire of kindred beings. Used with priestly care, sentences can perform that most essential sacrament: kindling hints of meaning beyond the dulled – and often damaged – diction that too often circumscribes us.

"When the time comes to lose them..."
(Reading Montaigne)

We should have wife, children, goods, and above all health, if we can; but we must not bind ourselves to them so strongly that our happiness depends on them. We must reserve a back shop all our own, entirely free, in which to establish our real liberty and our principal retreat and solitude. Here our ordinary conversation must be between us and ourselves, and so private that no outside association or communication can find a place; here we must talk and laugh as if without wife, without children, without possessions, without retinue and servants, so that, when the time comes to lose them, it will be nothing new to us to do without them.

Michel de Montaigne, "On Solitude"

I

When I was growing up in Northern Ireland, speedometers were regarded as unnecessary and dangerous accessories on a bike. I was forbidden to have one and envied boys who did. But even though it rankled, I could see the sense of this parental prohibition. Cycling down the road pell-mell, eyes glued to the dial, willing that red indicator needle to edge ever further up the scale, legs pounding the pedals furiously, crouching close to the handlebars to minimize wind-resistance – such rapt attention to speed meant a perilous disregard for traffic and pedestrians. In such circumstances, accidents were inevitable. Fortunately, none of my contemporaries suffered anything more than minor mishaps, despite a few close shaves. They were unrepentant, reckoning, in the foolhardy arithmetic of boys, that some trophy cuts and bruises were a small price to pay for being able to boast – improbably – that they'd reached thirty miles per hour.

Mileometers, by comparison, were considered safe, so my parents raised no objections when I got one. Mine was called a "cyclometer" (we never used the more technical-sounding "odometer"). It consisted of two parts: a little spur, designed to register each turn of the wheel; and the counter – a grey metal barrel about one-and-a-half inches long containing four rings of numerals, set side by side, visible through a rectangular window. The counter was mounted on a bracket on the front wheel-shaft, the spur was affixed to one of the spokes. Each time the wheel went round the spur clicked against the counter's mechanism and slowly turned the numbers. I don't know what portion of a mile is represented by one full revolution of a bicycle's wheel, but these were the increments by which, click by click, this slowly burgeoning measurement swelled.

The accumulating evidence of distance covered was a compelling novelty at first. But apart from this brief, initial phase, when I glanced down frequently to see how far I'd gone, I soon forgot the mileometer was there. The only other times it called attention to itself, in the distracting manner of a speedometer, were on those odd occasions when I happened to notice transitions between readings that seemed epochal in their own small way (from 99 to 100, for example), or if for some reason I wanted an exact measure of the distance between a journey's start and end.

I can still remember the pleasure of taking the virgin cyclometer out of its box, its four unsullied zeros lined up behind the pristine glass of the counter's tiny pane. I had a sense of achievement in gradually notching up those first few miles, and then a sporadic feeling of surprise mixed with satisfaction whenever I noticed how far I'd traveled. All those little bike rides that were so much a part of daily life back then – to friends' houses, to the shops, a race across the fields, going bird-watching, cycling from home to school and back – seemed to amount to something when they were put together and considered as a single measurement.

I can't remember now what my final tally amounted to, or what happened to the cyclometer, but I'm sure that all four rings of numbers were in use before I dismissed such a gadget as too childish an accessory to warrant transfer to the racing bike I bought when I was sixteen.

II

We all start with the corporeal equivalent of the cyclometer's virgin zeros. Then time ratchets up the hours and days, inexorably turning the wheel of our passage. Whether we look at it or not, the numbers on our life-counter are always turning, always moving towards that moment when they'll stop. Calibrated in years, a few of us call three numerals into play by the time we're done. But for most, two numbers are enough to mark the total distance traveled. Tragically, for many, a single figure suffices to record the brief duration of their lives. Of Michel de Montaigne's six children, only one survived beyond infancy, his beloved daughter Léonor.

No doubt these repeated infant bereavements, the death of his close friend Etienne de La Boétie, his own near-fatal riding accident, and the warfare, sectarian killing, famine and plague that beset France at this time (nearly half the population of Bordeaux succumbed to the black death in 1585) all contributed to Montaigne's intense sense of mortality. But I suspect there was also something in his individual cast of mind that made him vulnerable to having his awareness of life's brevity, its susceptibility to accident, honed to such a particular edge by his experiences – experiences that were by no means unusual for someone living in sixteenth century Europe. At that time, according to Saul Frampton, close to half the children born only required a single numeral to record their span of years. Average life-expectancy wasn't much over thirty. As Terence Cave points out, "the precariousness of life was no abstraction." Montaigne's writing is indelibly imbued with a sense of this precariousness. He was ever-mindful of the numbers on his life's mileometer, aware of their uncertain continuance, unknown total, and inevitable end. Reading Montaigne it sometimes feels like being on a bike whose clicking cyclometer is a constant refrain. Here is prose laced with a vivid realization of life's flow and transience. "I do not portray being," Montaigne says, "I portray passing."

Such passing means change not fixity. Montaigne recognizes his own "unstable posture" and suggests that anyone "who observes carefully" will "hardly find himself twice in the same state." His careful introspection finds him by turns: "Bashful, insolent; chaste, lascivious; talkative, taciturn; tough, delicate; clever, stupid; surly, affable; lying, truthful; learned, ignorant; liberal, miserly and prodigal." His essays explore the "gyration and discord" of this flux of impermanent states. Montaigne's patient soundings provide navigation charts that are sufficiently accurate still to be of use today to anyone seeking to understand the varied currents of the self. His life exemplifies the fact that, as Lydia Fakundiny puts it, "You are what you do with your time." Whatever he did, however his time was filled, it was done with a lucid awareness of time's passing and an unfailing interest in the experiences it contained. Kenneth Clark once described Leonardo da Vinci as "the most relentlessly curious man in history." Montaigne would surely have run him a close second.

III

One of the reasons I'm drawn to Montaigne is because there's an almost Buddhist feel to his outlook. His is a sensibility attuned to what followers of this great tradition refer to as *anicca* – impermanence – something so fundamental to our experience that it's regarded as one of three so-called "marks of existence." The other two – *dukkha* and *anatta* (roughly speaking, suffering and the fact that the self succumbs to change) – also find echoes in Montaigne. Taken alone, this could easily give the wrong impression – of a somber, if not morose, "sick soul" (to use William James's designation), someone preoccupied with the fleeting nature of our being, the unavoidability of pain, and the imminence of extinction. Yes, Montaigne is acutely aware of our finitude – he never loses sight of the turning numerals on life's cyclometer – but the impression that comes across is of a man of warmth and good humor, a genial conversationalist with endless curiosity about the world and an irrepressible zest for living, however hard the circumstances that attend it may be. "The surest sign of wisdom," writes Montaigne, "is constant cheerfulness." I find the Buddhist elements in the *Essays* attractive not because of their emphasis on impermanence, suffering and death, but because of the way in which Montaigne looks at these inevitabilities with an unclouded eye and takes them in his stride. His manner not infrequently recalls the robust, good humored serenity of Buddhism at its best.

Buddhism and Montaigne might seem an improbable, eccentric linkage built only on the shaky foundation of my personal idiosyncrasies – the fact that I happen to be an essayist who's been influenced by Buddhist thought. I find it reassuring, therefore, that one of the most perceptive modern commentators on Montaigne – Sarah Bakewell – also reaches for a Buddhist touchstone. She points to the way Montaigne seems sometimes to have achieved "an almost Zen-like discipline; an ability just to be." One of the reasons the *Essays* have exerted such an appeal over the centuries is that they record the outlook of a man who's able just to be, yet without shutting his eyes to uncomfortable truths. Rather than wearing the usual blinkers of custom and routine and drifting through life without thinking much about it, as so many of us do, Montaigne proceeds with a clear-sighted deliberation that's impressive. His was a life lived in pretty much continuous awareness of death – the kind of awareness that Philip Larkin expresses with magisterial, if chilling, fluency in his poem "Aubade." Montaigne's realization of time passing, his ability to "see what's really always there," namely that our lives are rushing to their end, is integral to the watermark of his personality; it pervades what he writes. For me, much of the appeal of Montaigne lies in the way in which, as you turn the pages of the essays you can hear the incessant click-click of life's cyclometer. Yet instead of being paralyzed or disheartened by this death-watch beetle in his timbers, far from reaching for some convenient set of blinkers or distractions, Montaigne surveys our doomed human vessel with a kind of dispassionate compassion that's slow to judge, quick to smile and question, determined to inquire. Instead of taking time's passing clicks merely as a countdown to disaster, Montaigne is fascinated by the cargoes that they carry. Reading his essays is like hearing the pounding of our mortal metronome parsed into meaningful rhythms.

IV

When the numbers on Montaigne's mortal cyclometer clicked round to September 13th 1592 his course was run. He died on that date (of quinsy and complications relating to that horrible affliction). Nearly four centuries later, Graham Good's *The Observing Self* was published, a book subtitled "Rediscovering the Essay." Appropriately, the opening chapter is devoted to Montaigne. According to Good, "Anyone who can look attentively, think freely, and write clearly can be an essayist; no other qualifications are needed." These are deceptively simple qualities to ask for. But I only need reflect on how often my looking is inattentive, my thinking chained to some dull presupposition or other, my writing muddled, to recognize the difficulty of the criteria Good lays down. And it becomes instantly apparent on reading Montaigne that he possessed these elusive attributes in abundant measure. (As an aside, I find it interesting that Good, one of the key modern authorities on the genre, is himself a Zen Buddhist and that he's recently explored the question "Could there be an affinity between Buddhism and the Essay?")

Sometimes I think of Montaigne as standing within a kind of impregnable palisade that, moment by moment draws more tightly round him. Like every individual, he's encircled by time's stockade. Our little fortresses of hours and days, the capsules of duration in which we draw our every breath of being, bear us through – define – our existence, but garrote us in the end. Time's cord loops round us, at once umbilical and lethal. Its lifeline-noose lays down iron laws and imperatives common to us all – but there's sufficient variation in its weave and texture, in how it falls upon us, how we wear it, to nurture the rich spectrum of diversity that enriches our humanity. One of its laws is that we are each alone; one of its imperatives that we seek companionship. It is the creative tension of solitude seeking company that powers one of our strongest drives: the urge to communicate. This is a powerful motive behind Montaigne's writing. "No pleasure," he says, "has any savor for me without communication."

In part, I think Montaigne's personality was cut into its particular shape by a kind of constant abrasion. His heightened awareness of the wash of time against him, the way he was always conscious of the click-click of life's cyclometer, acted like water or wind or sand on stone, smoothing and wearing the intimate landscape of his person into the unique features it displayed. Of course we all undergo such erosion – the impact of the world around us, how family, friends and strangers lay the touch of their influence upon our lives; the way our own biology hardwires us. I'm not sure what mesh of factors sets the level at which we're self-aware, or aware of time's passing; the extent to which we feel solitude and a desire to reach beyond it, but if Montaigne is anything to go by these key indices are all closely interlinked.

I've come to picture Montaigne consulting his life's cyclometer with the same frequency and intensity as my boyhood friends looked at their speedometers. But whereas their preoccupation with going as fast as possible made them blind to what was going on around them, Montaigne's preoccupation with life's passing led to more acute perception and, far from inculcating any kind of disregard for others, it enhanced his interest in them. It's these qualities that give Montaigne's prose its enduring appeal. They combine to form a kind of key that lets him unlock and throw open the shutters we usually close across sights we find unnerving, distasteful, commonplace or embarrassing. Whatever he looks at – sadness, friendship, sleep, smells, vanity, "the unruly liberty" of his penis – Montaigne's honesty is engaging. Throughout the essays, his readiness to lay things open on the page, his unflinching examination of idiocies, atrocities and intimacies, his preparedness to subject himself to the same scrutiny he brings to bear on others, is disarming. It creates an affectionate bond between reader and writer. Montaigne's is a voice that invites us to trust it. The humanity of its timbre makes light of the centuries that separate us.

V

My old cyclometer was calibrated on a simple scale, readily comprehended. Its four rings of numbers measured out distances it's easy to imagine. Even their maximum reading – 9,999 miles – gives a figure that the mind can encompass: the distance between France and Australia (or, to put it in terms more appropriate to a sixteenth century perspective, close to twenty times the length of the river Loire). A similar cyclometer geared to measure time would likewise give a manageable tally, graspable in straightforward examples. Click the numbers round to just a little over 400 and that's the stretch of years lying between Montaigne and us. Bring all four rings of numbers into play, set them to their maximum, and it only takes us back ten thousand years. Such measures don't challenge the comprehension, or stymie imagination's ability to generate pictures of what's meant.

Of course time's passing and life's fleetingness characterize our experience just as much as they did Montaigne's. But the cyclometers we have to face today throw our transience into even starker relief because of the scale we now know they're set to. We know, for example, that the Earth is around 4,600 million years old, that the first living cells appeared on it about 1,500 million years later. We know that the universe, of which our planet is so infinitesimal a part, came into being somewhere between 10 and 15 billion years ago. We know that, threaded through the immensities of space, there are hundreds of billions of galaxies. And when we turn to the stupendous array of microcosms surrounding us, innumerable cells, innumerable atoms lie beneath the simple visual structures we can see and touch. We also have a much more accurate picture of where we stand within the human swarm. "Worldometers" – a kind of global cyclometer website, its electronic counters clicking round continually – assesses current world population as over seven billion. The number of births and deaths on any given day is shown, likewise births and deaths per year. But what I find most arresting in the daunting array of numbers provided by Worldometers is the facility to estimate an individual's place in terms of where they fall in the long line of people who have lived since humanity began. When I was born I was the 76,136,299,830th representative of *Homo sapiens* to appear.

It's easy to be unnerved by such multitudes, to feel any sense of individual significance swept away as we recognize how minutely fractional a part of the species we are – the proverbial dust speck or sand grain or whatever other icon of irrelevance appeals. In this blizzard of other lives, each of us stakes out our tiny claim of time and space, pirouettes within it for an instant, obedient to our desires and fears, affections and regrets. And then we vanish – we have to bid goodbye to whatever relationships we forged, whatever achievements we accomplished, whatever possessions we accumulated, "When the time comes (as it will come) to lose them." Surrounded by inconceivable numbers of others, we are yet each of us alone, sequestered in the solitude of individual existence.

Click, and at any moment we can take readings from the cyclometers that are whirring all around us. We can look at the numbers that show our age, the temporal distance that we've traveled. Spin the counter and we're gone; our time is past. Spin it in the other direction and we've yet to be. Montaigne was right, surely, to insist that "it is as foolish to lament that we shall not be alive a hundred years from now as it is to lament that we were not alive a hundred years ago." From any personal perspective, the vastness of time is almost entirely characterized by our absence. Lament may be foolish, but wonder is not. Stand back and spin the cyclometer so that individual history blurs and species-calibration comes into play. We're soon back to when humanity had yet to hatch from its pre-hominid precursors, and beyond that to when life was no more than unicellular. Or switch to a geological scale and spin the massive numbers that it bears: go back a million years, ten million, a billion, or go forward by the same. These dizzying readings are hard to grasp beyond a vague apprehension of annihilating extent and duration. Our tiny mark is easily overlooked, so vast is the canvas on which it's painted.

VI

If, after leaving Montaigne's chateau, you head towards Menesterol and Mussidan, then drive east along the busy A69/E70 for nearly 60 miles, turning off for Montignac, you'll soon come to one of the most famous Stone Age sites in Europe – Lascaux. It's a drive of about an hour and a half through the beautiful Dordogne countryside. I like the fact that as he sat in the round tower of his library, this cave of treasures lay waiting to be discovered only 85 miles away. The magnificent Paleolithic art at Lascaux is thought to be over 17,000 years old. There are almost 2,000 painted forms in the caves, showing animals (by far the largest group), one human figure and various abstract marks, mostly dots and squares. Lascaux was discovered accidentally in September 1940 by 18-year-old Marcel Ravidat and three friends. An unpromising hole they stumbled on turned out to lead into another world – an interlinked series of caverns, the walls and ceilings of which were resplendent with images that are now so much a part of our common cultural heritage they more or less define what we understand by prehistoric art (though the caves themselves have been closed to the public since 1963 to avoid visitors' breath further damaging the colored pigments).

It's been suggested that the paintings may have served some kind of astronomical function; that they show the moon's phases and provide rudimentary star charts, attempts to plot and orientate our position, to map where we are in relation to the heavenly bodies above us. Whatever their stellar significance, it's certain that these magnificent artworks represent a reaching out, an attempt to find navigable meanings, touchstones to help us plot a course through life. That's a property they share with the essays that would be written millennia later less than a hundred miles away.

Montaigne extended hospitality to anyone who called at his chateau. With some temporal sleight of hand, it's easy to imagine him inviting the ancient Lascaux artists to sit down and talk with him over a glass of wine. He'd have been interested in surmounting the communication barrier that lack of a common language would have interposed between them, interested in asking about their art and what it meant, interested in their mode of dress, their diet, customs, beliefs, sex life, body odor. Montaigne would have relished trying to understand them – as he tried to understand cannibals, cripples, thumbs, cruelty, drunkenness, sleep, ancient customs, liars, and a host of other topics. In each case, he would further understand himself in the process. He was ever obedient to one of the educational principles he laid down – that we should "rub and polish our brains by contact with those of others."

When the Lascaux paintings were done, it's unlikely the world's population was much over a million. Our swarm has grown enormously since then: 100

million by 3000 BC; 250 million by the time of Christ; around 450 million during Montaigne's lifetime; the stupendous current total. Each of these millions lived as we do now; sheathed in their solitude, shaped by experience, garnering memories as local and particular as those of my boyhood cyclometer. We each reach out to others, strive and falter. All of us perish. Whatever number time ratchets up on our individual mileometers in terms of days and years, whatever we dream and dread, every person who has ever lived adds the solitaire of their precious life to the great sum of humans there have been. We are all spurs on the species' wheel clicking round its numbers.

VII

Despite the torrent of lives to which we each contribute the single droplet of ourselves, we lack the seamlessness of liquid. Instead, we're marooned in our own quiet pool; the inalienable, detached solitude that rings our person giving us space to be the individuals we are. However much we're part of stupefying measures of time and number, there is about us an aura of private singularity; workable specificity; the impregnable fastness of the individual psyche. Montaigne speaks out of, and into, precisely that nerve of solitude.

According to Graham Good, "At heart, the essay is the voice of the individual." That, I think, is why we listen to it. Individual voices are pitched at a level we can savor, whereas the full chorus of the human swarm would be overwhelming. In *Middlemarch*, George Eliot famously speculated about what it might be like if we could hear grass grow and the beat of squirrels' hearts. Such heightened perception would, she warned, be more than we could bear – "and we should die of that roar which lies on the other side of silence." The sound of seven billion voices is a daunting prospect. Yet, contained in what Richard Chadbourne calls "the most famous" of Montaigne's assertions – that "Each person carries the entire form of the human condition," there's a suggestion that, through any life, we can eavesdrop on every life.

My boyhood cycling companions staring fixedly at their speedometers, Montaigne's short-lived infants; the Lascaux artists; those in plague times whom Montaigne witnessed digging their own graves and pulling the earth over themselves in mortal desperation; George Eliot, Graham Good, whoever's eyes are now upon this sentence; any of the billions of us swarming across the globe – *everyone* – acts as a kind of portal. Discover how to open us, and you're led into panoramas that are incredible in what they can reveal. Explore our story even just a little way and we're soon taken into astonishing vistas. This is what conjures essays. Like philosophy, they begin with wonder. Montaigne, the masterful originator of the genre, was adept at opening the portal of the seemingly ordinary and seeing the extraordinary dimensions just behind it. He may have had a simpler purview than the one confronting us today, but he had a keen understanding of the way "all subjects are linked with one another." That being the case, he laid down a dictum that resonates through the history of the essay: "Any topic is fertile for me. A fly will serve my purpose."

Montaigne's essays provide images as compelling as any Lascaux bison. Reading them, we tap into the same vein of human endeavor that led our Stone Age precursors to blow colored pigment through hollow bones, creating art that still moves us. Such diverse efforts connect us to one of our most fundamental urges: to seek meaning; to understand ourselves. In that connection we may, perhaps, find some comfort to blow through our own mortal bones as we face up to what we can't evade "When the time comes to lose them."

*   *   *

"Solitude" isn't the kind of thing I normally think about, at least not directly. My writing stems from specific objects and events; it's firmly anchored in the particular. I'm wary of the approach taken by previous generations of essayists where – preceded by "on" or "of" – some wide-ranging topic is announced and readers are treated to a few pages of amiable enough reflection, but pitched at a level of such generality as to be close to vacuous. I find a few such pieces perceptive, some of historical significance, but the majority of no interest whatsoever. It amuses me – though not enough to compensate for reading what's tedious – that their prepositional "on" is so far off the mark. In terms of my attention, this kind of "on" triggers a swift turning off.

I was uneasy, therefore, to find myself writing an essay for *Reading Life* that took an "on" essay as its main point of reference. The cyclometer was an intuitive, preemptive countermove against being drawn into the kind of essay whose day, I think, is done. Some part of my psyche, seeing me poised to plunge into dubious waters, threw me the memory-nugget lifebelt of the cyclometer – something hard, specific, definite, rooted in the particularities of time and place that define me; an antidote to any breezy abstractions that "on" might tempt me into making.

Of course the way that "on" means "off" rarely applies to Montaigne. He's an exception to this – as to so many – rules. In any case, you can't judge his essays by their titles. The relationship between them and what he says is loose, tangential, vague – sometimes close to nonexistent. (In part this is due to what Patrick Henry calls "façade titles", which were "designed to trick the censor into missing the hidden, heterodox, or otherwise subversive subject.")

Although it's tempting to present this essay as an echo of Montaigne's of the same title, that would be misleading. An echo suggests a mirror image, something that paces out the same essential shape, albeit at a distance. It is a kind of aural shadow. Echoes wear the livery of repetition, even mimicry; they carry only the residue of a sound already made, rather than making their own original contribution. Although my musings on solitude were occasioned by reading Montaigne, I hope what I've written does more than echo what he says. An echo would be poor homage to a writer I esteem.

Why "On Solitude"? It's not one of Montaigne's great essays, nor does it reflect a principal characteristic of his personality. Montaigne is the most convivial of men, "born for company and friendship" as he asserts himself. In "A Consideration Upon Cicero" – which is, in effect, the second part of his essay "On Solitude" – he says that he would have preferred letters to essays as the "form to publish my sallies," if only he had "had someone to talk to." The sense of the man that comes across in his writing is of someone genial and talkative who relishes company. Despite his retirement from the affairs of the world, it would be a mistake to see him as a recluse recording his thoughts in lonely isolation. Terence Cave is right to stress the conversational mode of the essays. "Although Montaigne often depicts himself thinking and writing in solitude," says Cave, "he always imagines his writing directed towards others." The essays aren't soliloquies. Rather, they're attempts to reach out and engage others in his ruminations. The sense of conversation, rather than monologue, is enhanced by the frequency with which Montaigne refers to – and quotes from – other writers. Nonetheless, despite all this chatty congeniality, solitude is an essential characteristic of Montaigne – as it is of every individual. How the unique torques and contours of our personality are shaped to form the gradients that make us, is clearly a complicated matter. It depends on a complex set of formulae involving numerous factors. But whatever the unique individual sum may be that makes us who we are, it's held in solution by the water of our solitude.

The title I've chosen for this essay is taken from Montaigne's words about marriage, family, material possessions, and "above all health." He sees the value of such things, but also counsels awareness of the fact that we shall, inevitably, have to part from them. I hope the haunting resonance of his seven words "When the time comes to lose them..." – the ellipsis pointing to our inevitable fate – will act as reminders of our essential solitariness and our need to clad it, albeit temporarily, in the kind of warm reflective apparel that Montaigne provides so richly.

Tracks
(Reading footprints in the snow)

I

I've learned two new words this week – "sett" and "clough" – and take them with me as we walk in the snowy woods around the house. A sett is a roughly shaped rectangle of flat stone used for paving. Compared with cobbles, setts are larger, less regular; they don't possess the same gently rounded uniformity. The narrow streets of Heptonstall, the nearest village to the house, are paved with setts. Their uneven slab patchwork underfoot accentuates the sense of quaintness, antiquity, and hardness already created by the tightly huddled houses, built in the same local stone. Its dark-grained hue allows no hint of mellowness.

A clough is a steeply wooded valley, its incline sufficiently extreme to make it almost a ravine. The house has terraces cut into the clough on which it's built and looks out at an equally steep rise of land on the other side of a small river. The river runs along the base of the deep v-shape formed by the gradients that flank it all along this tree-stippled gorge. From the house you can sometimes hear the river and so infer its presence from that, or from the river-suggestive lie of the land. But the steepness of the slope means that it's only when you walk further down the clough that the glittering ribbon of water actually becomes visible.

There are seven others walking with me. We proceed slowly, taking care. The snow is sufficiently deep in places for us to sink suddenly up to our knees or further, but the paths we mostly keep to, though slippery, are either cleared or topped with a hard-packed crust that bears our weight. It hasn't snowed since we arrived here four days ago, but it's stayed cold enough for the land to keep its wintry cladding, however unseasonable this seems for England in late March.

One part of the clough we're walking through is cliffed with bare rock in a little dell. So many giant icicles have formed in this miniature, quarry-like gully that it has the air of some kind of improbably pretty magic grotto, a suitable abode for frost-spangled sprites and fairies. Inevitably, some of us stop to photograph it. But the spell of the place – the moment – is impossible to catch in any image.

The dry-stone walls bordering the steeply sloping paths and fields have acted like snow dams. In some places the wind has herded such deep accumulations against them that it will take days to melt, even when the temperature begins to rise. In other places the wind has blown the ground clear of all but a whispered remnant of white, like the thin dusting of icing-sugar on a cake.

Turning over my two newly acquired words as I walk, I'm pleased to find that their contiguity in mind is echoed in the landscape. Some of the steps and paths that vein the clough with the navigable routes we follow are beaded with setts. Finding their dark, solid bulk underfoot, visible here and there where the snow has thinned enough, is like catching glimpses of the broad, muscled backs of fish in a river, their solid forms effortlessly suspended just beneath the surface of the water.

These narrow, sett-studded thoroughfares were built to facilitate the tread of workers' feet to and from the riverside mills. These are long deserted and mostly in ruins, but substantial traces of some of their buildings remain, clustered around the foot of two massive stone chimneys that are visible from the house. Not only are the chimneys still standing, they appear more or less intact. At first glance through the trees they're easy to miss, despite their size; their resemblance to gigantic branchless trunks bestows a kind of camouflage. When you get nearer, their scale and symmetry betrays them as something made, not natural. These stony remnants – like the name "Weavers' Square" in Heptonstall – provide clues to the history that has left its script written on the landscape: this area was once at the center of a thriving wool industry.

My interest in words is shared by my companions. The fact that we deal in them rather than the more tangible commodities that led to the building of the house where we're staying and the now derelict mills whose chimneys are visible from its terraces, provides a ready symbol for the sea-change that has washed through this place over the last few centuries. What we're intent on weaving is very different from what the weavers of Heptonstall made on their looms – though I hope we bring to our task a care and industry and concentration that they would have recognized; vital elements in our craft as in theirs.

II

We're staying at Lumb Bank in the North of England. This is how the house is described in the information folders left in every bedroom:

> Lumb Bank is a fine example of a twenty-acre Yorkshire mill-owner's estate. However, it dates back to the late medieval period, with the current development built in two stages during the mid- and late- Georgian period.

Whatever its origin and early history, the place is best known now for wordcraft, rather than anything to do with mills. Lumb Bank used to be the home of poet Ted Hughes, who was born in the nearby village of Mytholmroyd. He bought the property in 1969. Twenty years later it was acquired by the Arvon Foundation, a charity that promotes creative writing. Arvon now run Lumb Bank as one of their residential writing centers.

I'm here for a week as one of the tutors on a writing course. Cancellations due to snow have whittled the group down to less than half of what the house can accommodate. Some have traveled a considerable distance to be here. Those coming from Switzerland, Belgium and a long way south of London make my six-hour journey from Scotland seem short. None of us have met before, but the mix of personalities works well. Everyone is seriously committed to advancing their own writing, and seriously interested in what they can learn from, and contribute to, the writing of others in the group. But this seriousness is leavened with a ready sense of humor and an appreciation of the rare privilege of being able to spend time at this literary haven, temporarily freed from the routine distractions and demands of everyday life (like the other Arvon centers, Lumb Bank deliberately eschews TV and internet).

Though not slavishly, we follow the pattern Arvon recommends for all their writing courses: mornings are for workshops, afternoons are when students focus on their own writing and have individual sessions with tutors. Evenings are devoted to conversation and readings. In the middle of the week a guest writer visits. On the last evening students read from what they've written during the course.

As so often when I'm supposedly the teacher, I learn a lot. I'm impressed by the quality of the work that emerges and by the dedication people bring to the mysterious, compelling process of putting words together on the page or screen. Amidst the claims of home and family, the demands of careers, the difficulties – in some cases – of prolonged illness, the pressure on time and energy from all sorts of other commitments, everyone somehow manages to sustain a writing life. Watching them write as we sit at the large wooden table in the dining room, I'm struck by the thought that pens and keyboards act like shamanic devices; ritual implements that mediate between one world and another. Through them, imagination, perception, intellection – all the gathered energies of the psyche – are channeled into a communicable form. Via the densely coded fibers of language, we call into being in our notebooks some token of ourselves. Reading out our warp and weft of words we offer this to others, watch and listen as it falls upon the fabric of their mind and they respond with a reciprocal giving of themselves. It's as if writing allows a way of running nerves direct from one life into others; jump-leads through which we can share the strange, compelling electricity of our experience. Frequently in the course of the week I'm reminded of an observation in Strunk and White's *Elements of Style*:

> Creative writing is communication through revelation – it is the Self escaping into the open. No writer long remains incognito.

For the most part we just write; read what we've written; comment, reflect, revise; talk about what we're attempting and how the harnesses of composition can sometimes chafe, sometimes allow us – seemingly with incommensurable effort – to pull loads of such astonishing weight and texture that our accomplishment ambushes us with one of those moments of delighted surprise that stud the writing process. But one morning, instead of settling straight away to write, we start the day by walking in the snowy woods around the house. As we set off, "sett" and "clough" are still fresh in my mind from a conversation that was sparked by their appearance in a poem written – and read out – on the first day of the course. Neither word is yet bedded down by familiarity and use so that it fits smoothly, unnoticeably, into the accumulated silt of my word-hoard. Instead, they both jut out, keep catching my attention, so that I have a sense of being accompanied as I walk by two spectral companions, verbal ghost-hounds that dash and sniff through my thoughts with a kind of puppyish exuberance.

We're not just walking – though there'd be nothing wrong with that, particularly on such a fine morning when the sun and snow combine to add a special luster to the already lovely woodland around Lumb Bank. We're walking with a view to writing. The idea – suggested by one of the group – is to find some object that appeals and to use it as a starting point for a piece of prose or poetry.

III

Since I'm tutoring the course, I'm exempted from having to find an object to write about at the morning's workshop session. But I'm a beachcomber at heart and am susceptible to the power of objects to nudge narratives into being. I'm fascinated by the potential even the most commonplace things possess to spark a thread of thought, begin a story. I know from my own writing how often it's some found article that offers the way into a stratum of telling; provides a kind of shaft or trapdoor into those webs of words that lure our attention into the mazes of their unfolding. As it happens, nothing I can pick up and carry with me catches my eye on this occasion, but I'm powerfully struck by something I glimpse as we're walking.

We return to the house at the agreed time, having gone our individual ways after a communal beginning. On the long wooden table in the dining room, alongside laptops, notebooks, a scattering of pens and coffee cups and discarded scarves and gloves, there's now a selection of objects: a small block of stone evidently broken off a sett; a lichen covered twig; a sprig of holly; two pebbles; a feather. As the students write their object-related pieces, I scribble notes in a cheap school jotter. I'll eventually develop these untidy musings into the words you're reading now.

What's struck me on the walk is nothing extraordinary – until, that is, you look past the camouflage of the mundane. It's just our footprints in the snow. Whatever we write when we're back in the warmth of the house, we leave a more poignant and pregnant signature on the ground outside via this natural script that issues from us automatically, effortlessly, with every step we take. It may lack the deliberation of our compositions, but there's an eloquence about our tracks that's hard to match in words.

The poignancy of our footprints lies in the way in which transience is so compellingly suggested by them. Here's the unique impress of a person, warm, alive and breathing, the weight of their body, their vital substance, pressing down to leave behind, like a perfect scale fallen from a butterfly's wing, a delicate trace of their presence – and of their absence. For a footprint is innately bilingual. It speaks on the one hand of someone's being here and, on the other, of their having gone; the intertwined mysteries of being and not being are corded into each tread as surely as the patterns on the sole of whatever footwear shods the walker's feet. The tracks bear with them the certainty that they're fated to disappear as soon as the snow thaws – a moment which, however cold it is now, can't be far away. Given their inevitable short-livedness, it's hard not to move from footprints to our own mortality; they are potent reminders of life's fast-melting nature.

It's not just the obvious temporariness of our footprints in the snow that flags up this wider sense of finitude. Our transience is also emphasized by the fact that being here together at Lumb Bank is just a brief association. We've been thrown together for a few days only. Once we disperse, return to our ordinary lives, we're unlikely ever to see each other again. This is one of those fleeting meetings, one life with others, which will not be repeated. Our passage through the days is routinely littered with goodbyes that are as final as any uttered on a deathbed.

The tracks are pregnant in part because of their indelible poignancy, the way they interlace with and emphasize our evanescence. But the sense they convey of being heavily laden with a significance that goes beyond their purely visual form, also stems from the way in which they're so suggestive of the individuals who left them. Looking at the size of a footprint, noticing the pattern of the tread, the angle and depth of its imprint, the way these steps were laid here on the ground, is to realize that each one is the unique call-sign of the feet-ankles-knees-thighs-crotch-belly-torso-shoulders-arms-and-head that together pour the weight of someone into the precise mold of their particular gravity, so that every print resonates with an intimate sense of person. It's not just the raw weight of meat and bone and sinew pressing here that makes these tracks. Their specificity is molded by the coefficients of age and race and gender; the looped intricacies of character, circumstance, relationship. The tracks give plaintive voice to the fact of fleeting lives, leaving behind as momentary testament these whispered traces in the snow; fugitive witnesses to their passing.

IV

In the cowboy films I watched when I was a boy, my favorite character was always the tracker, a solitary figure usually cast as taciturn, mysteriously expert, tough, and frequently morose. Trackers tended to be inscrutable, unpredictable, liable to go their own way, stubbornly determined. What I liked best about them was their independence and self-sufficiency, the way they could see things at a glance that others didn't notice. They could read the minutiae of a landscape, tell from the subtlest signs what had happened there. To me, they made the cavalry and cowboys, the gunslingers and ordinary braves and squaws seem like illiterates, blind to what was written in the world around them. Trackers could sniff the air as discerningly as whiskey blenders nose a malt. When they tasted the earth they were as alert to its flavors as any geologist. Even the slightest crease in a blade of grass acted like a compass needle for them. With their ear pressed close to a canyon's stony floor, they could detect sounds – vibrations – imperceptible to ordinary listening. Trackers seemed able to catch invisible letters borne on the breeze and reassemble from them an alphabet that allowed them to spell out what the wind had seen as it blew across landscapes that remained blankly inscrutable to others. Fluent in some ancient earth-language that everyone else had forgotten, trackers were able to decode its secret scripts and read from them the story of who had passed through a place, and what they had done there, however empty of information the surroundings might appear. Trackers were so utterly in tune with things, so much a part of the land, that they were securely at home in the world for all their outsider status in the eyes of others. Trackers possessed a rooted fixity denied to those other stock characters in Westerns who, by comparison, seemed superficial, unanchored to anything more substantial than their own flimsy stereotypes. I know, of course, that my romanticized, exaggerated image of the tracker is a stereotype too – but it was one that held in its delineation something that seemed worthwhile, unlike the superficial posturing of the usual heroes and villains.

After our object-seeking walk in the snow, we sit and write, clustered around the large wooden table that dominates Lumb Bank's dining room. From its place on the wall, next to a gold-framed mirror, a large photograph of Ted Hughes looks down at us. There are also framed hand-written copies of some of his poems hanging in a line along another wall, neat exhortations of completion, totems of the elusive finished article towards which all of us are struggling: the written word cast exactly as its writer wants it. The students write about the various objects they've collected and I think about the footprints we've left in the snow outside. Looking at the people gathered silently together in this room, I pair the marks their treads have left with what I know about their lives. Of course I don't know much, just what's emerged from conversation, from reading what they've written and discussing it with them, and from what the eye can see – glimpses and hints of other lives. I'm no expert tracker in the mold of my childhood film heroes, but I'm powerfully reminded of them when I realize how much a footprint holds.

For all our commonalities of form and fate, I picture life's register of experiences cutting the notches of its particular unfolding – moment by moment – into our soles, each according to our individual pattern, so that even if we happened to be identically shod and followed the same pathway exactly, no two of us would leave behind the same trail to mark our passing. Unlike my idealized tracker, I can't make many point-by-point connections between these footprints in the snow and the specific lives that left them. In my tracking, it's imagination rather than literal decoding that offers the key to understanding what our prints portend. The reading that imagination offers can't make the boast of being a faithful transcription of individual particularities, but there's surely a sense in which it offers perspectives that are more in tune with the contours of our lives than are the shrinking cartographies that are all our everyday diction normally allows. Our ordinary vocabulary, with all the ready labels it imposes, downplays the nature of things; our usual cadences of naming tend towards such a degree of simplification that it sometimes seems more akin to distortion. Often I feel I'm reading our life-spoor as ineptly – as crudely – as the most obtuse cavalry sergeant, unable to see beyond the cul-de-sac of rules and regulations; the gridlock of conventional perspective with its attenuated, blinkered vision.

V

When I look at the tracks we've left and think about what's invisibly written in them, an entirely different picture emerges from the one that immediately strikes the eye – the simple geometrical designs cut into our boot soles. Instead of any combination of circles, chevrons, triangles and squares, I imagine footprints showing within their outlines no mere cut symmetries designed to bolster grip, but all the footfalls an individual has placed upon the earth distilled into one concentrated pattern. This composite print – occupying dimensions of reflection that make light of the confines of literal space – includes the embryo's ungrounded, floating tread; the tiny barefoot prints of the newly born, not yet laid upon the earth; the toddler's first steps; the youth's, the adult's; steps taken shod and barefoot, eagerly, reluctantly, in pleasure and in pain; our walking lives, each step accompanied by whatever thoughts and feelings were harbored in the fastness of our being at that moment as we moved from one day to the next, progressing from our infancy to our end, step by step. Written into this imagined mosaic tread-of-treads is the unique signature impress of a life; one individual's existence coded into a dense concentrate and announced in every tread. Each footprint sings out the delicate weave of a biography from its inception to its unthreading.

Examining the complex configurations left by such prints, it's possible to decipher far more than the secret story of one life. Looking closely at our tracks via the optic of an informed and inquiring imagination, the years cascade away, peel back time's crusting, so that the present reveals layer after layer beneath it, reaching back beyond even the embryo's ground-virgin foot. A further story – a continuation of the story – lies coiled within the visible prints left by every individual as they tread the course of their lifespan. This is the hidden spring in our step, the nerve that sparked us into being, the livewire of our lineage pulsating with the species' voltage. Considering it, it's clear that we're like icebergs in the amount of us that's evident; our lives are only jagged points momentarily breaking the surface of the sea of being. Beneath them our back-story burgeons into a bulk that dwarfs the tiny portion that we think of as ourselves.

Before the embryo's foot formed, there was a nub of undifferentiated flesh poised to quicken into specific parts. Before that nub cohered into existence in the conjugal coalescence of constituent egg and sperm, it was something held implicit in the two individuals who came before it. Their footsteps led them to walk together for a while, led to their mating and the issue of the entity whose tread – years later – would catch my eye in the snow around Lumb Bank. But that's to track things quickly back only a little of the way, to follow the trail just around the first bend of its meandering. An expert tracker could pursue it further, not only following the intricate twists and turns of an individual life to the two progenitors who begot it, but – tasting the air, reading the earth, kneeling to check the angle of inflexion of each life's trodden grass blades of circumstance

– the trail could be followed further back through the knots and whorls of that couples' lives, their togetherness, to those who, in turn, walked the earth before them, sparking the next generation into being. Our tracks lead back for centuries, today's footprints connecting with those that came before, all of them part of the complicated tangle of lifelines that proliferate into our multiple-peopled story; the heavy tread of heritage.

The tracks in the snow that caught my eye that morning offer a portal into nothing less than human history, itself only one brief trail in the spoor that life has woven. Within its signature shape, each footprint suggests a spiraling back through the eons, back to the 1.5 million-year-old footprints that are the earliest yet found to display our modern foot's anatomy; back to the 3.7 million-year-old tracks of *Australopithecus afarensis*, found in volcanic ash in Laetoli, Tanzania; back further until our recognizable print edges into nothing we would recognize as even proto-human, as we go back through the millennia towards the mystery of beginnings. There is so much more in the script our tracks have left than we could ever write down, however long we sat together at the wooden table in Lumb Bank's dining room. If a footprint held the cargo of its story literally, rather than imaginatively, it would leave a tread that was meters – miles – deep, sinking through earth and stone as readily as we sink in snowdrifts. A tracker might kneel before such tracks in stupefied amazement – even awe – left reeling and disorientated by the supersaturated wealth of clues and signals they contain.

VI

Of course Lumb Bank possesses trails of its own, traces of august passage that literary trackers like to follow. To sit in the Library, knowing this is where Ted Hughes, Seamus Heaney, Philip Larkin and Charles Causley sat together to read through all 30,000 entries in the first Arvon International Poetry Competition (won by Andrew Motion, who succeeded Hughes as Poet Laureate), is to have a sense of placing your own foot into an impressive set of found prints, testing for fit and seeing how different your tread is compared to what came before. With Ted Hughes's portrait photograph and poems on the walls, and the knowledge that once the house was his, there's also a more than occasional wondering about the life he lived here, a curiosity about the course it followed. Did he ever stand in exactly this same spot where we now stand, looking out the window, gazing at the same view? What occupied his mind, what moved his heart, as he stood here, his body warming the same space that's now warmed by us? Given his marriage to Sylvia Plath, her tragic, shocking suicide, and all that's been written about them, it's perhaps inevitable that one's thoughts touch particularly on their relationship, speculate about the textures of its alignment and derailment; how their personalities and bodies fitted snugly together, how they strained and jarred. Since Plath is buried in Heptonstall churchyard, only twenty minutes walk from the house, many of those who come on writing courses follow the steep path from Lumb Bank to the main road and then down the sett-flagged main street of the village in order to find the poet's grave. Why? To pay their respects – or just stare and speculate at what's become a kind of local attraction? Do we merely succumb to the fatuous magnetism of celebrity, attractive even in death (perhaps magnified by death), or is it something else that draws us?

The cemetery is in deep snow throughout our time at Lumb Bank, so that it acts as a kind of absorbent page, recording the steps of every visitor like an untidy swarm of smudged vowels and consonants, inarticulate in their wanderings and overlappings. I find it oddly moving to discover when I'm there a selection of the same tracks that I'm familiar with from the marks our group has left in the woods around the house. Thinking about these tracks in the snow, clustered at this modest grave – through whose icy covering some dwarf narcissi are showing their yellow blooms – I'm reminded of a question asked by one member of our group before we left Lumb Bank on our object-seeking walk: "Are we all going in the same direction?" The question is meant in an immediate, practical sense of course – are we going to walk together as one group or each go our separate ways? – but it elicits a joking reply pitched at a different level altogether. The dissonance occasions laughter. This ability to smile at what might leave us trembling in terror, is surely one of our more admirable human traits. For we are all going in the same direction; our tracks lead inexorably to the same full stop that punctuated Sylvia Plath's life, as it punctuates every life; that final period beyond which our voices fall silent.

On the headstone, below "In Memory Sylvia Plath Hughes 1932-1963," there are two lines of verse:

Even amidst fierce flames
The golden lotus can be planted

Opinion differs as to the provenance of these words. Some suggest the *Bhaga-vad Gita*, others Wu Cheng'en's great sixteenth century work, *Journey to the West*. Occasionally they're attributed – I think mistakenly – to Ted Hughes himself. When I read them, I'm reminded of lines from Plath's "Morning Song" (in *Ariel*, posthumously published in 1965). "The golden lotus" summons back to mind her image of "a fat gold watch":

> Love set you going like a fat gold watch.
> The midwife slapped your footsoles, and your bald cry
> Took its place among the elements.

The tracks we weave through the elements, the tick-tock steps of our life's gold watch, the patterns that our footsoles trace from birth to death, are an infinitesimal filigree in the spoor of our species. Even our best poet-trackers are hard-pressed to map the route we follow, or to chronicle the nature of our journey. Often, the contours we are bound to elude even the most carefully composed tracings. Words are denied the oxygen they need at the temporal altitudes our steps lead to and issue from.

We could spend a lifetime attempting to decode the natural hieroglyphics left by our trail. But it remains uncertain if our footprints provide any kind of alphabet with which we might spell out meanings beyond the ad hoc patterns created by our steps. Does our human thread, spun across such daunting distances of time and space, in the end admit of any more intelligible alignment than whatever shapes our lives weave out? Are the cluster of tracks our slapped and cradled footsoles make upon the surface of the planet just the jumbled letters of happenstance, or can they be parsed into declensions that tap into seams of significance beyond our ordinary tread?

VII

Alongside "sett" and "clough", another verbal ghost-hound scampers round my thoughts all the time I'm staying at Lumb Bank. It is, undoubtedly, the name of the house that has summoned it. "Lumb" has awoken from memory the old Scottish saying: "Lang mae yer lumb reek." "Lumb" (sometimes simply "lum") means chimney, "reek" is smoke, "lang," "mae" and "yer" are Scots dialect versions of long, may and your. To say to someone "Lang mae yer lumb reek" is to wish them well, to hope they enjoy long life and prosperity: coal burning in their hearth, breath in their life-fire for as long as possible. I'm not sure if the area around Heptonstall is far enough north in England for the Scots "lumb" to mean chimney here as well. Perhaps that word in the name of the house draws on a different grid of local reference of which I'm ignorant and means something else entirely. No one in the house seems to know, but given the presence of the two tall mill chimneys on the steep bank of the clough just below the house, it seems plausible to think of lumb this way. In any case, whether or not it means chimney in Yorkshire makes no difference to the word's awakening from its slumbers in my memory the Scots saying I first heard years ago – uncomprehendingly – when I was a student in Edinburgh. Like an ill-trained dog that will not come to heel, that barks and worries when it should be still and silent, I find "Lang mae yer lumb reek" echoing through my mind with a kind of raucous, mocking irreverence as I stand at Plath's grave. It barks out the sure knowledge that all our fires are as temporary as our footprints; that all our tracks lead to the same destination.

If you visited Lumb Bank now, the snow would have melted, our tracks would have vanished, there would be no trace of us. Our trails into the house and out of it again have gone. Since then, scores of other writing groups have inhabited the place. We dispersed on a cold, sunny Saturday, each of us returning to whatever life-niche we'd temporarily left to be there, placing our steps, one before the other, in the lifelines that we follow and create, obedient to the weave of pacing that our particular tracks of circumstance and personality demand. All of us, I'm sure, feel invigorated by the time we've spent here. But of course it's impossible to predict how the writing life of each of us – of anyone – will develop. As Joseph Brodsky once observed:

> If you are in banking or if you fly an aircraft, you know that after you gain a substantial amount of expertise you are more or less guaranteed a profit or a safe landing. Whereas in the business of writing what one accumulates is not expertise but uncertainties. In this field, expertise invites doom.

Our time at Lumb Bank was not intended to foster "expertise" – that would indeed have been folly. Instead, it offered a setting in which to experiment with creative uncertainties – and to benefit from the company of others used to working with them.

Since returning, and writing about the footprints we left there, I still sometimes think of setts and cloughs. But the way I view them now has changed. Instead of paving slabs and steeply wooded hillsides, I think of words and the gradients of the mind and heart they let us chart. We make tracks upon the snow-blank page and screen, carefully fit our setts of words together into sentences, lay down ways through our inner worlds of thought and feeling so that others may follow, should they be so minded, and so that we ourselves may have a clearer sense of direction, better understand and celebrate the slants and tilts at which our psyche's cloughs are angled on this strange life-walk that we're pacing. As stone setts are more durable than footprints, so I like to think (or is this just a writerly conceit?) that words are as durable as stone, and that what we weave in language's tough filaments will long outlive us. I imagine the tread of others, intimate, exact, uncertain, placing their weight upon my word-setts when I'm gone, as I've placed my weight in the tracks marked out by those who came before me. Their steps – like mine, like yours, like everyone's – part of the same umbilical fire we leave reeking in the human chimney, kindling smoke signals we all recognize so well but struggle to interpret.

Sonatina for Oboe and Bayonet
(Reading *All Quiet on the Western Front*)

I

I was surprised when my daughter, Laura, told me she was reading *All Quiet on the Western Front* at school. Erich Maria Remarque's great novel of the First World War seemed a curious choice for children of her age. It's a long time since I've read it, but my memory of the story wouldn't make me rush to share it with ten and eleven year olds. This impression of unsuitability was confirmed when – spurred by Laura's news – I dug out my old copy. It's no collector's first edition, just a battered Mayflower paperback from 1963, translated from the German by A.W. Wheen. The cover illustration shows soldiers' bodies – I counted seven – strewn in the mud of a trench that's topped with coils of barbed wire. Below the title and the author's name, the picture centers on a corpse's out-stretched hand. It's shown in close-up and seems almost to be reaching towards the reader, as if to pull them in. Nearly touching the fingers there's a butterfly. The artist has portrayed it in mid-flutter, undecided whether to alight on the hand or on a nearby strand of wire. The sky is blue with just a few white wisps of cloud. Standing head down, by itself, reins trailing, there's a horse a little way beyond the lip of the trench. It looks uninjured, if dejected, but it made me remember an incident in the book where horses are horribly wounded in a bombardment. Their screaming unnerves the men more than the cries of their fallen comrades. One horse, its belly ripped open by shrapnel, gets entangled in its own unravelling innards, trips on them and falls.

The cover illustration on my copy, and the memories it brought back, fuelled my concern that *All Quiet on the Western Front* was the wrong choice of reading for my daughter's class. The less gruesome livery in which Laura's book was clad did little to allay my worries. Her edition – published by Vintage for World Book Night 2011 (in Brian Murdoch's 1993 translation) – isn't visually disturbing in the least. Its cover only features an artful image of a poppy. But what about the text within? Was it as shocking as I remembered? I resolved to read the book again before making a final judgment.

II

This intention to re-read Remarque might never have been realized and I might just have forgotten about the whole thing, had I not received an unexpected prompt. Laura is a keen musician and practice is a daily part of her routine. She's learning violin, oboe and piano and tends to alternate between them in terms of having a favorite instrument. No doubt her interest will fix eventually on one. At the time of reading *All Quiet on the Western Front* the oboe is in the ascendant. One evening after she's finished playing and is kneeling on the floor, disassembling her instrument, she asks me:

"What's a bayonet, Dad?"

It's not so much that she doesn't know at all; more that she wants clarification for the hazy picture that's formed already in her mind. Reading *All Quiet on the Western Front* has resulted in regular word-lists for homework, with pupils charged to find the meanings for a cluster of unfamiliar terms: mess-tin; Verey light; munitions; barrage; sniper; shrapnel; hemorrhage; gangrene; amputation; annihilation. "Bayonet" has already featured on one of these lists.

I try to provide as straightforward an answer to her question as I can:

"It's a long knife fitted to the end of a rifle."

"How big?"

"Almost as long as your oboe."

"Oh."

I know how hard it is to build up from words alone the full concretion of an object. How many in her class have seen, let alone held, a rifle or a revolver, felt the weight of an infantryman's weaponry? How many have heard live gunfire, handled a gasmask, tried on a metal helmet? So, remembering the old bayonet that I have, I ask (not without misgivings):

"Would you like to see one?"

"Yes!"

After some rummaging I find it. It's something I bought years ago in an antique/junk shop, obedient to that common impulse – a kind of dark magnetism of blood – which draws so many boys to weapons. There had been numerous bayonets for sale, alongside swords, spears, cutlasses and daggers, a grim cornucopia of blades stacked on the floor beside an old oak roll-top desk, on which was sitting one of those white china heads phrenologists used to show which sections of the skull supposedly correspond to different emotions. The bayonets were in different styles and sizes. They ranged from ornate to plain and represented various nations and dates – but they were under-run by one fearsome common denominator of intent: all were variations on the selfsame theme of stabbing your enemy to death. The one I bought – appropriately for what Laura would be reading years later – was labeled "German, Mauser, WWI."

I show her how to draw the blade and slide it back into its narrow metal scabbard. She takes the bayonet from me and examines it intently – first weighing the sheathed blade in both hands, taking in the heavy compactness of bayonet and scabbard combined. Then she draws out the blade with first-time awkwardness. It's as long as her arm held straight from wrist to shoulder. She touches the tip carefully, then her fingers explore the sharpened edge and the smooth indented runnel that runs the full length of the blade. After sliding it back into its snugly fitting scabbard she puts the bayonet on the floor beside her. She's silent for a moment and then asks:

"Do you think this one's ever killed anyone, Dad?"

Her question is the one that I'd expected. It's what I'd asked myself when I first bought the bayonet, my purchase of it prompted – at least in part – by a powerful curiosity about its complicity in death. It's that complicity, I think, whether realized or just waiting in potential, which bestows on weapons the somber gravity they exert. I have no satisfactory answer to her question.

"I don't know."

"Is that blood?"

She's found some discoloration on the wooden haft. I've wondered about it too.

"Perhaps. I'm not sure."

Then she tries out some other possibilities.

"Maybe this one was made at the end of the war and was never used."

"Maybe. But it doesn't look in mint condition."

"Or maybe it's been in lots of battles."

"Maybe."

Though it can be frustrating not to know, perhaps it's just as well we can't read from touch alone the history of the things we handle. If we could, who knows what laments and frenzied war cries this old bayonet might sing out? Who knows whose flesh this blade ripped and gouged, or what emotions its wielder felt as they used it – horror, fury, exhilaration, guilt, remorse?

III

The picture of a little girl kneeling on the floor between an oboe and a bayonet makes a powerful cameo that lodges in my mind, freezing into a kind of icon of incongruity that's at once symbolic and interrogative. It symbolizes vividly the way in which our world is riven by the coexistence of opposites: gentleness and brutality; compassion and cruelty; beauty and ugliness; creativity and destruction; peace and war. These polarities can pull apart any equilibrium of meaning we try to lay between them. Their sudden alternations act like artillery rounds, pounding the semblance of order on which we build our lives.

As well as symbolizing opposites, this icon of girl with oboe and bayonet also raises questions about innocence and honesty. When should children be told about the ugliness of which our species has shown itself (continues to show itself) to be so routinely capable? To what extent should we try to shelter those in our charge from life's horrors? Where does the dividing line run between protection and coddling; between information and violation?

In the early pages of *All Quiet on the Western Front*, Paul Bäumer, the German infantryman from whose perspective the novel is told, reflects on the brutalizing harshness of the training regimen to which all recruits are subjected. The outcome? "We became hard, suspicious, pitiless, vicious, tough," he says. But then adds, "and that was good; for these attributes were just what we lacked." Few of these attributes are ones that parents would wish to see fostered in their children. We would rather that they learned to play musical instruments than how to stab with bayonets. But if we concentrate too much on the gentling refinements of music, art and literature, shield children's eyes from the gross violence that runs throughout our history, may we not thereby weaken them, leave them ill-equipped to face life's harsher edges? Later in the book Bäumer talks about feelings which "might be ornamental enough in peacetime" but which serve no purpose at the front. Without wishing to impose some kind of battlefield curriculum, is enough attention given to fostering feelings that are more than merely "ornamental"?

Deciding when it's appropriate to share with children a knowledge of the horrors of history (which of course reach into the present too) is, I know, very largely a question of degree – the fine judgment of how much to tell and when. Individual variations in intelligence, awareness, empathy and toughness erode the credibility of any general catch-all rule that seeks unvarying universal application. "Ten year olds shouldn't be taught about bayonets" is certainly not a restriction I'd endorse. I'm less sure, though, even in a culture of incessant media exposure to violence, if children of this age should be encouraged to read the kind of detail about bayonet use that's provided in Remarque's book:

> It is best to stick a bayonet in the belly because there it doesn't get jammed, as it does in the ribs.

> The sharpened spade is a more handy and many-sided weapon; not only can it be used for jabbing a man under the chin, but it is much better for striking with because of its greater weight: and if one hits between the neck and the shoulder it easily cleaves as far down as the chest. The bayonet frequently jams on the thrust and then a man has to kick hard on the other fellow's belly to pull it out again; and in the interval he may easily get one himself. And what's more the blade gets broken off.

> During the day......we overhaul the bayonets – that is to say, the ones that have a saw on the blunt edge. If the fellows over there catch a man with one of those he's killed on sight. In the next sector some of our men were found whose noses were cut off and their eyes poked out with their own saw-bayonets. Their mouths and noses were stuffed with sawdust so that they suffocated. Some of the recruits have bayonets of this sort; we take them away and give them the ordinary kind.

To listen one moment to such accounts and the next to the notes of an oboe playing Bach or Mozart, to hold in the mind simultaneously the most sublime music and the bloodiest horrors, is to savor the perplexing flavor of life, shot through and through with so many bittersweet contrasts it's hard to know whether to rejoice or retch. I'd not want things saccharined with some Bowdlerized version of events that would knit a dulling gauze of denial and pretence, drape it across what happens, have us believe only a sanitized version of the human story. But it tears my heart to see a child grappling with these painful incongruities, knowing there is little or nothing I can do to help. This is how we humans are – make of it what you will. Trying to account for our conflicted nature is hard enough; trying to change it harder still.

IV

Of course my icon of little girl with oboe and bayonet is far from the only symbol of the way in which the cords of gentleness and violence, ugliness and beauty – and all of life's other opposites – are tightly braided together and laid down like nerves in the bedrock of our experience, charged with the voltage of their difference. The butterfly close to alighting on the corpse's hand that's foregrounded in the cover illustration of my copy of *All Quiet on the Western Front* acts in a similar manner, showing in one glance, in a single conceptual breath, the tight-woven contiguity of delicacy and brutality, the graceful and the gross; how the living and the dead are bound in close proximity.

The illustrator was surely drawing on, and alluding to, an incident in the book. At one point Remarque has us see butterflies through Paul Bäumer's eyes:

> One morning two butterflies play in front of our trench. They are brimstone butterflies, with red spots on their yellow wings. What can they be looking for here? There is not a plant nor a flower for miles. They settle on the teeth of a skull.

I don't know why the artist substituted a hand for a skull, chose to include only one butterfly instead of two, and made it look more like a cabbage white than a brimstone, with black spots on its wings instead of red and the wings themselves colored closer to white than yellow. This seems a pointless deviation from the text. But at least the essential symbolism is unchanged: life in the midst of death; beauty amidst ugliness; delicacy touching the brutal aftermath of battle.

Different symbols will appeal to different people. For me, the contrast between oboe and bayonet is particularly potent; particularly unsettling. In part, this is doubtless due to seeing them in my daughter's hands; the presence of a child between them further accentuating life's daunting incongruities. But the things themselves seem almost like distillations of difference, so massively dissimilar are their functions. It's as if the objects have been formed from a dense concentrate of opposing features standing in stark contrast to each other – oboe and bayonet slowly dripping their radically unlike essences to form the artifacts that bear these names. One is a finely worked wooden channel that allows the living breath to be sculpted into sophisticated gyres of music; the other a sharp metal plug designed to be rammed into someone's body so that their breath is stopped forever. Put musical instrument and stabbing instrument side by side, contrast the way in which breath is trained to play an oboe and the way it's used to make a bayonet thrust, and there's a jarring enough disjunction to derail any philosophy, any theology, that's only based on vacuous pieties or wishful thinking about how we *ought* to be, instead of being founded on the perplexingly uneven, stony ground of what we are.

Feeling the sharp flints and smooth pebbles of our humanness underfoot, our capacity for bloodshed and for beauty, the haunting melodies of an oboe often seem a more appropriate response than anything words can deliver. Yet – a disturbing thought – to what extent does the great music that moves us, draw elements of its texture from that side of our nature for which a bayonet can stand as emblem? Even (especially?) the most beautiful refrain, rooted in the bedrock of our spirit, draws from there a water that has but little claim to purity. Thinking back to the antique/junk shop where I bought the bayonet, selecting it from the stack of blades clustered on the floor around that old roll-top desk, I remember the white china head that sat above them, marked out with that lacework of black lines and letterings in phrenology's now discredited mind-mapping. How close might oboe and bayonet sometimes be, supposing we could really chart the oceans of the mind, mark in their complex currents, reefs and trenches? I suspect we harbor all manner of disturbing contiguities within us.

V

Having reread *All Quiet on the Western Front* in light of the knowledge that it was prescribed for Laura's class, I still can't decide for sure whether it's unsuitable reading or not. If I'd been the teacher charged with making a choice from out of the twenty-five titles selected for World Book Night, I think I might have played safe and opted for something else – perhaps Mark Haddon's *The Curious Incident of the Dog in the Night-Time*, or Philip Pullman's *Northern Lights*, or maybe Seamus Heaney's *Selected Poems 1966-1987*. But playing safe is at best a questionable educational strategy, at worst a kind of cowardice. If, come each November, we ask children to wear poppies and remember, it's surely important to give them some idea of just what it is that they're remembering. *All Quiet on the Western Front* could be seen as one way of looking behind the poppies and understanding what they symbolize. In the edition Laura's class was reading, the translator, Brian Murdoch, adds a useful "Afterword" which would help enhance such understanding.

It provides background on Remarque (1898-1970), particularly about how he was reviled by the Nazis. In 1933 his works were banned. Misinformation was disseminated about his supposed Jewish connections and the "fact" that he had evaded military service in the First World War. Remarque went into exile. His books were publicly burned. His sister was sentenced to death on trumped up charges. At the trial she was told "Your brother has unfortunately escaped us – you, however, will not." She was guillotined in 1943.

Remarque's book is, of course, a novel. It isn't a simple documentary – if we allow to pass unchallenged that naïve fiction which supposes truth-telling is ever straightforward. But it's clear the incidents he describes were based on his own and others' experiences of trench warfare during World War I. The characters and what happens to them possess that authority of the authentic which only comes from drawing on real life. It's worth remembering that Remarque himself, and his first English translator, Arthur Wheen, were war veterans – both of whom were injured on the battlefield.

As a parent, I hope my daughter never has to encounter in real life many of the things mentioned in *All Quiet on the Western Front*. It would not do to underestimate the repulsiveness that's integral to Remarque's topic:

> Officers' brothels; bayonet practice; disemboweled horses; gas victims who 'cough up their burnt lungs in clots'; men fouling themselves in terror; bodies reduced to 'mincemeat and bone splinters'; 'corpse-rats' growing fat from feasting on the dead; vicious hand-to-hand combat; dismembered corpses blasted into trees, their body-parts hanging from the branches like grotesque fruit; skulls blown open; soldiers attempting to run with their feet cut off.......

To try to shield children from too early an exposure to life's horrors is the natural protectiveness of love in action, an enfolding of what we cherish within whatever comfort we can give. But of course there comes a point where such protection edges into something else; it becomes closer to denial than to nurture. Unless we're careful, caring can shade into the dishonesty of blindfolding, if not outright censorship.

I'm still not sure when it's right for children to be introduced to a book like

All Quiet on the Western Front. But the more I consider this, the less inclined I'd be to try to formulate some single invariant age before which it's frowned upon and after which it's deemed OK. Such an algorithm might work for machines; it doesn't work for individuals. Laura herself is adamant that although it's what she describes as "a very, very sad story," she and her peers were ready for it – in a way they would not have been (in her assessment) the year before. Perhaps instead of worrying about whether ten or eight or twelve or fifteen constitutes some watershed of readiness, it would be better to be concerned with the fact that too many people never read the book at all.

Describing a Thought-Path
(Reading a path along which I cycle nearly every day)

What descriptions – or good ones anyway – actually describe is consciousness, the mind playing over the world of matter, finding there a
glass various and lustrous enough to reflect back the complexities of the
self that's doing the looking.

Mark Doty, *The Art of Description*

I

Even in term time, in the middle of the day, it's rarely crowded. In the
early morning, when I cycle, it's unusual to meet anyone. Sometimes
there's a jogger, or dog-walker, or one of the university porters going in to work.
But mostly the path is deserted and I have it to myself. It runs for several hundred yards between farmland and playing fields. On the playing field side, a
dense coniferous hedge borders the path. Cherry trees are set into its dark foliage like pillars. There are maybe thirty of them, planted at regular intervals
along the full length of the path. Sometimes, on breezy mornings, they remind
me of the wooden stakes that were sewn into the canvas windbreak that we un-
furled around us, when I was little, on family picnics at the beach. When the
wind is strong, the hedge is blown into canvas-like bulges, straining between
their cherry stakes. In a gale, it's almost like a long ribbon of sail with the cherries
resembling a flotilla of masts holding each billowing section in place.

A seven-strand wire fence, strung between chest-high wooden posts, runs
parallel to the hedge on the other side of the path. It marks the boundary between path and fields. When the wind is strong enough to flex and curve the
sections of hedge between the cherries, the wires sometimes sing eerie, plaintive
notes. Whenever that happens, I think of the fence as a kind of unearthly seven-stringed instrument whose invisible player places ghostly fingers along the
frets of the posts, subtly altering the volume and modulation of the wail.

The path is as well surfaced as a road. It's lit by streetlights, and is just wide
enough to take a car – though vehicles, other than bikes, are prohibited. At one

end of the path there's a village-sized cluster of student halls of residence; at the other, a sports centre. From the sports centre it's just a short walk to most of the university's science departments. Mostly, the path is used by students taking a shortcut between living quarters and lectures, but it also offers cyclists an appealing alternative to the main road.

The routes I take in the morning vary. I'm cycling for exercise – and pleasure – before I start to write. It's not as if I'm forced along one track of iron routine dictated by a daily commute. But despite this freedom, almost invariably, whatever route I decide to follow, it will at some point incorporate the path. Though it took a while for me to recognize the fact, the path has become a special place for me, somewhere that exerts a kind of magnetism that I find perplexing yet irresistible. My motive in writing about it here is straightforward: I want to try to describe and bring into clearer focus the nature of the path's appeal, and so begin to understand why it keeps drawing me back.

II

In part there's nothing mysterious about this. At the level of conventional superficialities there are enough factors to offer a plausible, commonsense explanation of the path's attraction. Straight, well-lit on dark winter mornings, smooth surfaced, no cars, few pedestrians, and on only a gentle gradient – it offers a short stretch of well-nigh ideal cycling terrain. Not only that, but for someone interested in natural history like me, the path is close enough to countryside for it to be a fruitful locus for the sighting of creatures that don't venture into town. I've seen hares, weasels, and foxes here. The birdlife too is varied. Cycling along the path I've spotted goldfinches, yellowhammers, curlews, oystercatchers, herons, sparrowhawks, owls and more. The verge that runs along the farmland side of the path is dotted and clumped in midsummer with untidy arrays of wildflowers – making a nice contrast with the regularly spaced cherries on the other side, and the dark uniformity of the fir hedge that grows between them. However, although they no doubt contribute to its appeal, these two characteristics are scarcely unique. They're found in lots of other places that, whilst appealing, possess no special power of attraction. Its cyclist-friendly nature and the richness of its flora and fauna cannot by themselves explain the pull the path exerts. To understand the gravity of its attraction I need to look elsewhere.

III

In trying to understand what draws me to the path with a force beyond anything its obvious features can account for, I've come to the conclusion that what lies at the root of it is an illusion of separateness, simplicity, and drama. What I mean by this is that the path paints on a manageable scale pictures that, in their naturally occurring form, are drawn on so large and intricate a canvas it's hard to bring them into focus.

Of course I know that paths can't paint pictures. Putting it this way is simply a shorthand device to indicate how, in this particular instance, the alchemy of place and person works. It's clear, I think, that places can affect us in all kinds of different ways. The predictable permutations involved in this equation provide the readiest examples – how, for example, standing on a summit amidst a magnificent mountain range can be inspiring or belittling. But I'm more interested in the mundane, and often mysterious, micro-climates that affect us in our everyday locations, so that in some we feel content, whilst others nudge us towards moods of longing or disquiet.

For reasons that no doubt stem partly from my particular personality, not just from the characteristics of the path, cycling along it prompts a more than usual degree of thoughtfulness. In this frame of mind I often remember Aristotle's comment about philosophy beginning with wonder. Does the path provide the kind of wonder that prompts me to philosophize? I'm wary of using a term that's become a territory colonized by academic specialists. I'm sure my musings on the path would be viewed askance by professional philosophers. They'd be likely to dismiss them as idle daydreaming, lacking the rigor of their craft. But regardless of whether it gives rise to something that could be called philosophy, wonder is also associated with the realization that the ordinary is extraordinary (though which comes first, the wonder or the realization, is a hard knot to unravel and I'm happy to leave it firmly tied). The point I want to stress is simply that the path is strongly conducive to seeing how what seems unremarkable is, in fact, anything but.

IV

I've resisted the impulse to attempt the kind of description that privileges appearance – which would try to convey in words as fully and accurately as possible the visual impressions that the path lays upon an observer. Likewise I've avoided focusing on any of the events that I've witnessed on the path. Yes, I've given a few details about its length and width, location, what flanks it on each side. But of the richer, more specific textures that are contained within such features, or the things that happen in the milieu they provide, I've said nothing. This deliberate strategy of avoidance must seem strange. If I want to explain why the place is special to me, surely it would be better to home in on its unique particularities instead of, as it were, standing back at the safe remove of talking about such obvious features as its hedge and fence, its streetlights, and tarred surface.

It would certainly be easier to choose some eye-catching detail and focus in on it more closely – mine the rich ore it offers and refine it into words. The moonlit morning when I saw two fox cubs playing a kind of tag, for example, running repeatedly between field and path, their energetic squirming under the lowest strand of the fence evidently an integral part of their game. Or the morning I so nearly collided with two students cycling without lights and going hell-for-leather down the path in erratic zigzags, one sitting on the crossbar, one pedaling furiously, both singing loudly, evidently drunk, or high, or both, and completely oblivious to the world around them. I don't think they even noticed I was there. Or I might look more closely at the wildflowers I mentioned earlier – map in words the patchwork of shapes, scents, and colors made by vetch and campion, willowherb and dandelion, daisy, clover, and all the other species that richly braid the fence-side verge. Or I could recall to the page the nine wave-smoothed stones – clearly brought from the nearby seaside – that someone once placed dead centre of the path in a perfect circle – a hazard for cyclists, but a promising nucleus around which speculation could be woven about who and why.

Such events and objects are readily enough recounted, and it's tempting to highlight them – because they're easier for me as writer and you as reader to grasp than the path's more abstract attributes. But to dwell on what surrenders to words with so little resistance would be a distraction. I may struggle to understand it, but I know that the path's power to keep beckoning me back does not reside in anything that meekly submits to list and label.

V

Harder to describe than any fox cub gamboling in the moonlight is the way the path gives the impression of being separate from its surroundings. Of course this is an illusion. Like any place, the path is firmly embedded in its milieu. It is part of the continuum of presence that constitutes the world – for it's impossible to abstract anywhere from where it adjoins and leads to; to turn it into something cut off and self sufficient. Everywhere is next to somewhere else. Time and distance may join hands to make it seem as if places can be pushed apart, made separate, but the world unfolds the varied tapestry of its surface without breaks: desert becomes grassland, becomes mountain, becomes jungle, becomes river, becomes city, becomes marsh, becomes sea, becomes glacier, becomes tundra, becomes forest. There's no detached segment; no independent, standalone locus that exists by itself unconnected to the environing topography.

But although it's clearly part of the uninterrupted tread of what's here all around us, although it's conjoined with what comes before it, beside it, with how the world unfurls beyond it, although it's simply a feature of the landscape hereabouts, an unimportant detail of the local environs rather than something broken away from them, the path still conveys a sense of singularity and separateness. It feels more apart from things than part of them. I'm not sure how this illusory sense of separateness is conjured, how the path appears to be detached, discrete, almost a self-contained unit. Perhaps it stems from the way its straightness draws the eye along it, or the fact that its hard surface running between fields acquires an emphasis via the contrast between tar and the grass to either side. But since such things are scarcely unique, there must be other factors operating. Sometimes I think the path resembles a thick black line that someone has ruled across the land. Maybe the deliberateness of that act, the underscoring it embodies, imbues the path with a kind of extended exclamation mark, demanding attention more forcefully than what adjoins it.

However it is generated, this sense of separateness bestows upon the path the semblance of a stage which kindles a strong sense of platform and performance. What plays out upon its surface is thereby marked, made special, set apart from the workaday buzz of things happening all round it. Maybe the hedge, with its regularly spaced cherries and streetlights, together with the fence on the other side, act together to form a kind of elongated proscenium arch, framing the path in such a way as to give rise to a sense of anticipation, a feeling that something will happen on it; that it's a space for unfolding drama.

Naturally, I realize that this sense of disjunction between the path and what's around it, the feeling of mise-en-scène that seems to hover in the air so that whatever happens along its thread becomes something to pay particular attention to, could simply be unique to me. It may be that my reading – or mis-reading – of this place is just an idiosyncrasy, an individual quirk rather than any intrinsic quality that the path possesses independently of me. I'm not sure what others feel as they walk or cycle here. Whatever the reasons behind my sense of path-as-stage – and I can't pinpoint them beyond the blurry possibilities I've just outlined – I think it's the sense of drama thus engendered that keeps beckoning me back.

VI

A drama needs actors. But I've stressed as one of the path's characteristics the way in which, at the time of day I cycle along it, there tends to be no one there. In fact this is precisely what helps transform what might be unnoticed minor roles into something much more eye-catching. If the path was regularly thronged with people, I suspect that none of the bit-parts involved in such crowd scenes would draw the eye. It is the rarity of seeing someone, and the fact that, in the early morning, they are usually alone, that underscores the drama of their presence. The path's emptiness gives rise to a sense of waiting, anticipation, the feeling that something is poised to happen. Built into it as path qua path is the expectation that there will be walkers on it; if none of them are there, there's the hush before a curtain rises.

Dramatic emphasis is also given by the straightness of the path and the fact that – on those rare occasions when I do meet someone – they often appear on foot at one end of the path as I'm just starting to cycle along it from the other end. This means that the spotlight of attention is fully on them; they are the unchallenged protagonist upon this narrow podium – so that it is speculation about their story that occupies my mind as the distance between us closes. And, as a kind of echo or corollary to this, when I'm alone on the path the spotlight shifts to me and I become more self-conscious of the role I'm acting out upon the boards it offers.

Sometimes, I think of myself as a theatergoer who has let his attention wander, or even dozed off, somehow becoming oblivious to the dramatic events raging on the stage he's meant to be watching. Only in real life it's worse than this.

It's bad enough for an audience member to absent himself in slumber; for an actor to do so is even less excusable. And yet this is surely the mode in which I stumble through many of my days. Unlikely though it may seem, the path acts as an antidote to such sleepwalking. It wakes me up again to the nature of the drama that I'm part of – a drama in which everyone has a starring role. Being on its tar-ribbon stage, seeing others appearing there, feeling the sense of expectation that its emptiness creates, all this helps peel away the blindfolds that are woven into place by the lulling rhythms of routine.

When we pass someone in the street, it's something so ordinary, such an often repeated occurrence, that it's easy to overlook it, to scarcely notice it and certainly not to recognize what's really happening. We tend to focus only on a few superficial specifics of the moment and fail to take into account the way they're tightly stitched into something that's far from being ordinary. When such a passing happens on the path, it's as if the true texture of things becomes apparent, the blur of the commonplace gives way for a few moments to a lucid glimpse of what lies behind it.

VII

A long, straight path on which a person appears for a while then vanishes again, carries with it obvious symbolic resonance with our situation. It has the potential to remind us of the elemental coordinates that plot our position with more durable, if less palatable, accuracy than the usual grid references by which we locate ourselves – name, nationality, relationships, religion, interests, profession, qualifications, political allegiances, wealth, and so on. Instead of these costumes that we wear, this is a stage that stresses the naked facts of finitude; the raw truth of our situation. We appear momentarily on life's path, live our brief quota of days upon it, and then vanish into the same enigmatic and terrifying nothingness from which our existence was drawn.

Obviously, the parallel is not exact. The path is a simple, if not primitive stage that can only point to the nature of the story that it mimes, rather than imitate its intricate unfolding in any detail; it is only lit by streetlights, not by some great Pole Star of being. But, for me, its value – the fascination it exerts, the quality that keeps drawing me back to cycle along its length – lies in the way the path heightens my awareness of the life-threads we are all un-spooling through time and our place upon them – fleeting, ephemeral – like blossoms of a day that bud and bloom and wither upon their ancient branches.

Such is the angle of perception at which this little stage sets my mind that our lifelines become almost tangible and I can picture the person walking towards me starting out as an embryo and growing as they come closer. When they pass, I picture them becoming stooped and old until, at the path's end, they falter, fall and lie still. Or – if the path is deserted – I see myself launched along it as if it was a kind of composite birth canal, life-path and terminus, where the stages of development, the stations of our aging, are emphasized in miniature, speeded up, shown in the microcosm that the path creates.

Sparked by this image of an individual's lifespan – shorn of its variations so that its major themes are more apparent – another picture frequently ignites in my imagination when I'm cycling here. Its stations of progress are less clear, its unfolding more complex than a single person's route through life. This image gazes back beyond the embryo, beyond the chain of fusions over generations, those repeated collisions of egg and sperm that dot the route everyone takes to wherever life has placed them. It pictures our species unraveling into the ones that preceded it until, eventually, some distant point of ignition is reached where life first came into being. This is our back story, the path that all of us followed, the path taken by every individual who appears here, on this strip of tar down which students walk, their heads filled with equations and ideas, questions, hopes, desires, and fears. This is how all of us got to here. Each cyclist, or jogger, every dog-walker is like a portal that opens into the depths of the lineage behind them. Despite our heritage, for the most part we cut the umbilical of history that binds us to this centuries-long unfolding. We may leave a stump that links us to the generation immediately before us, or to the one preceding that, but the spiraling back through the aeons that knits us into being, that constitutes the deep-time of our history, is only rarely acknowledged. It's as if we work on ourselves the same illusion that the path seems to work on my perception of it, making it seem somewhere apart and separate. So we live as if cut off from all but a tiny fraction of our bloodline. But we are no more separate from what surrounds us, what precedes us, what follows us, no more independent of our milieu, than the path is independent of the environment in which it's set.

VIII

The path's stage should, I know, be miles long to better mimic what it has the power to suggest. And even though they'd all need to have the same origin and end, the routes it allows upon its surface should be multiple, diverse, different, instead of just having one single straight line of tar. This would more closely shadow and present the variety of lives it's possible to lead as we act out our individual dramas on the pathways offered by the world. But the value of the path for me lies in the fact that it represents, rather than attempts to replicate, key aspects in the story of our existence. Indeed, if it lost its simplicity, I suspect that much of its appeal would vanish; it would become merely an indistinguishable part of things, a tiny fragment of capillary network, absorbed into the fine detail of life's body. As such, it would lose the capacity to point to the arteries that pulse through our existence, swollen with the blood of being.

Usually, it's the sense of being part of a lifeline that the path enhances. It makes me think about an individual's conception, birth, life, and death. It emphasizes the fact that whoever I meet on the path is also at some point on this dramatic journey. Clearly we always occupy some point on the transit between conception and death, but it's as if the path acts to electrify the arc of our trajectory through time, making its presence more tangible than it is in the ordinary run of things.

I'm often prompted by this intensified feeling of occupying some point on our individual odyssey to think about the way in which its four main stations – conception, birth, life, and death – have been visited and revisited so many millions of times, and how each of the actors on the path – everyone – is part of a line that stretches back through repeated performances of this quartet to some veiled moment of beginning when life first hatched from the mute substance of the planet. Since then, encore and variation have seeded time with life's diversity, populating the aeons with a dramatis personae whose scale is hard to grasp. In a gale, when the fence's seven-stringed instrument is wailing out its eldritch notes, I sometimes think of it as a kind of life-music, an unnerving anthem demanding our allegiance as it reminds us of the essential mystery of being. It brings to mind Kobayashi Issa's haunting haiku:

> What a strange thing,
> To be thus alive
> Beneath the cherry blossoms!

IX

Sometimes, too, I think about how the tiny segment of existence that's constituted by the path isn't really so small if you take account of more than its obvious dimensions. If you picture not just its length, breadth, and surface, the only inches-thick layer of tar, but instead consider the total depth that underlies it, the full height that rises over it, then a very different image of the path emerges. If you imagine the path-stage lifted all along the strip of its obvious surface and then set upright, it can help the mind to picture these massively enhanced senses of above and below: simply imagine this upright column of path extending up like a beanstalk, down like a root, rupturing the containments within which we normally think of it. Instead of a line drawn on a surface it becomes a kind of wall stretching indefinitely towards what seems never to be there – a floor and ceiling to anchor it to comprehensible dimensions.

Thinking like this reminds me of the way – when we were children, aged maybe ten and seven – my brother and I used to speculate about where we'd get to if we just kept on going. We weren't so interested in the terrestrial version of such a supposition, We'd pretty much grasped the fact that the Earth was round, so that if we set off from wherever we happened to be and continued in a straight line we'd eventually end up back where we started. Such hypothetical circlings of the world, though incredible, didn't catch our imagination in the same way as the idea that if we went straight up, into the sky, into space, among the stars, we'd just keep on going. With a terrestrial circumnavigation we could picture ourselves beading the planet's surface with our progress. It would be an astonishing journey, but the mind could grasp it. We knew about bird migration, the way in which the swallows that came each summer had made the great trek from Africa. The disparity in scale between such tiny birds and such great distances helped us to picture in our mind's eye what would be involved if we set out one day and determined to keep on walking until we came full circle. But the idea of such epic journeying, however much it contained the allure of faraway exotic places, was less interesting to us than the fact, as we understood it, that if you went up and continued into space you'd just keep going on forever.

It's clear there's space above the path. Less obviously, there's space below it too – for once the path's realm is extended downwards, dropping through the varied strata of soil and rock and metal, the depth of earth that underlies it would eventually be exhausted and we'd emerge at the other side of the globe and so also into space below in the same way as above. Considering the path in these terms, I sometimes wonder about all the entities and objects that have populated it across time. What has it witnessed when its territory is thus massively magnified by the amplitude of above and below, both extended indefinitely into space? What has moved beneath the surface that we think of as the path? And above it, far above where the line of tar is situated, what has played out in this segment of being over all the aeons it has been there?

X

Coming down to earth again, the path also makes me think about all the paths we've followed since *Homo sapiens* first emerged, and all those paths paced out by the shadowy pre-human hominids in whose footprints we trod before our pathways diverged. As our numbers have spiraled into today's billions, we've covered the surface of the planet with an ever increasing density of tracks, marking out the ways we've followed – all the paths and bridleways and roads that we've impressed with the momentary weight of our presence and passage. We are a path-making species – and not just in the literal sense of the footfalls we leave on our accustomed routes. We also look for ways through life, seeking out pathways of value and meaning that might confer upon our time here a deeper sense of sense than that conferred merely by our basic wants.

If thinking of the drama acted out upon the little stage of my thought-path, if bringing to mind a picture of it massively extended up and down, if considering our history spiraling back into deep time with the pattern of our species' paths a dense filigree marking only the most recent centuries is not enough to strike a spark from mind-flints so dulled by routine that they cannot see the path as any more than just a path, think of the fact that everyone who walks or cycles here is themselves a colony of paths. There are within us mazes of intricate routes in the brain, delicate tracks and channels that host the play of thoughts, the glimmer of feelings, the networks of consciousness that make us who we are. Sometimes I think of the neural pathways that go past me, no more than an arm's length away, as I cycle on the path. What invisible impulses are moving on them at astonishing speeds as I and their bearers plod our slow ways through the external world? As we approach each other along this narrow ribbon of tar, what thoughts are approaching each other, held within the hive of pathways in the head? The speed of movement on those inner routes makes walking and cycling along this strip of tar seem almost static. How do the paths we traverse in the world impact upon what moves along the pathways that our thoughts and feelings follow? And how does what passes along these hidden neural routes affect the way in which we understand what happens, who and what we see, as we go along these several hundred yards of tar laid down between farmland and playing fields? Everyone I pass when I cycle here will have an intricate network of pathways etched into their brain. In part these are shaped by time, carved into the particular species-shape we occupy by centuries of evolution and development. In part they are molded into our unique variations on these basic themes by a complex cluster of individual factors. How free are we to walk the paths we want, to think thoughts that we can truly call our own? Are we ourselves pathfinders, path-makers, path walkers – or more like tiny cobbles that are themselves just part of some great route laid down by forces that have no more regard for us than we have for fragments of gravel underfoot?

XI

It would fascinate me to know how others view my thought-path. How do these several hundred yards of tar bounded by hedge and cherry trees on one side, by seven strands of wire on the other, appear to the elderly dog walker who's sufficiently hard of hearing to be startled when my bike appears beside him? How does the Japanese student view it who, anytime I've seen her walking here, is talking intently on her phone, seemingly oblivious to her surroundings? What about the jogger who wears the same red hooded top, whatever the weather? Or the overweight, balding man of my age who never responds to a smile or a "good morning" and seems lost in some desolate inner world of his own? How does a fox cub read it, or a weasel? How does the path strike the robins and blackbirds that nest in the fir hedge? What sense of the place is imparted to the embryos carried invisibly along its narrow length, swaddled in the fastness of their mothers' wombs? Do any of the people who walk along it see the path in ways similar to me? And do any of us see it the way it actually is?

It isn't easy – in fact the philosophers tell us that it isn't possible – to strip away the texture of our individual outlook and see things as they really are. Kant's contention remains unassailable – that we are confined to the world of phenomena; the noumenon is beyond us. Caught in the mesh of our unique personality, like flies caught in a series of densely interlocking webs – life-history, physiology, language, all the things that make us who we are – we're powerless to brush aside the gossamer strands of our particularity and see things as they are in themselves without us, freed from how we frame them.

If I wanted to describe the path as it is in itself, I know this would be impossible. However carefully I cast my words, however close my account might draw to the actual lineaments of the place, its accuracy would already be compromised. Yes, I can set out the basics of what's there, note what's hard or soft, large or small, and attach much the same labels that others would for colors, shapes and quantities. But beyond such superficial herding into categories, the world soon strays into the diversity of our individual readings. It's just as well, then, that my intention here has not been to attempt to paint something realistic, a literal portrait, so that tree by tree and flower by flower, fence post by fence post, and moment by moment the words on the page tick off each constituent part of the scene, corresponding to what's there with slavish exactitude, obedient to every jot and tittle that lays itself upon the senses. Far from seeking such impossible equivalence of the verbal and the actual, my concern has been to try to depict and unravel the spell the path has cast on me.

I'm interested in the path less as a fixed objective place set in the landscape, something anyone could see and walk along, more as a runway along which the imagination can take off into a realm of ideas. The ideas are invisible to any observer; they have no place in the raft of obvious qualities that impinge upon the senses. And yet it is the ideas rather than the raw substance of the path as it falls upon our perception that have come to dominate the way I see it. In a sense, seeing what isn't really there has come to dominate my view of the path, defining what I think of as its essential substance.

XII

On misty mornings, the moisture heavy in the air, the dark foliage of the hedge between the cherry trees is festooned with cobwebs. Of course they're always there – we just don't see them. Ordinarily, their strands are invisible. It's only when they're heavily beaded with a misting of tiny water droplets that their existence is revealed. When I think of how little an ordinary account of walking along the path catches of the tread of what is there, the cobwebs often come to mind. They offer a readymade natural symbol for the way in which there's far more there than we can ever see; that there are hidden dimensions in what seems so straightforward we normally pay it scant attention. The intricate lacework of strands in these cobwebs – arrayed in their thousands, their millions, all along this line of hedge – are suggestive of the host of connections and interrelationships whose mesh is sutured onto every second of even the most mundane moment.

The mist comes on still mornings when there's not a breath of wind, so that the moisture-laden air clings to what it touches, draping it in coats of cloudy breath that the slightest breeze would soon disperse. Despite the stillness, looking at the mist-revealed cobwebs always makes me think of how a strong wind plays haunting notes upon the seven strands of fence wire opposite the hedge. And I realize that if the nature of things has any note or anthem that could sing out something of its essence, it would approximate more to the strings of countless cobwebs being plucked than to any of the singularities that are sounded by the wire. It is as if the simple notes made as the wind whistles through the fence's strands point to the hedge that runs parallel to it, indicating the real texture of the world's music once we start to listen to it. I can conceptualize and describe – could even write out on a score – the wind-song as it plays upon the wires. But the complex intricacy of sound created as air currents flow and buffet their way through a myriad of cobwebs, plucking and bowing their millions of strings, mocks such simplistic notation. In this line of cobwebbed hedge, facing the seven-stranded fence, I realize there's a haunting metaphor for the transaction language offers. It translates the plenum of the world into something we can grasp – but what it gives us is, for the most part, utterly remote from what is there.

Containing Agostino
(Reading a copy of Alberto Moravia's novella)

I

Linguistics and philosophy have much to say about the manner in which reality and language interrelate: how we talk the world into sense; how it forges on the anvil of the tongue an imprint of itself. But for all the labors of scholars in these disciplines, it remains difficult to determine whether words are the bedrock metaling the roads of understanding we traverse, or the signs that tell us where to find these routes; or if they operate both as map and territory, at once pointing out the way and helping to create it. However the precise alignment between world and word is set, a key function of words involves containment and control. We use them to divide one thing from another, to parse into separate objects and instances what would otherwise be an unmanageable rush of experience. Sometimes, though, this function fails – the masks of our labeling slip and the world shifts momentarily into a different perspective: boundaries blur, things run together, connections rip through the flimsy curtailments erected by the names we give.

Essays often start in these moments of containment-meltdown and are, perhaps, words' rearguard action, an attempt to subjugate the new perspective with a redrawn verbal cartography so that some measure of containment may still be brought to bear. Writing holds the promise of handling the burgeoning fluidity that follows in the wake of containment-failure, making it pool behind an account which tries to dam and channel with new diction the unfettered interconnections that have melted the ice of our usual categories, cracking with an array of veining fissures what had seemed smoothly fixed and settled. Faced with a momentarily estranged world shot through with ice-breaking vistas – vistas which our normal workaday use of language does not comfortably accommodate – we can either fall silent, try to ignore them, or attempt to recalibrate the parameters of containment. This last strategy allows us to continue to cast our verbal nets – but this time in a way that draws in a different catch of meaning from the stolid, unexamined certainties that ordinarily hold things frozen in their grip.

According to the Zhou dynasty Taoist master Chuang Zi:

> A fishhook only exists because of fish. A rabbit trap only exists because of rabbits. Words only exist because of meaning.

Unlike fishhooks and rabbit traps, though, which procure for us something pre-existent and independent of them, it's not always clear whether – or to what extent – words' quarry exists before their traps are sprung. Another conundrum emerges when we consider the different meshes in which it's possible to weave our verbal nets. Which caliber retrieves (or creates) the most accurate picture of the world? How – to focus on the matter at hand – should *Agostino* be seen? Given the wildly divergent meanings that can be hooked from this one small book, which wordy tackle – the icy idiom of ordinary discourse, or an essay's snare of fissure-catching/causing vocabulary – is best geared to lure a measure of understanding within our grasp?

II

Although it's often hard to spot those hairline fractures in the commonplace that herald containment-meltdown, that moment when words no longer seem able to bear the load we put upon them, in this instance it was easy. The initial fault-line lay in two names signed inside a slim, grey, hardback volume. One was my own, under which I'd written "Edinburgh, March 1980." The other reads: "E.R.S. Fifoot." The book that bore these signatures was Alberto Moravia's *Agostino*. The copy sits beside me now as I compose these sentences, sentences that are trying both to trace the fault-lines and contain them via a more encompassing account. Or, to put this in another way, I am at once examining how traps set in the scale of ordinary language failed, and attempting to reset them, but this time hooked and sprung according to a different key.

My copy of *Agostino* is a first edition of the English translation by Beryl de Zoete, published in London by Secker and Warburg in 1947. The book originally appeared in an edition of 500 copies in 1944, with two lithographs by Renato Guttoso. There's no dust jacket, just the oddly designed hardcover, patterned all over with abstract grey and white whorls and shadings – except for a plain cream margin on the spine. I'm not sure of the exact artistic technique used to produce the striking effect of this design. It looks like a form of combed marbling, but how far it follows the usual steps of what its early Persian practitioners nicely termed *ebru* (cloud art), or what the Japanese refer to more prosaically as *suminagashi* (floating ink, describing the main process involved), is hard to say. However it was done, the pattern gives the appearance of a close-up black and white photograph of some intricately crevassed and wooded winter landscape seen from space. I bought the book at a library sale in Edinburgh when I was a student there. It has sat neglected on my shelves until recently. Over thirty years would pass between signing my name on it and actually reading this assured, novella-length exploration of an adolescent boy's sexual awakening during a summer holiday spent with his beautiful widowed mother at an Italian seaside resort.

Perhaps part of the appeal of books lies in the way they simultaneously suggest constraint and freedom. On the one hand, a book conveys order and control in the disciplined neatness of all the marshaled lines of print that it contains. Its compact, rectangular solidity has no ambiguity in terms of boundary or extent; it's clear where books, considered as objects, begin and end. They are straightforwardly labeled units easily identified as such. On the other hand, even before we read it, we know a book gives access to another world, that its author can lead us into all sorts of mazes of meaning. It can take us deep into the past or the imagined future; transport us to a different country, an alien culture. Books can lure us with fantasy, place a wealth of information before us; they can offer intimate explorations of other lives, weave tales that slake our thirst for stories. A book's clear-cut shape, the immediate impression it gives of being something unproblematically bounded, separate and discrete, the fact that it's such a familiar object, something that surrenders readily to identification and labeling, in fact belies its nature as an entryway into far less easily mapped dimensions than those presented by its raw impress upon the senses.

III

The way in which text and reader interact is fascinating. Their relationship in some ways mirrors in little that between world and word. How much reader and writer each brings to the equation that results in meaning being generated remains unclear, nor do we fully understand how marks made on a page can light up the mind with the hidden incandescence of thoughts, feelings, imaginings and memories. However it happens, such ignition is of comparable significance to our species as the discovery of fire. It would be interesting to know how much our reading molds the psyche, to map the way in which its isobars thread through and help determine our inner weather. But it's hard to see how such an intimate cartography could ever be drawn beyond the uncertainties of introspective speculation. Fortunately this doesn't matter in the present case, for with *Agostino* I'm not concerned with how much (or little) Moravia's story impacted on the shifting meteorology of my psyche. My interest is focused rather on how the book as object, not as written text, sparked a containment-failure; how what had seemed entirely straightforward momentarily became something that ruptured the usual labels reached for in categorizing it, such that continuing to think of it merely as "a hardback first edition of the English translation of Alberto Moravia's *Agostino*" looked at best superficial, at worst a blinkering distortion designed to prevent a more interesting, albeit unsettling vision from coming into focus.

I bought the book largely because it bore E.R.S. Fifoot's signature. At that point I only knew he was the University Librarian. It appealed to me as a postgraduate student to have a volume on my shelves that belonged to the unmet person in charge of an institution in which I spent so much time and whose rich collections had such an impact on the inner weather of so many selves – my own among them. I'd heard of Alberto Moravia but at that point hadn't read any of his work, so a reasonably priced hardback edition of one of his novels was also an appealing prospect, regardless of who its previous owner had been. Though I have no memory of packing or unpacking it, the book must have traveled with me from Scotland to Ireland to Wales, and then back to Scotland, as I changed jobs and locations between 1980 and 2012. Occasionally I noticed it sitting on a shelf as I looked for some other volume. I always intended to read it but repeatedly postponed so doing as other books intervened and other priorities took precedence over reading.

IV

On winter walks through woodland when I was a boy, I'd always stop at stacks of cut logs and prize off the loose dead bark to see what creatures might be sheltering beneath it. The most striking finds were hibernating queen wasps, their sleek black and yellow hulls deadly as hidden missiles lying snug in secret silos, cached beneath a dull coffining of wood. When *Agostino* split at the fracture of my and Fifoot's names, its quotidian guise of second-hand book was sloughed off like some flimsy sarcophagus to reveal beneath it the quicksilver of emergent complexity, as striking as some gigantic gleaming scarab. Once revealed, its presence – majestic, mysterious and monstrous – defied containment in the deadwood bark of ordinary prose.

What awoke this hibernating scarab? Why did those two signatures act like sharp steel wedges, splitting the wood of ordinary containment as thought tapped them further and further into it? Perhaps it was the ghostly shadow of Fifoot's life lingering in his written name, or the sense of all the turnings in my life that had brought me to Edinburgh in March 1980 and led me away from there again. It could even have resulted from the fact that the book had been in my possession unread for so long that reading it pointed to the enormous dormant potential of script; the fact that meaning can lie in wait for us for years, perhaps indefinitely, stowed safely in the hold of writing. Just as some seeds are capable of propagating centuries after they form, supposing finally the conditions needed for germination occur, so books can retain their potency for centuries after they're written. This power of dormancy confers upon them a kind of live current. Maybe in this case its voltage was enough to spark the kind of containment-failure that changed the leaden categorization of *Agostino* as "book" into something far less certain and constraining.

Though Moravia's novella has much to recommend it, I don't think it was anything to do with what he wrote that caused *Agostino* to take on the properties it did. This was a case of the unwritten book, of factors quite separate from those the author intended, acting on the mind. Whatever caused the alchemy that happened, as I held it, began to read it, the book seemed less and less a bounded, familiar object safely named and fixed within the accustomed realm of the everyday, and more and more some kind of mercurial nexus, a fragment of meteorite intruding on this world from another. I came to see it as a mysterious node linking disparate individuals and giving access to a cascade of connections. These connections swept away the anchoring curtailment of "book" and formed a network whose scale and gravity was enough to pull the present into orbit around its compacted tangle of lives, places and events.

V

Instilled in any signature is a sense of the writer's individuality. Signing your name is like leaving a kind of fingerprint; a unique trace of who you are. I never met Erik Richard Sidney Fifoot, but his signature – and the little I did know about him – prompted me to find out more. Fifoot ("Dick" to his friends) was born on June 14 1925. Public school and Oxford educated, he served in the Coldstream Guards from 1943-46. In the Orders of Battle for March 30th 1945, when his regiment was engaged in crossing the Rhine in the final days of World War II, Fifoot is listed as a platoon commander. He's already been awarded a Military Cross, a medal intended to mark exemplary gallantry in active operations against the enemy. To his MA in Jurisprudence, Fifoot added a Diploma in Librarianship from the University of London, and his career after returning to civilian life was that of a successful academic librarian. He worked at university libraries in Leeds and Nottingham before coming to Edinburgh in 1960. He remained there until he was appointed Bodley's Librarian in 1979, holding this position in the Bodleian Library in Oxford – one of the premier posts in British librarianship – until 1981. Four years after the end of the War, he married Jean Thain. They had two daughters. His main published work is *A Bibliography of Edith, Osbert and Sacheverell Sitwell* (1963, second edition 1971). Fifoot died on June 24 1992. He's remembered fondly by colleagues, one of whom described him as "a scholar with a heart." Photographs show a refined, almost ascetic looking figure cast in precisely the kind of mold one might expect from Berkhampstead School, Oxford and the Coldstream Guards. In my student days in Edinburgh he was an august but distant figure, rarely glimpsed, someone about whom I knew little beyond the bare facts of his name and position as University Librarian. It was only years later, prompted by his signature on the book, that I sought out the details of his life.

His penciled "E.R.S. Fifoot" on *Agostino* is like a dropped glove still warm from being worn. The gently fluent contours of the name act as a kind of electrocardiogram, their lines charting in their rise and fall a tiny remnant of his life. The signature came to strike me almost as a solidified pulse, a fragment of some stalagmite of self, recording in the unique fixity of its shape the echo of a vanished life. This little segment of fossilized pulse, the heartbeat of a life frozen into the rigid framework of a handwritten name, seemed to tear the fabric of the commonplace. The rip once started was aided and abetted by my own name and "Edinburgh, March 1980," since to my knowing eye that place and time and my occupancy of them carried so much weight in the subsequent unfolding of my life. It was almost as if Fifoot and I had become jagged shards of stubbornly irreducible particularity, puncturing with their insistent presence the little dam walls of generalization built into "book."

Although the first breach in the hold of ordinary containment was caused by these signatures, it might have been a manageable enough leak if it had merely been confined to Fifoot and to me. Two lives introduce a wealth of detail, connection, and complexity – but one that is still bankable via the economics of ordinary discourse. But our names sank shafts in the hard skin of the everyday that quickly led into a warren of fault-lines, each one leading on to another, their linkage creating a bewildering density of other times, places, lives. Sometime prior to my buying the book, Fifoot must have held it as he signed his name. Connected to the pencil in his hand, as if it was a conductor's baton, was the whole complex symphony of who he was: his conception, birth, childhood, schooling, soldiering, marriage, fatherhood; the dreams he dreamed, the words he spoke, his hopes and fears. In the same way, my pen writing "Edinburgh, March 1980" pointed to my antecedents and origins, my descendents and end, the warm moments of being that I've occupied.

The fact that our eyes had – assuming he'd actually read the book – scanned the same pages, read the same words, helped to slip the moorings of containment by prompting an awareness not just of Fifoot and of me but of the unseen community of readers whose spectral presence had, like ours, temporarily lit with the warmth of their attention the paths traced out by Moravia's prose – not just in this copy of the book but in others, whether in translation or the original Italian. Each constituent life in this invisible community of *Agostino* readers, embedded in its own unique context of connection, association, limitation, led from one to another in a chain-reaction that quickly moves beyond the confines of books and readers to issue in a blaze of sentience, dotted with the disappearance of each mortal individual – for death's serial annihilation of our fires is as much a part of us as our umbilical cords. Fifoot's pencil, my pen came to resemble less any conductor's baton than some sort of lightning conductor, sending to earth in this small book the colossal charge of history, prehistory – time itself, the very fact of being. "Book" is quickly scorched with something well beyond its ordinary hold.

VI

One of the things I've always liked about second-hand books is the way they hold the spoor of other readers and how, following their tracks, a sense of almost tribal complicity can sometimes be kindled, despite the solitariness of reading as an act. For some people, the imperative of ownership makes them erase or score out other names, or obliterate them with bookplates, covering over all the tracks of those who've passed this way before them. Only with the unchallenged emblazoning of their own name can they celebrate a volume's being part of their domain, their private property. That approach has never much appealed to me. I prefer to sign my name alongside previous owners and hope that others will do likewise in the years to come, as the book continues to travel through time, long outlasting any individual reader. With *Agostino*, it came to feel as if the book was already covered in hundreds of signatures, though only two are visible, and that each one led off into a tangle of connections. Picking up the book, I half expected to have to tug hard before it could be wrenched free from the liana-like clusters of stories in which it was embedded, the tendrils of a billion moments wrapped tightly around it, suturing the book to a mesmerizing spiral of lives.

The resonance of touch seemed to come alive, almost to acquire a voice, as I held the book in my hand and imagined all the other hands that had held it before mine, that will hold it after my touch has gone cold; the other objects those hands touched in their turn, the other hands they'd clasped, the other bodies caressed. Fifoot's grip, soon to be dusted with a librarian's familiarity with books, would most likely have come to this one as a young man, the echo of armaments and love-making still fresh upon it. From 30 March 1944, when he crossed the Rhine, until that unspecified March day thirty-six years later when I bought the book that had once been his, is not much longer than the time between my buying and reading *Agostino*. Add the two together and it's little short of Fifoot's lifespan. But the book seems freighted with a weight of days that quite capsizes such brief measures of duration. "Book," instead of enwrapping, containing, defining in the usual way, fails to find its ordinarily secure purchase and slips off *Agostino*. Uncovered, this little object's nakedness points to a kind of beckoning whirlpool; a portal into the shift and flux of being, out of whose filaments our lives are knitted and unraveled. How can we map its nature and extent without merely falling back on the curtailing superficialities of ordinary diction? Just beyond the boundaries of the commonsense perspectives in which it's usually held,

Agostino seems like a kind of talisman of far horizons whispering insistently of other times, other lives, other places and how all of them, however much words rule them out of sight, are as close-fettered to us as are we to them.

VII

Putting *Agostino* back on my bookshelves felt like setting a live ember amidst highly flammable material – for much of what applies to this book applies to others too, each one trailing with it an invisible network of exposed nerves, their fibers pointing beyond anything the neat confinement of author-text-reader can contain. Every book – every object in the lexicon of things we use – comes smudged with an alphabet of touch, is stained with a bloodline of association. The contagion of connection, once caught, spreads like wildfire and threatens any sense of containment with vistas it is hard to encompass. Even the plain wood of a bookshelf thus infected comes to seem pregnant, heavily swollen with the story of its origins, deep-structure, manufacture, use – awakening the long history of plant-life, the dance of atoms, the transient lives of those who felled and shaped and bought and sold this thing.

One of the volumes I happened to place Agostino next to was Edward Armstrong's *Birds of the Grey Wind*, first published four years before Moravia's novella. In the course of this lyrical – and philosophical – celebration of Northern Ireland's countryside and birdlife Armstrong suggests that:

> There is a profound poignant joy in experiencing contact with naked reality, life stripped of artificialities and reduced to its elementals.

I warm to such a viewpoint. But it's easy to limit "elementals" to the kind of things that Armstrong had in mind – earth, sea, sky, day and night and the weathers they bring to fall upon us. These are, of course, of fundamental importance. But are there not also less obvious elementals? Can we not encounter "naked reality" in the ordinary things around us as well as barefoot, climbing a rock face on remote Rathlin Island, the Atlantic crashing below us, as per the context in which Armstrong was writing? Is it not the elemental aspect of *Agostino* that refuses containment in anything as bland as "book?" Is it not something akin to a tiny corner of "naked reality" that we glimpse through the pinhole apertures of the signatures my copy bears? No wonder it's difficult to find words that work; no wonder we fall back so readily on the worn tackle of our quotidian masking vocabulary and the lifelines of simplification it throws us.

VIII

Unlike essays, where the essayist can wander in and out of the text at will, writers mostly absent themselves from fiction and it is the narrative alone that claims attention. That's something I welcome – who wants the author's shadow darkening one's reading of a story? But in the case of *Agostino*, a trace of Moravia's life has been implanted in the book, courtesy of an introduction by Ian Greenlees. Greenlees recounts how he was in Naples in May 1944 and received a phone call from an American friend who had just entered the small town of Fondi and found Alberto Moravia and his wife emerging from hiding to greet the Allied troops. They had taken refuge there nine months previously, fleeing the growing likelihood of arrest. Moravia had been opposed to Mussolini's Fascists and, being half-Jewish, was in considerable peril. Inevitably, these sparse details and others I already knew of Moravia's life (the tubercular disease that had led to a lengthy period of confinement in childhood, his choice of nom-de-plume, his time spent in America, the reception accorded to his other novels at home and abroad) were drawn into the current of lives that seemed to surge through *Agostino*. It also made the book into a kind of wartime artifact, speaking of the destruction visited on Europe, the terrible fate of so many of its Jews, the way in which writers and librarians and shopkeepers and teachers, parents and children, wives and husbands, were caught up in the maelstrom. It was strange to think of Fifoot crossing the Rhine as a platoon commander while Moravia and his wife hid in Fondi, neither party aware of the other, still less of how the book would eventually link them. For me, such things more or less eclipse the novella Moravia labored to produce. The story *Agostino* tells me is far removed from the simple one its author wrote.

Greenlees makes the suggestion that "*Agostino* is perhaps the most mature work" in Moravia's oeuvre. He also quotes a comment of Moravia's which I find arresting:

> I believe a novelist is not worthy of the name unless he succeeds in creating a character who does not resemble himself.

I'm not sure if this is true, but it made me think about the criteria for success in the very different genre of the essay. Perhaps no essayist is worthy of that name unless he or she succeeds in creating objects which do not resemble their usual descriptors but are instead depicted in that elemental rawness which shows how little, in the ordinary run of things, we allow them to resemble what they in fact appear to be.

Scrimshaw
(Reading a whale's tooth)

One of the most treasured remnants from my childhood is a whale's tooth. It was given to me in exchange for – and as a distraction for losing – a tooth of my own. The gift was from my dentist, Mr. Wilson, about whom I wish I could remember more. It was the first time I'd had a tooth out and I was scared. But Mr. Wilson more than lived up to his reputation of being good with children. After the extraction, to distract me from the blood and pain, and the shock of having a part of myself excised, disconnected from my body and left beside me bloody on a metal tray, he put the whale's tooth in my hand – its icy density completely unexpected – and said that I could have it in exchange for my tooth. Even in my distressed state, I could calculate the excellence of such a swop with a little boy's unfailing playground logic.

Resembling a tiny elephant's tusk, the tooth fits snugly in my grip whenever I lift it from its accustomed place on my desk. Four and a half inches (13 cm) long, it curves and tapers to a strong, smooth point. Grasped in my hand so that an inch of point escapes the fist, it's like a primitive stabbing dagger. It fills the hand with the same cold weight as a gun. At the end where the tooth would have been affixed to the jaw, a kind of gummy, fleshy residue fills the center of the tooth. There's still a hint of pink about it, the kind of organic matter that would make some people say "yuck!" But it's quite dry, completely hard, and emits no odor I can detect. There are a few cracks and imperfections on the tooth, but despite these it feels smooth. The creamy ivory surface, yellowing at the tip, has the slight sheen of a natural enameled glaze. At one point, about an inch and a half (4 cm) from the tip, someone has cut an X. Where its lines intersect a tiny hole has been drilled.

Mr. Wilson's surgery was on the first floor of a building that stood on a busy street corner in the center of Lisburn, the town near Belfast where I grew up. The waiting room offered a splendid vantage point from which to watch the bustle of people and vehicles outside. Though there were magazines and children's comics arrayed on a table in the middle of the waiting room, I was never tempted by them. Their pristine state suggested that I wasn't alone in thinking that the windows provided far more entertainment. My image of Mr. Wilson himself is vague and I don't trust it. I remember him as a small, dark-haired man with a broad forehead accentuated by a receding hairline. He was invariably dressed in a white, short-sleeved clinician's tunic. The tunic is accurate enough, but I'm suspicious of the person I've put into it. He looks too like Desmond Morris – author of *The Naked Ape*. I suspect that somewhere in the inscrutable workings of the memory a picture of Morris – either from a book jacket or his TV appearances – has been superimposed over Mr. Wilson because of some superficial similarity between them. This has effectively obliterated my recollection of what my childhood dentist really looked like.

The most striking thing about Mr. Wilson to a child's eye, and what has remained as his signature feature ever since, something far more deeply incised on memory that anything about his face, was the nicotine staining on his fingers. In those days dentists didn't wear gloves – and of course his hands came in for close inspection as he plied his trade. His thumb and the first two fingers on his right hand were glazed to the same shade of yellowed ivory as the tip of the whale's tooth. I can still recall the pungent aroma of tobacco, stale smoke, soap and disinfectant that always emanated from him.

In the immediate aftermath of the extraction, my jaw was gently clamped on a wad of lint to staunch the bleeding, my heart was racing, and my eyes flitted between the whale's tooth, grasped like a trophy in my hand, and the metal dish beside me with the dreadful pliers and my own forlorn tooth, its roots indecently exposed, drawing my gaze repeatedly to their desperate, defeated nakedness. I was in no fit state to engage in conversation and can't imagine having asked Mr. Wilson anything. But – again demonstrating his skill with kids – he kept up a beguiling banter and, anticipating the question I most wanted answered, explained how the tooth had come into his possession.

A whale had appeared in Belfast harbor, he said, and seemed to be in great distress. The harbormaster, a grizzled sailor with years of seafaring behind him, was fluent in the language of cetaceans and asked the beast what ailed it. "Toothache" was the answer given – caused of course by eating too many sweets (even then I recognized the heavy-handed moral of the story). Knowing that none of the Belfast dentists had the skill to take on this unusual patient, the harbormaster advised the whale to swim eight miles up the River Lagan to Lisburn, where his friend Mr. Wilson would come to the quayside and do what was necessary. The whale sped off and Mr. Wilson, having been phoned by the harbormaster, gathered up his biggest implements and walked down to the river. Soon he saw a huge spout of water being sprayed from the whale's blowhole as it powered up the river. Slowing gently, it came to a halt and nudged its bulk alongside the town's dingy wharf, as big as any barge that had ever berthed there. When it opened its fearsome mouth, Mr. Wilson reached in with an enormous pair of pliers and pulled out the offending tooth. The whale thanked him and went on its way. He even produced an outsized pair of pliers to illustrate his story. What function they served I can't imagine; they were far too large to accomplish any feat of human dentistry.

Of course, even at seven, I knew this was a tall tale. Quite apart from a harbormaster who spoke Whalish, or a whale able to survive in freshwater, the river Lagan has been turned into a canal for several long stretches between Belfast and Lisburn, with the insuperable barrier of lock-gates. I knew whales didn't eat sweets or seek out dentists, and the picture of Mr. Wilson reaching into one's mouth and pulling out a tooth was absurd. But it was a good story, well told, and I had the enticing prop of a real whale's tooth clasped in my hand. It was like a token brought back from some magical world that almost proved its existence. Deliberately far-fetched, Mr. Wilson's fantastic narrative did what it was designed to do. It transported me away from my present surroundings and kept my mind from dwelling on my pain.

Did he have lots of whales' teeth, or a collection of other animals' teeth, so that he could present one to every child after an extraction? If I'd kept him as my dentist, and had had more teeth removed, might I have built up a collection of dental curios – teeth from sharks, lions, horses, tigers, snakes, each one accompanied by its own fantastic story? Or was the whale's tooth just a one-off gesture, a single impulsive act of which I was the privileged recipient? I was never to discover. That Mr. Wilson was good with children was widely acknowledged – and it's certainly a quality I'd attest to. But my parents gradually came to suspect that he was too kind with his junior patients. Reluctant to cause them pain, he sometimes avoided treatment that, however unpleasant, was necessary. I don't know whether my parents' suspicion was justified – but when I changed dentists the new one embarked on an extensive program of fillings and kept tut-tutting that they should have been attended to long ago. He was a pleasant enough man, but he had none of Mr. Wilson's panache. A dentist who uses a whale's tooth as an analgesic is a hard act for anyone to follow.

How did Mr. Wilson really get the tooth? I'd love to know, but this has become one of those quotidian questions, once straightforwardly answerable, that has turned into an insoluble mystery. I moved away from my home town shortly after my eighteenth birthday and so lost touch with all the little networks of local knowledge that might have provided clues. Mr. Wilson himself died years ago and I know no one who remembers him any better than I do. The surgery on that first floor corner site has long gone – the building converted into offices. There's no one I can ask, nowhere I can go to find an answer. All I'm left with is the durable presence of the tooth, my memory of his giving it to me, and a spectrum of possibilities spun by the imagination to account for his having such an improbable object to hand. It's impossible to know for sure how closely any of these possibilities match what really happened.

"Scrimshaw" – a strange word, of uncertain origin – refers to drawings engraved on whales' teeth or bones. Often said to have originated on whaling ships in the eighteenth century, something that sailors did to occupy their leisure time on long voyages far away from home, it's hard to say if this can be regarded as a genuine beginning, or if the sailors were influenced by what they saw engraved on Inuit artifacts, a practice in that culture that dates back several thousand years. Whatever its origins, dictionary definitions of scrimshaw are careful to withhold any approbation that might come from describing it as an art. It's presented as the naïve, if not crude, pictorial efforts of unsophisticated seamen – artisans at best – not the creative work of artists. *Chambers Dictionary*, for example, defines it as: "a sailor's spare time handicraft, as engraving fanciful designs on shells, whales' teeth etc.: anything so executed." Sometimes the designs are indeed fanciful – an improbably well endowed sweetheart, a mermaid, a unicorn – but often scrimshaw features meticulously accurate studies of the ships on which the scrimshanders (the name for practitioners of scrimshaw) were working. The brutal business of hunting whales is also a popular subject. It seems a cruel irony that many of the teeth and bones were inscribed with scenes of the slaughter and butchery that procured them. Scrimshaw is done with a needle or fine blade, and the cuts are then stained black – color is unusual – traditionally using soot from the galley stoves, or gunpowder, mixed with a little whale oil. Ink was too rare a commodity on whaling vessels to waste it on such fancies.

Apart from a few natural lines and scratches, and the small X with the tiny drill hole at its centre, the whale's tooth Mr. Wilson gave me is as unmarked as it would have been when it was in the mouth of the whale that bore it. But the way it strikes me now often makes me think that its pale ivory surface is covered with a dense black tracery of scrimshaw. Some of the pictures in this imaginary engraving show how the tooth came into the hands of a Lisburn dentist. They give all the lost detail of the milieu he occupied, the people he associated with, and what led to the moment when he placed the tooth in a tearful seven-year-old's hand. Like fingerprints that record the whole genealogy of human touch upon it, the whorls of this imaginary scrimshaw picture all the lives – mine included – in which the tooth has featured, tracing out the connections that explain how it passed between us and became embedded in our histories, part of the mosaic of what happens, a dot in the pointillism of being.

Yet for all that these pictures of human involvement trace out complex networks of cause and effect and relationship, they are the most straightforward part of the swirling black lines I imagine cut into the tooth's surface. What most of them picture, following the usual tradition of scrimshaw, has to do with the vessel and the voyage – meaning, in this case, the whale and its life-story. It's incredible enough to think of where this tooth has been since it parted company with the mouth that bore it, how it has been passed from hand to hand in a little web of transactions – gifts, purchases, findings, takings – each hand representing a unique biography, densely filled with its own secret interiorities and publicly observable unfoldings. But how much more incredible is the story of this little prop itself, quite independent of any human dimension.

The tooth's proximate beginning lay in the mating of two whales. An egg and sperm, smaller than the dot of ink above this i, melded together in the clasp of fertilization. Embedded in the womb, like an ember buried within the warm tonnage of its mother's fleshy tinder, this new glint of life-fire burned within the strict containments of all the preset fuses that channeled it into the incandescence of an embryonic orca – for the tooth is from a killer whale; it's too small to be a sperm whale's (the scrimshanders' favorite). As the female swam with her pod, hunted, played, ate, excreted, powered through miles of ocean, her sleek torpedo form sometimes reaching thirty miles per hour, unseen inside her a silent orchestration marshaled her calf's cells into ribs and fins and eyes and skull and teeth and vertebrae, each part of its complexity dovetailing gracefully with the next, the body blueprint unpacked and joined together with elegant precision so that, after seventeen months gestation, the calf was born.

Somewhere in the waters of the world, in a moment that would have taken little longer than Mr. Wilson's extraction of my tooth, a new killer whale swam free and nestled beside its mother, registering in its brain for the first time the exterior dimensions of her bulk. Entirely dependent to begin with on suckling fat-rich maternal milk, the young whale grew. A hardness within the jaws gradually ripened and the teeth erupted, punctuating the gums with their lethal interlocking rows. The calf took solid food, learnt to hunt. Its size and vigor rapidly increased. It grew to around twenty to thirty feet and would have weighed between eight and ten tons. The tooth that Mr. Wilson gave me will have closed with deadly force on the live nutritious flesh of seals and other prey as this streamlined wolf of the sea ranged through the waters with its pack – orcas hunt in pods of anything from just a handful of individuals to thirty or more. How many lives will this single fang have bitten into, helped to change from creature into carcass?

Since killer whales inhabit all the oceans of the world, it's hard to tell where this one swam – but since the species is most numerous in the Arctic and Antarctic, it's likely that the tooth will have felt against its hardness the icy flow of waters there. Was it a female or a male? Did it bear or sire offspring? How long did it live? What were the circumstances of its death? Again, I encounter a cluster of questions that would be straightforwardly answerable given the right perspective, but in the here and now that defines my encounter with the tooth they are shrouded in the mystique of the unanswerable.

All of the drama of individual genesis and development is implicit in the cold lump of organic matter with which the whale's tooth weights my hand whenever I pick it up. It's easy to forget, because of its stillness and silence, its hard, stone-like inertness, that this is a remnant from a life of blood and breath and furious activity. Carved into the microscopic circuitry of this little meteorite, fallen from planet Orca, there's the DNA coding that structured this life-form into the precise shape of its species' specifications. Traces of the individual drawn from that coding still ghost about it, suggesting echoes of a unique life-story played out in the ocean as we play out ours upon the land.

Behind the whale that spawned the tooth are its parents. Behind them are theirs, and beyond that, taking in an immensity of time, there's a paired line of antecedents going back some 60 million years to the land animals whales once were. And, stretching back from them, there is the continuance of a bloodline whose beginnings are rooted in life's first eruption on the planet. The genealogy of the killer whale – like that of any creature we encounter – leads finally to the same destination: that moment of naked singularity, the great beginning, the point at which there was something rather than nothing. One thing leads back to another and before long we are floundering in oceans of time that make the whale's watery world seem like a raindrop by comparison.

"The whale's tooth on my desk" can be described – dismissed – like that; six words that draw the thin film of familiar diction, like oil on water, across depths that are difficult to fathom. The whale's tooth, like many of the things around us, is a silent conspirator in the illusions that we weave. For the most part they wear without complaint the names we give them, the shorthand by which we routinely attenuate their identity and significance. But the truth is that we deal in wonders every day. Sometimes they break out of the confinements we put on them; our fire blankets of ordinary discourse fail, incinerated by what we've thrown them over.

Sometimes I feel like pounding the tooth with a hammer to make it yield up its secrets, but I know that when it smashed all the fragments would each one still withhold its story and simply replicate the enigma of its being. Sometimes, the tooth clasped tightly in my hand, I imagine squeezing it like some hard udder until the milk of its essence is forced out to fuel my pen with the right phrases to describe it. But I know that any blood extracted from this tooth-stone would be like invisible ink and that anything I wrote with it on the page would take me no further in grasping its essential nature. Sometimes I think the atomic structure of things better reflects their nature than the bland, static surfaces we're conscious of. Perhaps the orbits of electrons, the spaces yawning within the deep structure of things, provides a richer source of metaphor for what faces us than the visible artifacts constructed from such surreally miniature building blocks. But it's hard to see a solid object like the tooth as, essentially, composed of a kind of particle-stippled emptiness, however much this may be the natural scrimshaw tattooed into the structural essence of everything around us, including us.

Looked at in one way, the tooth is just a remnant from childhood, an eccentric curio of little value to anyone but me. Looked at in another way, it feels almost like a relic, something made near numinous by the wonders it's festooned with. Like the Buddhists of Sri Lanka and their famous Temple of the Tooth, built to house what's said to be one of the Buddha's incisors, perhaps this essay is my way of enshrining the whale's tooth, placing it in the verbal equivalent of a jewel-studded reliquary. Or, far from such reverence, perhaps I've been acting more like the eponymous hero in William Golding's novel *Pincher Martin*. To avoid facing the fact that his ship has sunk and that he is drowning, Pincher Martin constructs in his imagination a bizarre dreamlike island based solely on the topography of one of his own tongue-explored teeth. Dazzled by the store of memories and stories and possibilities suggested by the whale's tooth, am I guilty of weaving mere illusions? Sometimes I think the time to put childhood things aside is overdue and that I should just grasp the tooth in my hand for one last time, take it to the sea and throw it in, watch as it vanishes into the salty amniotic from which we all began. More often I'm content to let it sit and gather dust on my desk – and to marvel every now and then at how much more is held within it than even the most intricate and extensive scrimshaw of words could chronicle.

"Coincidences, Graces, Gifts..."
(Reading Seamus Heaney)

When I was growing up in Northern Ireland, people were thought to come of age at 21. I'm not sure when, or why, this was revised downwards so that, today, 18 is regarded as the point at which we step over the threshold of dependency on parents and become fully fledged adults: independent, sensible, accountable, mature. I don't know how well I cleared those hurdles. In fact, as I grew older, I came increasingly to suspect that – the raw chronology of aging notwithstanding – there's a sense in which none of us ever properly grows up. Certainly the violent events in Ulster that cast such shadows on my youth did not suggest much sense or maturity in society at large; accountability that simply blames the other side is surely childishness at its worst.

One of the more lavish presents I was given when I came of age was a cheque for £21 from an uncle well enough off to lay down a pound for every year. It was a considerable amount in those far-off days. I used it to buy hardback copies of Flann O'Brien's books, at that point my favorite author. My uncle was not best pleased when he discovered how I'd spent his largesse. It wasn't that he disapproved of books – though he shared a widespread family view that I read too much. It was the nature of the books, or, more pointedly, the religio-political affiliation of their author, that sparked his disapproval. Nothing was ever said of course, as is typically the case in Northern Ireland. But despite the absence of any direct comment about my purchase of O'Brien's books, a heavy sense of disagreement with my choice, condemnation, angry disappointment at the way I'd let people down, was effortlessly conveyed by terseness, silence, look – that potent dialect of mood in which everyone was schooled to deadly fluency long before the age of 21.

To me, Flann O'Brien was the writer of such brilliant works as *At Swim-Two-Birds* and *The Third Policeman*. To my uncle, O'Brien's literary accomplishments meant nothing. They came a long way second to the fact that he was a Fenian or a Teague (these offensive words for Catholic were used more or less interchangeably in the Protestant patois of the day). That meant his books were unsuitable for anyone from "our side." Buying them indicated a worrying lapse of tribal solidarity on my part. It suggested, at the very least, poor judgment and, at worst, that I harbored turncoat tendencies. It made my uncle look at me askance.

Telling him about my new O'Brien books seemed demanded by the courtesy of saying thank you for his gift. Perhaps if I'd been a little more mature at 21, I'd have expressed my gratitude more strategically, without disclosing exactly what I'd bought. But at least I had the sense not to share with my uncle the (guilty?) knowledge that on the same shelf as my O'Brien collection there were the books of another Teague writer I esteemed, Seamus Heaney. I knew that if my uncle had seen the Heaney books what he'd have noticed wouldn't have been the titles, or the slim, poetry-indicating girth of the spines, but the name "Seamus." Like "O'Brien," but even more so, "Seamus" signaled membership of the opposing tribe. To Ulster Protestant ears, it's an indelibly Catholic name. "Seamus" would have acted as a red rag (a green one really) to the bull of my uncle's prejudices. It would have made me even further suspect in his eyes.

*   *   *

The only time I met Seamus Heaney was in Belfast, on June 30 1987. That was the day on which UVF gunmen murdered James Keelan, a Catholic living with a Protestant woman in Ballysillan. Such killings became common coin in the currency of sectarianism that, for a time, looked set to bankrupt life in Northern Ireland completely, flooding the ordinary transactions of our little day-to-day decencies with a counterfeit economy of tit-for-tat exchange: one brutality met with another; revenge confused with justice; anything that spoke of accommodation, tolerance, forgiveness reviled as weakness or betrayal of your side. I mention Keelan's killing in the same breath as my meeting with the poet, not because there's any real connection between them beyond their happening on the same date, but because, from my perspective, Heaney's poetry and the poison of Ulster's Troubles are intimately intermingled. I don't mean by this that Heaney's writing was principally about the Troubles, or that his was a political voice raised in response to the carnage, but simply that, for me, his work provided a source of antidote to the social venom of the times. As the bombings and shootings of the Troubles raged, Heaney's measured voice provided a kind of haven. It spoke out not for one side or the other but for ordinary, essential human things that transcended the bigotry and hatred; it provided a kind of rosary, beaded with day-to-day occurrence, object and affection.

I can date meeting the man exactly. But when it comes to my first encounter with his work, I'm less certain when that happened. Sometimes when I buy a book, I sign my name in it and often add the place and date. But with my Heaney books, not all bear such citations. The earliest one to do so is *North*. In this, Heaney's fourth collection, I've written "Chris Arthur, Belfast, September 1975." But I'm quite sure it was some years before buying *North* that I first became acquainted with his poems. My copy of Heaney's first collection, *Death of a Naturalist*, published in 1966, only has my name signed in it. I've no recollection of the date of purchase, though the place was almost certainly Belfast too. Judging from the handwriting of the signature, I'd guess I was fourteen, fifteen, or maybe just sixteen. This would mean that I first encountered Heaney's work sometime between 1969 and 1971 – precisely the point at which Ulster's violence was clicking into gear.

*　　*　　*

Although the age at which I first encountered Heaney's work suggests school as the likely mode of introduction, I'm certain this was not the case. This wasn't because Protestant schools were avoiding a Catholic writer – though they're capable of that – but simply that Heaney's reputation wasn't yet fully established when I was a pupil. It was a close call. I left school in 1973 (I can still remember helping to crisscross the classroom windows with clear tape to minimize glass shrapnel in the event of explosions). Only a year later, Penguin Education brought out a book that was to prove popular in UK schools, *Worlds: Seven Modern Poets*. It was designed to introduce contemporary poetry to younger readers and Heaney was one of the seven poets featured. The selection of his work in *Worlds* is accompanied by a series of photographs by Larry Herman. These show Heaney and his family and scenes of rural life. As Geoffrey Summerfield puts it in his editor's introduction, the photographs are not intended as "illustrations" but as reminders "that poems, like poets, come out of the world we know, and that that is where they belong." One photo strikes a very different note from all the rest and gives a telling clue about the kind of world anyone living in Northern Ireland came to know in the 1970s. It shows Heaney passing through the metal-gated fence of a city centre security cordon, probably in Belfast. He's pictured just inside the barrier, raising his arms to be body-searched by a waiting soldier. Including this image was a good way of showing how the

Troubles intruded, sounding a discordant note right next to ordinary domesticity and scenes of peaceful daily life. Looking at the photo I'm reminded of the scores of times I passed through such security checks myself. They were designed primarily to prevent incendiary bomb attacks. Often, I was in Belfast to browse the bookshops. Had I been searched on some of those occasions and asked to open a suspect package in my pocket, it would have contained one of Heaney's slim volumes: incendiaries of a different sort.

Death of a Naturalist was published three years before I left the first school I attended. This was Friends' School in Lisburn – a Quaker establishment, as its name suggests. It's a pity I hadn't known Heaney's first collection when I was there, because one of the poems, the wonderful "In Small Townlands" is dedicated to – and about the work of – Colin Middleton, who was our art teacher at the time. We never appreciated his exceptional talent. In fact I don't think we even thought of him as an *artist*, merely as the person who tried to teach us art. Heaney's poem might have helped correct our philistine blindness. Or perhaps, in the efficiently cruel way of children, we'd just have taken a tribute poem as further evidence of eccentricity; fresh ammunition for taunting someone we considered odd. Whenever I read the poem now, a picture of Middleton comes to mind. Likewise, if I try to remember the artist's face it's invariably accompanied by some of Heaney's words. The two have become inseparably conjoined. The last verse in particular is closely interwoven with Middleton's disconcertingly acute stare, which felt as if it peeled through our immaturity to some underlying bedrock more worthy of his attention:

> His eyes, thick, greedy lenses, fire
> This bare bald earth with white and red,
> Incinerate it till its black
> And brilliant as a funeral pyre:
> A new world cools out of his head.

*   *   *

How do we find the writing that speaks to us? How do we decide which books to attend to and which to ignore? Beyond the sanctioned syllabus of texts laid down at school and university, what are the factors that mold our reading lives into the unique shapes they manifest, twining around us invisibly and offering what can seem almost like magic portals into topographies that extend (and alter) the landscapes of the self? More specifically, how did a Protestant boy growing up in Northern Ireland happen to stumble into an acquaintance with Flann O'Brien and Seamus Heaney, such that their nudge and clasp of words, the torque and spin of language as they forged it, embraced him, opening vistas that seemed to legitimate and expand perspectives that were already tentatively dawning in his psyche?

I'd love to be able to trace out the pathways that led me to O'Brien and Heaney, and to those other books I came to think of as canonical in the reading life that happened alongside my real one, greatly influencing it and helping me to come of age. No doubt our literary fingerprints change over time, but the books we encounter with adolescent passion surely leave an indelible mark, however much they may be overlaid with other influences. Perhaps a few of the items in my literary canon were there due to school, or because they were already on the bookshelves at home, but for the most part I think my choice of reading resulted from chance discoveries, many of them made whilst browsing Belfast's bookshops – Mullan's, Erskine Mayne's, the APCK, Gardiner's, Eason's, and the University Bookshop at Queen's. Looking back, it's hard not to elevate such places into beacons of civilization, given what was unfolding in the streets around them.

As well as the serendipity of bookshop browsing, reviews in newspapers might be thought an obvious way of becoming alerted to books. But I'm not sure what age I was when I began to read newspapers independently, or to notice much beyond the headlines (which in Ulster at that time followed a predictable catechism of outrage and condemnation). The paper my father read every day – Sundays excepted – was Ulster's long-established *News Letter*, first printed in 1737 and still going strong today. But despite its venerable age, it carried only minimal coverage of the arts and almost nothing about contemporary writing. It would have provided few, if any, literary pointers.

Much more likely to have flagged up Heaney's work than the stolidly Protestant *News Letter*, was *The Honest Ulsterman*, founded by James Simmons in 1968. I subscribed to it for years and still have 40 or more issues sitting on my bookshelves. But the earliest one I can find is no.53, dating from November/December 1976, by which time Heaney was already an important landmark on my literary horizons. It could be, of course, that I've simply mislaid earlier issues; my books are "arranged" in a way that's closer to chaos than a librarian's strict order. Or perhaps these putative pre-1976 issues were lent to friends, discarded in periodic clearances, or lost in one of my many changes of address. I can't remember now when I first took out a subscription. But even if I could, and even if it was through this little magazine's vibrant pages that I first learnt about Heaney's poems, that wouldn't explain what led me to *The Honest Ulsterman*. How our particular, individual reading profiles are formed remains elusive. It's difficult to trace their genealogies. Like peeling an onion – only one in which all the skins are of the same thin, papery parchment of the exterior – if one book, or magazine, or friend's suggestion is the reason for reading something, behind it lie a whole series of interdependent antecedent causes. Even supposing it was possible to neatly peel back all the layers, without any crumpling, tearing, or omission, charting precisely and completely the way in which one thing underlies and leads to another, I suspect that what would be left at the end of this forensic process wouldn't so much be enlightenment as a pile of whispering, sloughed off skins that would only offer the ghostliest of hints about the nature of the snake that shed them.

*   *   *

Of course "A Magazine of Revolution," as the first issue of *The Honest Ulsterman* styled itself, isn't to everyone's taste. Although this rousing – or ridiculous – sobriquet was soon dropped from the masthead, even the magazine's unaccompanied name put some people off. Was it just for men? Only for Ulster-born writers? And, in any case, amidst all the partisan warring, with so many lies and half-truths abounding, was there much credibility in the concept of an *honest* Ulsterman? As Ruth Carr, one of the magazine's editors, put it, "The" was "the only non-contentious word in the title." Such concerns led to a modest re-branding. The name changed first to "*H.U.*," but accompanied by *The Honest Ulsterman* below in smaller print. Then "*H.U.*" came to stand alone, the two initial letters followed by periods to begin with, but then simply "*HU*" unaccompanied by any punctuation or explanatory subtitle. It was as if the rough-hewn tone of the original, plain-spoken title had been subjected to an unlikely distillation, transforming it into a kind of haiku-like Asiatic syllable that was at once question and assertion. Through all these manifestations I remained a faithful reader and was particularly pleased whenever Heaney's work was included. His poems became a kind of touchstone. Reading them, having his books to hand – particularly when I was living "across the water" as a student in Scotland – was at once a kind of affirmation of belonging, a statement of my Ulster provenance, and a distancing of myself both from the Protestant mainstream in which I'd been raised and the violence of the Troubles.

In addition to its main issues – and distributed free with them every now and then – *The Honest Ulsterman* published a series of poetry pamphlets. Seamus Heaney's *Stations* appeared in this series in 1975. In his introduction to the pamphlet Heaney writes:

> I think of the pieces now as points on a psychic *turas*, stations that I have often made unthinkingly in my head. I wrote each of them down with the excitement of coming for the first time to a place I had always known completely.

The Irish word *turas* means a journey, visit, or tour – usually in the sense of pilgrimage, particularly to a holy well. Doing the *turas* at a sacred place involves stopping to pray or meditate at various designated points.

Reading Heaney's verse I had – have – a sense of being taken to places I already know but getting to know them better. By no means all his psychic *turas* coincide with mine of course. But there are enough points of contact for a sense of ethnic, indeed almost familial, solidarity to be engendered; a feeling of kinship, if not brotherhood, despite the fact of my Protestant and his Catholic provenance and all the differences and tensions that entails in an Ulster context.

In her endnote to the final issue of *HU*, Ruth Carr notes how "in the wider context of things, the demise of a long-standing, local poetry magazine may seem less than negligible." Of course that's true. Compared to the agonies of Ulster's Troubles, a poetry magazine can appear beside the point – something filled with self-indulgent conceits; a fiddling while Rome burns (though I know how much some would jib at that comparison). Measured against the scale imposed by violently blighted lives, the family tragedies that followed bombings, shootings, burnings out, a poem is easily enough ridiculed as irrelevant, something out of touch with the brutal realities of living in such a time and place. I can sympathize with – but don't share – that view. Rather, I agree with Ruth Carr's assessment of the value of *HU*. She says, quite simply, that

> The voices that have spoken through its pages have shed light among the shadows.

That is no small achievement given the depth of the darkness that engulfed Northern Ireland. For my part, I know that in early adulthood the magazine functioned in the same way Heaney's work did. It provided a kind of buoy. It helped keep afloat a more varied and melodic note than the raucous repetitions of sectarianism that were sounding in the streets and in the press and that sought to drown out other voices in the grim tidal surge of adversarial dualism that came close to cleaving Ulster into two. Reading *HU*, as well as simply being a pleasure, was a way of declaring and strengthening a determination not to let myself be drawn by the magnetism of bigotry that tried to pull everyone into one side or the other. Its forces of attraction and repulsion crisscrossed Ulster society like so many intricate, treacherous tripwires. In a flag-flying culture like Northern Ireland, where union jacks and tricolors and Ulster flags vie for territory, I suppose *HU* was a kind of pennant of independence, a stepping back from the brink; a badge of allegiance to neither side.

*   *   *

However I was led to it, I certainly already knew of Heaney's work on September 21 1975, the first time that I heard his voice. Up until that date my awareness of him had been mediated through the silent world of print. September 21 1975 was the day before a UVF bomb and gun attack on McCann's Bar in Ballyhegan. It left Margaret Hale dead and eleven others injured. Again, I intrude this ugly fragment from the Troubles into my recollections of Heaney to stress the way in which my encounters with his writing took place at a time of violent unrest. The close contiguity of mayhem and poetry meant, perhaps inevitably, that one looked to poets for some solace from, or response to, the terrible events that were unfolding across Northern Ireland. Of course Heaney and the other Ulster poets were possessed of sufficient good judgment – maturity – not to allow themselves to be drawn into the conflict, in the sense of letting their voices be hijacked for the partisan ends of either side. I didn't look to Heaney for some kind of fatuous "solution," for words that might set straight what was so desperately awry. It was more that I found in his voice a kind of counterpoint to what was happening; a well of words not sourced in bigotry, not merely conjured for some sly political maneuver, not uttered in tit-for-tat point-scoring; not derailed by the unspeakable brutality at large (the Kingsmill massacre, the Shankill Butchers' murders, the attack on Claudy – the list of terrible examples is long). His was a voice speaking with lyrical authority about ordinary things that matter; things on which our humanity is founded – digging turf, thatching a cottage roof, peeling potatoes, being attentive to the life around us, whether in poplar trees or trout or otters, or in the gentle dynamics of a marriage, or watching parents grow old and die. It was a voice aware of, but never overwhelmed by, those venomous antipathies that threatened to sully and eclipse; that would deny the iridescent sheen of the mundane seen by the mind's eye (through the poet's agency) as something marvelous.

In September 1975 I was about to start the second year of my studies as an undergraduate at the University of Edinburgh. I was taking a degree in Religious Studies, specializing in philosophy and Eastern religions – a choice in large part determined by what I'd witnessed of the impact of religion in Northern Ireland. I wanted to see, and try to better understand, this aspect of human nature in a wider, non-parochial perspective. The turn East was sparked by reading Aldous Huxley, whose books sat cheek-by-jowl with those of Flann O'Brien, Seamus Heaney and the other ur-texts on my shelves. I guess term hadn't started by September 21. I remember clearly that I was at home, in my parents' house in Lisburn, listening to an old valve radio that would be considered a museum piece today. I was in that curious liminal stage of studenthood, living in an unsettled state of transit between parental home and shared flat in Edinburgh. Then, as now, I listened to a lot of Radio 3. As I listened to whatever music was being played that day, had the UVF killers who attacked McCann's Bar already planned their attack? Or was it a spur of the moment impulse that wouldn't occur until the next day? I still find it odd to realize that in all the years I was reading Heaney's poems, or looking at the work of other poets in the pages of *The Honest Ulsterman*, even as the cadences of their verses unfolded in my mind, others close at hand – perhaps people I passed in the street as I went to and from the Belfast bookshops – were planning murder and destruction.

I can't remember what the music was that I was listening to that day, but I'd guess it was some concert with an interlude between pieces. In that space of time Seamus Heaney's "Feelings into Words" was broadcast. I caught it quite by chance. It was a recording of a lecture he'd given to the Royal Society of Literature in London the previous October. I think I can best explain the impact "Feelings into Words" had on me via an observation made by Sven Birkerts in *The Gutenberg Elegies*, his profound meditation on the fate of reading in an electronic age. According to Birkerts:

In writing we grope towards what we think of as the inevitable wording, as though the prose were already finished in an inner place we can
just barely reach. And when we do succeed, when from time to time we
reach it, we know we are beyond revision.

As a writer, I know how hard it is to reach this "inevitable wording," to find a
form of words that matches what's "already finished in an inner place." And I
know the intense sense of satisfaction and completion that attends those rare
occasions when I feel I've succeeded in matching on the page what's written in,
I suppose, the heart. What I found extraordinary about "Feelings into Words"
was the extent to which Heaney, in that familiar Ulster accent that's so much a
part of my world, seemed effortlessly to delineate the contours of inner places
that I recognized.

1975 was long before the advent of i-player, YouTube, and other such devices
that allow the transience of something broadcast to be kept and reconsidered. If
I'd known in advance that "Feelings into Words" was coming on, I would have
taped it. But I caught the talk by accident in the midst of other listening. Impressed by what I heard and wanting to examine it more closely, I wrote to the
BBC to request a transcript. They suggested I should contact the Royal Society
of Literature, which I did – only to be told that the talk was due for publication
in a volume of RSL lectures, but not for a year or more. If I didn't want to wait,
they suggested contacting Seamus Heaney himself to ask for a printed copy. I
wrote to him care of his publishers and in due course received a friendly letter
saying he'd be pleased to send a typescript but that there would be some delay
because he was in the midst of moving house. "Seamus and Marie Heaney, Glan-
more, Ashford, Co. Wicklow" had been scored out on the letterhead with the
Heaneys' new address in Dublin written in. Not long afterwards the typescript
appeared, together with a note apologizing for not sending it sooner.

"Feelings into Words" was included in *Preoccupations: Selected Prose 1968-1978*,
published by Faber in 1980. My copy has my signature in it along with "Belfast, November 1980." Among the violent deaths that month were those of
Owen McQuade, a soldier gunned down by the IRA outside Derry's Altnagel-
vin Hospital; Oliver Walsh, a businessman killed by a landmine intended for
the security forces on the road near Lislea; Peter Valente, murdered by the IRA
as a suspected informer; Norman Donaldson, ambushed by gunmen as he left
Derrygonnelly police station. I know these names will vanish and be forgotten,

along with the many others in Ulster's catalogue of lost lives. But it seems important to list them, if only as a blunt reminder of the milieu in which poetry was read and written at that time. The names of those murdered in the Troubles constitute the irreducible specifics of its brutality, like jagged, awkwardly shaped pieces in some jigsaw that will not fit in.

I was particularly struck in "Feelings into Words" by Heaney's comment that:

> Finding a voice means that you can get your own feeling into your own words and that your words have the feel of you about them.

He then went on to suggest that a poetic voice is "very intimately connected with the poet's natural voice" and that voice can be thought of as a kind of fingerprint. I count myself among those many readers who are glad to have been marked by Heaney's prints.

*   *   *

Somewhere, perhaps, a tape still exists of me reading a whole selection of Heaney's work. I was asked to do this by a doctoral student at the university in Wales where I taught for many years. I've forgotten now what aspect of things he was researching – he wasn't based in my department; I knew him socially, and only slightly, not in any professional capacity. Whatever his topic was, he'd taken on board Heaney's view that "there is a connection between the core of a poet's speaking voice and the core of his poetic voice, between his original accent and his discovered style." The student thought he'd come to a better understanding of the poems if he heard them read in an Ulster accent, rather than in his own polished southern English diction.

There are, of course, all sorts of Ulster accent. It's not just voiced in a single, undifferentiated note that's the same across all six counties. There are regional differences – County Fermanagh and County Antrim nurture different subtleties of speech; class and education leave a heavy mark, as does the amount of time a speaker may have spent domiciled elsewhere, so that Dublin, London, New York, or in my case Edinburgh, lays its own unique net of sound across the pattern of indigenous inflexions. I tried to explain this, stressing that my accent wasn't identical to Heaney's. I think the student took my point on board, but his view – which seemed reasonable – was that my accent was much closer to the poems than his could ever be. In any case, reading them out loud with the presence of a tape recorder to keep me on my toes was a pleasure. I was happy to oblige. I hope I did the poems justice and that my voice – hijacked for the occasion merely for the sound of its native authenticity, not because it could speak about Heaney with any authority – was as "energetic, angular, hard-edged" as Heaney says the Ulster accent is; that it struck "the tangent of the consonant" rather than rolling "the circle of the vowel."

*   *   *

Another vignette that comes to mind, as I try to map the ways in which Heaney's words have touched me, involves P.V. Glob's *The Bog People*. I think one of the reasons why *North* had such an impact was because I'd read Glob's book a few months before turning to Heaney's compelling fourth collection. So, before I came to poems like "Bog Queen," "The Grauballe Man," "Punishment," and "Strange Fruit" I'd read what Glob says about Iron Age sacrificial victims cast into the bog, whose bodies have been preserved by the peat down to the present day. More to the point, I'd looked at the extraordinary photographs that make Glob's book so arresting. Years later, I stumbled on Jefferson Hunter's *Image and Word*, a study of the interaction of photographs and texts. I readily agreed with Hunter's view that Seamus Heaney's bog poems may be "the best poems ever written thanks to, if not actually about photographs."

Why did I decide to read Glob, or Hunter (or Heaney's *North*)? Again, the question nags of what determines a person's syllabus of private reading. I feel I'd understand more about myself if I could unravel into clearer order the reasons for my turning to the literary influences I did; explain why the verbal *turas* of my reading should have taken the stations that it has. Some books – Heaney's prominent among them – feel as if they've played an important part in making me the person that I am. Yet, for the most part, how I found my way to them remains unclear, nor can I fully measure the weight of whatever silt of influence they've deposited in my waters.

Did "The Tollund Man" in *Wintering Out* – published in 1972 – direct me to Glob's book? The opening verse of this poem has Heaney declaring:

Some day I will go to Aarhus
To see his peat-brown head,
The mild pods of his eye-lids
His pointed skin cap.

The Tollund Man – so called because his body was retrieved from Tollund Fen in Bjaeldskov Dal – is one of the most strikingly preserved of all the bodies retrieved from Denmark's bogs. Beneath one photo of him, with those "mild pods of his eye-lids" gently closed, Glob simply puts the caption: "The dead and the sleeping, how they resemble each other." This 2000-year-old corpse looks indeed as if it might still blink open its eyes, yawn, stretch and smile as it wakens from a centuries-long sleep. But according to my copy of *Wintering Out*, I bought the book at the same time I bought *North*. Both books have written in them "Belfast, September 1975," and my memory is of reading *North* first. In Glob's *The Bog People* I've written under my name "Belfast, June 1975."

Whatever led me to make these formative purchases in 1975, I'm glad I did. I was profoundly struck by how Heaney utilized the material in Glob's book to explore – even chronicle – local events. Those ancient sacrificial victims, their lives violently ended and fed into the maw of Mother Earth via the ready portal of the bog, somehow resonated with the sectarian slaughter in Ireland. In Heaney's adept hands, the Iron Age bodies suggested ways of orientating more recent killings. In *Station Island*, Heaney's sixth collection, there's a short poem entitled "Widgeon" which I think offers a potent image for the way in which the poet drew on P.V. Glob's *The Bog People* and the Iron Age rituals it surmised. "Widgeon" describes plucking a duck of that species, one that's been "badly shot," and finding its voice box "like a flute stop in the broken windpipe." The poem pictures the unnamed person who's plucking the duck blowing on the voice box and, unexpectedly, making "his own small widgeon cries." In Glob's catalogue of Iron Age sacrifices sunk in Danish bogs, it's as if Heaney has found a terrible, yet compelling voice box. In breathing his verses through its ancient chords of ritual execution, he makes a sound as plangent and haunting as any widgeon.

*   *   *

As a small boy, I'd spent time exploring the peat bogs around a family farm in Donegal, helped to cut and stack peat for fuel, retrieved – so that I could carve and polish them – the gnarled bog-oak splinters that were threaded through the peaty earth like bone fragments in some ancient charnel house. I knew the slurp and suck of sink holes, the smooth remnants from turf cutting; dark banks of earth left cleanly trimmed as pages. I loved the delicate white tufts of bog cotton that stippled the barren landscape with a crop of white fluffy heads that nodded and shook in every breeze, and the purple flowering heather that covered the bog as densely, roughly, as some giant creature's fur. All this meant that, even without reading Glob, I was already predisposed to warm to a mythos of the bog.

Years after buying *The Bog People*, *North* and *Wintering Out* in Belfast, I happened to be in Scotland, visiting the Far North Pottery in Balnakiel, near Durness. Like catching "Feelings into Words" on the radio, this was a chance occurrence, not something known about in advance and planned. There, in this bleakly beautiful northernmost tip of Scotland, I found some unusual pieces of pottery on display. They struck a mysterious, intensely chthonic note. They'd been produced by firing stones at a very high temperature along with the clay. The resulting objects had about them an ancient, almost volcanic quality. The stones crack in the kiln, melt and crystallize into something that seems a kind of distillation and reflection of immense inner processes. These artworks looked less like a potter's creation than something meteorite-like, retrieved from the secret core of a planet, speaking of inner places it's hard to reach. They hinted at hidden forces, powerful transactions happening within. To my surprise, the potter responsible for making these striking pieces had a familiar name: Lotte Glob. I asked if there was a connection and she told me she was P.V. Glob's daughter.

Looking at her powerful creations, I found myself wondering what Seamus Heaney might make of them. They seemed to occupy precisely the kind of deep-earth contour that might appeal to him. Indeed in some ways the pieces seemed already Heaneyesque, as if his poems had been fired at high temperature and taken on these lithic, crystal-spangled forms. With this thought in mind, when I wrote to congratulate Heaney on the award of the Nobel Prize for Literature in 1995, I mentioned Lotte Glob's work as something he might like to see. In the reply he sent – from Santiago de Compostela, where he was on holiday – Heaney thanked me for writing and said: "In fact I did meet Lotte Glob in Harvard...coincidences, graces, gifts..." I think that trinity well describes something of what I feel about the ways I've encountered Heaney's poetry; how it's fallen on my life: "coincidences, graces, gifts" indeed.

*   *   *

Despite the influence of the Ulster poets, Seamus Heaney preeminent among them, despite my youthful efforts maturing into poems published in *HU, Poetry Ireland Review*, the *Southern Review* and other journals, despite my featuring in Lagan Press's 2004 volume *Poetry Introductions 1*, which sought to "bring to public attention five new exciting poetic voices from the north of Ireland," as my writing has developed I've turned more and more to essays as my genre of choice. But one of the small satisfactions of my writing life, something that gives a sense almost of coming full circle, a return to roots, has been the way in which reviewers periodically compare my essays to Seamus Heaney's poems.

"A book of essays that is so thoughtful and perceptive (think Seamus Heaney's poetry in prose) that I wanted to underline whole passages," was *The Scotsman's* verdict on *Irish Willow*, my second collection. Kimberly Myers, writing in *Nua: Studies in Contemporary Irish Writing*, suggests that "For one familiar with Heaney's work, reading Arthur's essays will immediately suggest felicitous pairings." And in *Nordic Irish Studies* – a journal published by the University of Aarhus and so already steeped in Heaney (and Glob) associations – Irene Gilsenan Nordin observes:

> While there are strong reminders of Heaney, especially with regard to the linking of moods with landscapes, Arthur stakes out his own personal space, and reclaims the landscape for the Protestant sensibility, describing a terrain that is at times as immanent with a sense of the numinous and sacred as any Heaney landscape.

I certainly never set out to "reclaim the landscape for the Protestant sensibility." Apart from anything else, by the time this review appeared I inclined more to Buddhism than the precepts of my native Presbyterianism. Nor, when I think about it, am I even sure what "the Protestant sensibility" would be. But if I've succeeded in suggesting a sense of the numinous that's on a par with what Heaney invests in his sense of place, I'm well satisfied.

Given the way in which Heaney has touched my life, influenced my growing up, I'm both pleased and daunted when he's used as a kind of yardstick to measure what I do (fortunately, at least so far, not as a stick to beat me with). Of course it would be ridiculous for an obscure writer in an often overlooked genre to suggest his work is similar to that of a Nobel laureate, someone described by the *New York Times* in 1998 as "the most skillful and profound poet writing in English today." I have no pretensions to such eminence. I realize that comparisons are often drawn not because of any remotely Heaney-like quality in my writing, but simply because of our shared Northern Irish provenance. In addition, Heaney's reputation is now of such proportions, his literary standing so securely established, that there's a sense in which he's become a kind of juggernaut in the sea of Irish writing such that anyone sailing in it, even someone proceeding in the modest craft of the essay, must have their position plotted by reference to his colossus. Such points notwithstanding, I feel a kind of aboriginal pleasure when – through whatever "coincidences, graces, gifts" are involved – our names are put together. If he'd lived to see such "felicitous pairings," I wonder what on earth my Fenian-hating uncle would have made of them.

*   *   *

I wish I'd met Heaney properly. On June 30 1987 I was in Belfast and happened to be in the bookshop at Queen's University. It was one of my regular browsing/buying ventures to the capital's bookshops; ventures that have yielded such a rewarding mix of reading. What I hadn't realized – again, another piece of welcome serendipity – was that on that day Heaney was doing a book-signing for his newly published seventh collection, *The Haw Lantern*. Since I wanted the book anyway, I joined the queue and had my copy signed. Waiting in line, listening to him banter easily with others, then talking briefly with him myself, the impression that came across was of shrewd intelligence and warmth and humor; here was someone who gave the moment at hand his close attention. In his 2010 collection, *Human Chain*, Heaney includes the poem "Loughanure," written in memoriam for Colin Middleton (who died in 1983). The first verse pictures the artist's gaze:

> Smoke might have been already in his eyes
> The way he'd narrow them to size you up
> As if you were a canvas...

There was a similar element of intense sizing up in Heaney's own scrutiny of the eager individuals in that book-signing queue.

Why do we want copies signed by the author? Why do I value the letters

Heaney sent me? Is it that, for all our sophistication and skepticism, a poet can still seem like a kind of shaman, an intermediary between this world and some other, such that a token of his person may carry with it the promise of a spark of otherness? Or is it merely a case of being dumbstruck by the idiot allure of celebrity? I only know that in the case of books I feel have touched me – whether poetry or prose – I'm susceptible to the power of talismans originating from their authors. This is how I look on cards and letters from William Golding, W.G. Sebald, Heaney and others. Or perhaps "relic" would better describe than "talisman" how these things strike me, or even "icon," for there is in my reaction to them something not too far removed from reverence. Whichever term is chosen, I know such things are only words on paper and that to invest them with any significance beyond that is foolish – but I find it hard to resist doing so all the same; a case of the head knowing one thing and the heart feeling quite another.

*   *   *

What I've written here has been a personal appreciation. It's my own *turas* around Heaney; the stations of my encounters with the man and his work – how his poems have touched my life. It's not a specialist academic assessment that seeks a place in the burgeoning secondary literature about him. I'm neither an English scholar nor a literary critic. My knowledge of Heaney's oeuvre is incomplete, idiosyncratic, amateur. I've not mentioned several of his poetry collections at all, little of his prose, none of his translations. I'm not attempting to provide an objective assessment of his writing, or give an overview of his output. Instead, this is an ordinary reader's reminiscence and reflection; an attempt to chart how some of Heaney's work has laid down translucent beads upon me like a scattering of little lenses, or a shower of benign verbal rain that cleanses and refreshes. But for all the subjectivity and incompletion of what I've written, I hope I've managed to convey a measure of the impact Heaney's work has had, particularly in Northern Ireland, even among members of the other tribe.

What spurred me to sit down and write this essay wasn't so much Heaney's death on August 30 2013 – though I was saddened when I heard of it – but Charlie McCarthy's brilliant film "Seamus Heaney: Out of the Marvelous," screened a few months later on BBC4 (and available worldwide through RTÉ Player). Watching it prompted me to think about the poet and his influence on me. The film takes its title from part viii of the sequence "Lightenings" in his

1991 collection, *Seeing Things*. In this section of the poem an instance is recounted from the ancient annals that tells of how the monks of Clonmacnoise see a great ship above them in the sky. Its anchor accidentally catches on the altar rails and the ship is trapped. A crewman "Shinned and grappled down the rope/And struggled to release it. But in vain." Seeing his failure, the Abbot says: "This man can't bear our life here and will drown unless we help him." The monks free the anchor and the crewman is described as climbing back into his celestial vessel "Out of the marvelous as he had known it." The myth is heavy with a sense of mediating between two worlds and of how, seen from a different perspective, what we take to be commonplace can appear as marvelous. The application to Heaney's verse doesn't need spelling out.

It's a long time since I was 21. The books on my shelves have multiplied around that core of early texts in which Heaney's played such an important part. The uncle who looked at me askance and thought my purchase of Flann O'Brien's books so suspect, is long since dead. His generation has taken with them a burden of intransigence and bigotry that I hope mine has thrown off, or at least significantly lightened. It will take time for changes to bed in, of course, but things in Ulster seem more positive today than they did when I was growing up. I hope there's less of a sense of antipathy and opposition abroad, more a feeling of shared concerns. A book that appeared in 2012 should certainly help promote this, Patricia Craig's *A Twisted Root*. She styles this as an examination of "ancestral entanglements in Ireland." Craig seeks to counteract the way in which some people in Northern Ireland still believe "they are indissolubly one thing or the other" – Protestant or Catholic; British or Irish; Loyalist or Republican. Taking her own family history as exemplar, she shows convincingly how the bloodlines of Prod and Teague are anything but pure. Instead, they show a kind of checkerboard of allegiance, an intimate intermixing, family lineages with one foot now in one camp, now the other. Craig argues convincingly for "fusion rather than segregation, complexity instead of fixity." She shows how untidily history rearranges our loyalties and likings; how our heritage displays a definite mongrel mixing.

Towards the end of *A Twisted Root* – which takes its title from a line of Paul Muldoon's that characterizes history thus – Craig describes an incident at Belfast's City Cemetery in 2010. People had gathered there to rededicate the grave of local playwright Sam Thompson. Actor/director James Ellis has been invited to say something at the rededication ceremony – an appropriate choice since it was Ellis who supported Thompson's controversial play about religious bigotry, *Over the Bridge*, when it was first performed in Belfast in 1960, ensuring that it got a hearing despite widespread opposition. Elderly and unwell, Ellis gets confused and announces what an honor it is to be invited to unveil the grave of Seamus Heaney, whom he describes as "the greatest poet Ireland has produced." In fact Heaney and his wife are in the crowd, along with Sinn Fein's Gerry Adams and other prominent figures from Northern Ireland's political and artistic circles. After others have tried and failed to correct James Ellis, Heaney himself steps in to set things right. Craig describes his intervention as something done with "his customary grace and gumption." Perhaps in James Ellis's misdirected eulogy, Heaney had a foretaste of how his actual death three years later would spark similar comments about his poetic stature. In any event, I think this tragicomic incident is a good place to end my personal *turas*. It places the poet in a kind of liminal space between this world and the next, almost present at his own obsequies, and facing it with two of his most characteristic qualities.

Memory Sticks
(Reading three old walking sticks)

I

A visual description doesn't reveal much, but I'd better sketch the rudiments of one nonetheless to give the reading eye something to hold on to. The four walking sticks, dusty and unused, are propped in a corner beside a chest-of-drawers that stands just inside the front door of my house. The most striking of them is a traditional blackthorn stick of a type once ubiquitous in Ireland, though they're far less common now. It's three feet long and densely prickled with little spikes. These are the cut-off remnants of the numerous twigs that once grew out of the branch the stick used to be. There are over fifty of them, with all but the very thinnest roughly sharpened, as a child's pencil might be, bringing each amputated twig into a bluntly whittled point. The cuts reveal the rich brown color of the wood beneath the black bark that gives this thorn its name.

In fact, "blackthorn" often seems a misnomer. The abundant white blossom of *Prunus spinosa* is what is most noticeable each spring, illuminating hedgerows all over Ireland. Come summer, the green foliage masks the bare wood. In autumn it's the purple-hued sloe berries that draw the eye. Seen in winter, the density of the small outer twigs creates a kind of camouflaging penumbra of nondescript bushy grey around the thicker branches which lie darkly unseen within. It's only when you examine one of these thicker branches up close, cut free from its thicket, that the striking blackness of the bark becomes evident.

The prickled shaft of the blackthorn walking stick is fitted with a brass ferrule at one end. At the other, it's shaped into a smooth, egg-sized knob that fits snugly in the hand. Here too, echoing the color of the cut-off sharpened twig-stumps, the brown of the wood beneath the bark is clearly visible. The egg-smooth handle reveals a large enough expanse of naked underwood for its delicate graining to be apparent. These woody whorls always remind me of the lines on someone's palm – though I'm not sure if I reach for this comparison because of any immediate visual similarity. It may be, rather, because the stick's knobbed handle immediately makes me think of a hand grasping it, thus beckoning my pairing of wood-grain and palm-line.

The ashplant is a thicker stick, the sturdiest of the four. In contrast to the blackthorn, its wood is smooth and pale. The name, "ashplant" – which is what such walking sticks are always called in Ireland – reveals the type of wood it's made from. The handle forms an inverted L-shape with the shaft. On it are two polished knots of bony wood, like swollen knuckles. It's only here on the handle, in these two bare protrusions, that the grain of the wood can be seen. The rest of the stick is still skinned with bark, although there are various old scars, particularly near the base, that suggest even lighter wood beneath. It looks as if the stick was sometimes used to whack a way through brambles, or some other tough undergrowth, resulting in this network of scratches; cicatrices subsequently dulled over.

The two other sticks both have curved handles; they're shaped like children's candy canes. If you cut the shaft of the stick level with the end of the handle, you'd be left with a perfect "n" (or "u") of wood. Other than their similarly shaped handles, these two sticks are markedly dissimilar. One is individual, elegant, expensive; the other mass-produced, crude, cheap. The elegant stick is made of cherry wood and has a silver band around the top of the shaft. The end of the handle is also sheathed in silver. Though the metal's tarnished almost to black, if you look at these silvered additions closely you can just make out a filigree pattern that shows a repeated fern-like motif of delicately curved and looping lines.

The other curved-handled walking stick is the blandest of the four, with no obvious distinguishing features to set it apart from millions of others like it. It's one of the sticks made for, and supplied by, Britain's National Health Service. They're manufactured from coppiced sweet chestnut – a light, strong wood. The raw staves are steamed to make them pliable, the handles bent into shape, the shafts cut to whatever length a patient needs. Any roughness or irregularity is minimized by sanding down, so that the sticks are remarkably uniform and anonymous for something made from a natural material. By far the majority of these sticks are produced for the infirm elderly. Unlike the other sticks, which taper to neat, metal-cased points, this one ends in the blunt stopper of a rubber ferrule that's thicker than the stick.

Once in daily use, relied on, gripped tightly, leaned upon, the sticks haven't left their dusty station now for years. They're like redundant rolling stock shunted into a forgotten siding and abandoned there. The only time they're moved is when I remember – infrequently enough – to dust away the cobwebs that periodically loop around them. In part, the cobwebs are aptly symbolic. Their threads are like a ghostly echo of the way the lives represented by these sticks were once linked together. But the links between the lives in question were far tougher, more enduring. If the sticks braided themselves together into an intricately knotted woody plait it would mirror more closely than any cobweb could the way in which the lives of which they're remnants once branched through each other in a dense maze of not always comfortable connections.

II

Each of the four sticks has a voice. If you listen closely – as I too rarely do – they tell intricate, intriguing stories. For the most part, though, far from facilitating such telling, I use words to gag and stifle the voices of what's around me. Instead of giving language free rein to express the depth of history and the complexity of connection that's implicit in things, I use it to fix more securely into place the mundane camouflage with which we clad the world. Sometimes, language seems more like a fire-blanket thrown over the conflagrations that consciousness can spark than something that allows us to sketch and celebrate the streamers of incandescence that arc and spiral in such dazzling profusion from even the unlikeliest coals of being.

It's much easier to tag the sticks with an expected, simple caption and just continue on our way. Our ordinary fire-blanket diction functions like a covert narcotic to which we don't realize we're addicted. It sedates experience, hobbles it with a facile vocabulary; keeps it slumbering within bounds that are easily encompassed.

But sometimes things change. Of course it's not so much the things themselves that do. Rather, there's some shift in the register of consciousness so that the way in which everyday objects customarily fall upon the mind is temporarily overwritten by a new tempo and intensity of thought – where memory, imagination and speculation pool their voltage and braid together into a strong rope capable of lassoing far more from the world than we normally pull in. This new tempo and intensity burns off the quotidian, allows glimpses of a different order of perception; one whose outlook strains at our usual vocabulary, rupturing commonsense nomenclature, and forcing language into new alignments. It writhes and contorts, flexing into unaccustomed sentences as it tries to catch the rich shoals of meaning suddenly made manifest. Then it fades in its turn, smothered by the resurgence of the ordinary.

Before the tempo slows, before the intensity dims and the world falls back into its accustomed verbal halters, it's possible, if you attune your ear, to catch some of this other order of perception.

Three of the walking sticks came into my possession after their owners died. The fourth – the blackthorn – was a gift. All of them now have the potential, if I stop to listen, to speak not only of the lives with which they were once so intimately associated, but – I know it sounds unlikely – of life itself. The walking sticks belonged to my father (the ashplant), mother (the chestnut crook), aunt (who passed the blackthorn stick to me) and great aunt (the silver capped cherry): four lives that touched each other in various patterns of relationship and that also laid their touch on me.

Just as the sticks are tiny attenuated filaments of the trees they were cut from, and just as those trees were minuscule individual instantiations of the great species-thickets of ash, chestnut, blackthorn and cherry that have flourished through the centuries, so the networks of connection between my father, mother, aunt and great aunt, for all their burgeoning complexity, are yet no more than the tiniest segments cut out of the forest of connection that links lives together over time and, in its totality, constitutes our human story; itself just one thread in the fabric of being.

Of course I mostly see them, think of them, just as four old walking sticks. Or rather, I don't see or think of them much at all, beyond that routine notice of scarcely taking notice which quickly names and overlooks the things around us. But when – for reasons I can't fathom – consciousness shifts into a different register of perception, it's as if the sticks begin to rub rapidly together, kindling a fire of associations that soon blazes out of control. Its light brings into clearer focus the texture of time and place in which all of us are cradled.

III

My aunt, May, my father's sister, gave me the blackthorn stick one summer when I was visiting her in Donegal, Ireland's most northerly, and to me most beautiful, county. I was in my early twenties at the time. The stick was among the things she'd inherited when the generation before hers died and the dilapidated family farm near the village of Dunfanaghy was sold. The stick had belonged to her mother's last surviving brother, May's uncle (my great uncle) Willie, who had lived on the farm all his life. I met him only on a handful of occasions when I was very young. My memory of him is of a twinkling-eyed eccentric. On our first encounter he sat me on his knee – a slightly apprehensive little boy, unused to such immediate familiarity – and told me tall stories about the swans that occurred in great number on the farm's impressive lake, watching carefully all the while to see how much I believed. Then, seeing my eyes wandering to the glass-fronted cabinet of curiosities beside which we were sitting, he presented me with two of the treasures it contained: a blown swan's egg and an empty tortoise's shell. Remarkably, decades later, and after several moves, I still have them somewhere in the clutter of my study.

I'm not sure now if great uncle Willie really did strike me as eccentric on the occasions when I met him, or if I'm seeing him through a lens obediently ground according to the prevailing family view. The last time I visited Donegal – in the summer of 2007 – I fell into conversation with someone who'd been a neighbor of his when she was growing up. She recalled a good humored man, not much interested in farming, who was patient with children and always ready with a story. But she also (laughingly) recalled his advising her never to come visiting without wearing a bright red scarf or cardigan. This would ensure instant recognition from afar, he told her, and guard against him shooting her in error. Was that just another of his tall tales? Or was Willie given to taking pot-shots at strangers who strayed onto his land?

For all the close association the blackthorn had with him, held snug in Willie's grip as he patrolled his poor but scenic acres, it conducts little of the specific voltage of the life he led – I think a lonely one – in the wilds of Ireland's remote northwest. However hard I grasp it now, it tells me little about the kind of person he was. The three objects that constitute the totality of the material residue that passed from his life into mine seem each to reinforce symbolically a sense of loss. Two – the swan's egg and the tortoise's shell – are empty; whilst on the blackthorn's short length there are scores of cut-off remnants. Yet, despite the cul-de-sacs, hollowness, dead ends, this stick, like the others, can conjure an enormous imaginative fullness when I stop and recognize what it really is.

My aunt May was a tall woman, so Willie's stick required no cutting down when it came to her. She used it for some years before giving it to me. I was never sure whether, for her, the blackthorn was a statement of style, a support to be leant on, or a weapon to defend herself. Perhaps its use drew a little on each of this troika of functions. She always seemed robust, but maybe as she grew older what was carried first as an accessory eventually became an aid. As for a weapon, I've witnessed May on more than one occasion raise the stick threateningly at angry farm-dogs that ran barking towards her on her frequent walks in the lovely countryside around Dunfanaghy. She always held her ground, and the dogs – sensitive to authority – never pressed home an attack. Had they done so, I've no doubt she'd have wielded the blackthorn with deadly aplomb.

I'm not sure why she gave the stick to me. Perhaps a sense of history and tradition prompted the gift; wanting the blackthorn to pass to a third generation. Or maybe it was just that she was tired of it, preferred a less rustic-looking walking stick to match her always elegant attire. Or perhaps it was one of those unprompted acts of generosity that veined her life with currents of warmth – unpredictable, spontaneous gestures that, like sudden sunny smiles, could brighten up a day.

May died almost twenty years ago, my great uncle Willie a long while before that. When I take the blackthorn in my hand today and slough off the quotidian fire-blanket label of "old walking stick," when I stop to think about what it is I'm holding, it's as if they're standing at my elbow again, beckoning me towards a bracing walk around the enigma of vanished lives and once familiar places. They smile in complicity at the shared mystery of our existence. If they spoke, it would not surprise me more than it should if they recited together Issa's famous verse:

> What a strange thing
> To be thus alive
> Beneath the cherry blossoms.

IV

I can touch the ashplant, feel the ghost of my father's grip, hear the echo of his walk – his signature "drop-foot" limp, the result of a leg wound sustained when he was fighting in Africa in World War II. The rubber-ferruled chestnut stick, for all its mass produced anonymity, can sing a lament in perfect individual pitch about my mother's slow decline into decrepitude. The silver-banded cherry stick, like some magician's wand, can bring back into mind a picture of my mother's aunt (my great aunt) Ellie. I can hear her tap her way across the flagged kitchen floor of her County Antrim farmhouse, imperious even in white-haired old age. She rattles the dog's bowl impatiently with her stick. When the metal ferrule chinks discordantly on the chipped enamel, it sounds like the scolding of some ill-tempered wren. Ellie warns her much put-upon terrier that if he doesn't finish the food she's given him "the stick will eat it." That metal-on-metal chink might also act as call-sign of the uneasy relationship between my mother and her sisters and their formidable spinster aunt.

It's always easy to lapse into the lazy convenience of custom and stereotype. My great aunt Ellie's elegant, silver-banded walking stick readily slips into a symbolic ramrod role of predictable inflexibility; an accoutrement of her sternness – something that can be personalized to represent the dismissive way I learned to read her, the intolerance that was shown towards her old-fashioned formalities and strictness. But I know it would be fairer, more in keeping with the complexities that every life contains, to take this candy cane-shaped stick as the stalk of a question mark and place below it, as the completing dot of interrogation, all the memories it calls back about her.

Like so many of the things around us, these memory sticks are laden; tight packed with history's seeds – to the extent that the sticks seem sometimes like thick nerve fibers, braided together from the filaments of time. They act like dowsing rods; touch them and they tug the grip down hard, responsive to life's water coursing through the jigsaw of what happened, happens and will happen. Feeling them dip towards the gravity of unexpected meanings, I find myself thinking again of John Muir's famous remark (made in his 1911 book *My First Summer in the Sierra*):

> When we try to pick out anything by itself, we find it hitched
> to everything else in the Universe.

At first, the sticks may seem simply hitched just to the individuals most associated with them. But such straightforward isolation soon fractures into links and loops and intricately tied knots of connection between one person and another; between yesterday, today, tomorrow. Here and there, like now and then, are sutured together by so many threads of interrelationship that it's not long before the accuracy of Muir's fell point is felt.

I could beat memory with each stick in turn, transcribe all the scenes such goading might elicit, trace out the contours of love and longing, of tension and bitterness, of like and dislike – the undulating network of emotional altitudes upon which different personalities are arrayed. But even were this done with flawless fluency, it would still give no more than a hint of the whole from which these sticks are such tiny cuttings. Each one is part of our family tree – by which I don't mean just those pruned lines of familial descent that offer up one's truncated, simplified genealogy. Rather, they are parts of the Tree of Life, on whose branches our stories cluster in such dense profusion and interrelationship.

Perhaps it's just as well that the narcotic of the accustomed seeps into the bloodstream of our perception and diction as regularly as it does. To feel the full impress of the things around us; to let the mind savor the rich taste of being, unfiltered by our dulling labels, might break the delicate net of sensing with which we reap our little harvests from the world. Imagination's tensile strength is great, but perhaps even it would be stretched if each dull stick was seen as part of a living plant – rooted, twigged and leaved; and each plant was seen as just a single dancer turning in the complex ballet of eon-spanning processes and events – the Big Bang, evolution, photosynthesis, the seasons, day and night.

V

The sticks have about them now almost an air of lost property – as if they'd been left propped up against my hall chest-of-drawers by visitors who forgot to take them with them when they left. And I suppose to some extent they are things left behind, sodden with personal associations that will steadily evaporate in time so that, before long, they'll transmute from mementos into junk. Looking at them leaning together in their accustomed cobwebbed niche, I sometimes wish I could carve into them in some magical script that's denser with connotation than any language that I know, the fine detail of their stories, every fold and tuck of meaning.

It's hard to see more than a little clouded way into the kind of perspective such storytelling might allow, but it would surely soon arrive at the way our species has leant on the stout canes wood provides in order to grow into the stature that we have. Sticks of so many kinds have been like cultural bones to us, providing *Homo sapiens* with a kind of exo-skeleton. As well as fuel for our fires, think of how much of our history has been framed by wood – canoes and ships and spear-shafts; bows and arrows, rafters, doors and tables; pencils, paper, scaffolds, boomerangs and fence posts; coaches, musical instruments and rifle stocks; crucifixes, breadboards, chopping blocks; floorboards and bookshelves, coal and coffins – it would be a near endless list. Strip wood out of our grasp and our story would have staggered, gone down another path. My four sticks, as well as all the specificity they bear, tap into the tangle of this human-wood relationship.

Sometimes now I think of my four sticks as a kind of star cluster – part of some little galaxy. Their twinkle is caused by the way they alternate between the commonplace – dusty old sticks – and the incredible – entry ways to something that has about it a disturbing likeness to the kind of infinity the mind soon baulks at. Perhaps this starry image is what makes me think of a blackthorn bush at night, moonlight silvering its dark-skinned bark. I picture it growing, hard and compact, in a Donegal hedgerow, its branches angled by the prevailing winds that sweep in across the Atlantic. It will have seeded from some bird-dropped sloe-stone and then slowly knitted into shape, its wood fed by the sun and water of this place. Now and then a bird alights, perches on a twig and sings. Sometimes ladybirds and other beetles lightly tap their way along a leaf or branch. Day follows night; the seasons come and go; the weather touches the blackthorn bush with sun and rain and frost. Slowly the branches grow, following the same pathways and processes sketched out by all the blackthorns that have been. Each season the sloe-berries ripen, drawing from the earth the elements to hue them purple, swell them with their bitter-juiced flesh.

One day, a man comes. He cuts a length of branch. Stripping off the twigs, he shapes a walking stick; carving and polishing the egg-bulb handle and whittling the shaft's other end so that a ferrule can be fitted. Years later, after it has tapped its way along miles of Donegal fields and tracks and narrow winding roads, I hold it in my hands, feel the prickled shaft dense with its cut-off twigs. Then I replace it with its three companions to stand once more unnoticed by the door. And it seems to me that each one of them is like a kind of Zen *keisaku* – the wooden stick used by meditation masters to carefully strike those meditating if drowsiness or lack of concentration threatens to overcome them. For the most part, we sleep our lives away, the patter of our talk skitters across the surfaces of things; goes no deeper than a beetle's legs pittering their inaudible tattoo upon a blackthorn branch. But sometimes, as if woken by the strike of some invisible *keisaku*, we see things in a different light, hear the cacophony that rages all around us. Then we cut words from the tree of language, build them into sentences as stout as any stick and, supported by them, try to walk a little further than our customary routes.

Reading Life
(Reading J.A. Baker's *The Peregrine*)

I

Wood and glass dominate the room. It is uncluttered, light-filled. Its near emptiness is emphasized by the few objects that there are. There's a sense of deliberate simplicity about it; a honing to essentials – table, chair, bed. The absence of unnecessary frills and lack of any of that personal detritus with which so many rooms are littered – crumpled clothes, magazines, make-up, glasses, bags – might suggest it is unoccupied. But if you put your hand under the already straightened and creaseless duvet, you'd feel the vestigial warmth of a body's recent presence in the bed. Then, from the kitchen, comes the occasional sharp sound of cutlery chinking against china. A rich smell of coffee gathers strength, mixing with and soon overpowering the fainter aroma of pine which is gently all-pervasive in this place. The windows – almost floor to ceiling – open onto a slatted wooden balcony. The view is of lake and forest. No other houses are visible from here.

There are no ornaments. A few natural objects sit on three otherwise empty shelves fitted against one wall: a feather, some giant fir-cones, the sun-bleached skull of what was probably a fox, an oddly shaped stone on which a tracery of bright yellow lichen is growing. On a low table by the windows there's a paperback book. Its blue-grey cover depicts six birds flying across a stormy sea. The book's title is obscured by a notebook on which the reader has made half a page of neatly pencil-written notes.

A soft tread close at hand alerts you to her return, barefoot, across the floorboards, carrying a mug of coffee. She sits cross-legged, straight-backed on a large floor cushion, puts the coffee on the table ready to hand beside her, lifts the book, finds her place and starts to read again. The silence is broken only by occasional birdsong from outside and the soft whisper of pages being turned. The scene is still; the only noticeable movement comes from the steam rising from the coffee mug, the reader's gentle breathing, slight shifts of position as she turns a page, and the little rhythmic footfalls of her close-focused gaze as her eyes tread the meandering word-paths that the book unwinds before them.

*   *   *

A copy of the same blue-grey paperback book is in the hands of a re-fined-looking elderly man. His neatly trimmed white hair and beard frame an alert, humorously bright-eyed face. His gaze is drawn along the same word-paths taken by the barefoot reader, though neither she nor any of the other readers who have come this way have left any trace of their passing on the pages' gradi-ents and turns. Even seated in the confined space of a Boeing 757, this reader looks relaxed. Slim, casually dressed, a fit-looking perhaps near seventy-year-old, he has the quietly self-possessed air of a man who knows himself and – without any trace of smugness or pomposity – is content with who he is. The plane is only half full. The steady engine drone, overlaid with the more dilute and varied sounds of passengers' talk and movement, has become such an accustomed hum that it could almost pass for silence.

Thirty-thousand feet below, the Atlantic's waters are far less stormy than the way they're depicted on the book's cover – which reproduces a painting by wild-life artist Michael Benington entitled "Eiders in a Gale." The painting shows six eider duck flying close to the surface of the water. It would add a pleasing echo, provide a haunting resonance suggestive of connection – perhaps even hinting at a harmonizing meaning encompassing time's disparate elements – if, com-plementing these six eiders, six real birds happened to be flying far below. I like to think that as this airborne reader sits with the book in his hands, his fingers warming the painted image of the ducks, their real life counterparts are forging their way towards land. I'll refrain from inventing such a coincidence, though, lest it undermine the plausibility of the scene. It's sufficient to note its possibility without insisting that it happened.

*   *   *

A third scene can be introduced by widening the aperture of "Eiders in a Gale" so that its six flying ducks become mere dots in the distance as the pan-orama opens out and they're dwarfed by the surrounding immensity of sea. The size of the waves is emphasized by the boat that now comes into view, pitching and rolling its way through them, sometimes seeming almost stalled so little progress does it make, as if it was somehow – impossibly – stationary amidst the gigantic roiling furrows of water. If you wanted to explain the meaning of the phrase making "heavy weather" of something, pointing to this vessel would suffice. Its slow embattled headway is like "heavy weather" personified. Looking at the contrast between the waves' scale and power and the boat's vulnerable solidity amidst them, it seems incredible that their massive liquid tonnage, their conjuring of such gigantic curvatures of water, will not bend and dilute into utter surrender this little bastion of hard, self-contained linearity. The neat lines of hull and prow withstanding such pounding by the elements, battering against the boat in all the fury of their wild irregularity, strikes the eye as a precariously temporary triumph of order over chaos.

I've already used "Eiders in a Gale" to focus on the boat battling its way through this heavy sea. If we were able to extend the power already granted to this painting-become-cover-illustration, so that it becomes a kind of magic lens allowing us to zoom in, look inside the vessel, what would we see? The practised nonchalance of crew members; the way bottles and glasses in the bar, expertly battened down against just such conditions, clink and rattle in their restraints as harmlessly as wind chimes; the flashing lights from the row of gaming machines in the deserted entertainment lounge, the storm-dazed passengers uninterested in these tawdry lures, trying to hook them with promises of jackpot; a girl with the whitish-green complexion of sea-sickness sitting miserably by herself, sometimes glancing out at the sea, dabbing the corners of her mouth with a crumpled handkerchief; the muscular thrum and torque of engines and waves quaking their reverberations through every surface so that the whole vessel shudders and vibrates; a man walking unsteadily from bar to toilet, clinging to the handrails for support and smiling to himself at how difficult the simple task of putting one foot in front of the other has become.

Push all of these details to one side of the mind, their context-setting task now done. The person on whom I wish to concentrate is sitting there, in a corner of the lounge, braced against chair and table to steady himself against the continuous roll and pitch of the storm's violent buffeting. He sits with his back to the porthole, never looking out. His attention is wholly given over to the book he's holding. He's reading with such fixed intensity of purpose that it might make a perceptive observer suspicious that it was a pose; someone pretending to be engrossed in a book while in fact their thoughts are somewhere else entirely. This reader looks in his early twenties at most. He has dark, untidy, shoulder-length hair. His clothes are casual, verging on dishevelled. The guess that he's a student would be reinforced by glancing at the bulging rucksack that has been strapped into the seat beside him. From the shape of the bulges in the canvas, you can see it's packed with books. The fact is he's terrified of the waves and fears the boat may founder. His heart is pounding, his mouth is dry, his hands are wet with sweat. He's trying to take refuge in reading, following the book's word-paths as if they were a kind of lifeline, an umbilical of protection, offering escape to some inner place of safety.

II

That was the easy part of the picture I want to draw: three scenes that submit to straightforward enough depiction. What interests me is not so much what the eye can pick out or immediately infer as it scans each reader's setting, but the complex invisibilities of the processes behind the act of reading – that elegant and seemingly effortless decoding by which we can construct resplendent worlds of meaning from a density of small symbols clustered on a page or screen. Reading is like a kind of raising from the dead, or at least a wakening from deep hibernation. We pass our gaze along a line of print and each sepulchral letter blinks as sense awakens from it; each word-coffin turns into chrysalis as what was packed into it unfurls and hatches, comes to life again. More precisely, *something* hatches. Whether it was what the writer intended to greet the reader's eye is less certain. As George Steiner puts it (in *After Babel*) – "no two human beings share an identical associative context," there are "no facsimiles of sensibility, no twin psyches." This means that the way in which any word strikes the reading eye varies from individual to individual according to how it percolates through the unique alchemy of their personality and history. Even the same reader reading the same book at two points in their life is unlikely to take from it an identical harvest (as is nicely shown in Anne Fadiman's *Re-Readings* and R.S. Sugirtharajah's *Caught Reading Again*). We hatch the sense of every sentence that we read by gentle brooding at the fire of who we are. Such incubation draws its warmth from the inner strata that layer the self's secret interiorities. As such, it would be simplistic to assume that a writer simply lays down the path that readers follow, their steps obedient to every shift and change intoned by the authorial voice. Reading-writing is far more complicated – far more interesting – than such a vision of puppetry allows.

I want to try to trace out a few of the filaments in the dense network of connection that tangles and proliferates between writers and their readers; to see more clearly what our reading life involves.

*   *   *

The nameless, barefoot reader and her austerely stylish room have become a persistent image, repeatedly glimmering on the edges of my consciousness. Despite their growing familiarity, the fact that I've come to recognize them, they are more representative than actual. The book and its northern setting are real enough, as is the glimpsed Scandinavian reader who supplied the template for her barefoot doppelganger. They are all part of the world you can touch, talk to, visit; confirming their existence is straightforward. But although it's possible there is just such a room as I've described, although the glimpsed individual might go barefoot in it, it seems likely that the contours of this picture would only ever roughly correspond to the actual topography of her specific circumstances and all the complex undulations of its unique particularities. The image of the Spartan room and barefoot reader has come to symbolize for me – perhaps more concretely than it should – the shadowy form of readings yet to come: she is the reader of the future, poised to drink her coffee, take up the eider-covered book.

The reader on the 757 flight is entirely real, specific, actual – no wraith representing what is yet to come. He has a name, an address, a unique life-history. It was from information he himself supplied that I know he was reading the eider-covered book on a transatlantic flight from the UK to America. With a little effort I could provide more background detail – describe the reasons for his journey, give an itinerary of places visited, people met with, note times of arrival and departure, flight number, who he sat next to, focus in more closely on his appearance, personality, professional accomplishments. But the outline sketch I've given is enough, I think, to place this cameo scene within the wider frame of the picture I want to try to paint. This is the reader of the present – even if the present slips away at every moment and is no more fixed and static than a flock of eider ducks, or the movement of the waves they fly across, or the jet that outpaces them high above. He represents the close-at-hand, what falls within the boundaries of the recent – which is as close to now as I can get without focusing on the unknown eye falling right this minute – that is already passing – on the precise shape of this sentence.

My third reader – the seaborne frightened student – is also real. He's crossing the North Channel, that frequently rough stretch of the Irish Sea which separates Northern Ireland from Scotland. The boat he's on is one of the ferries that regularly plies between Larne and Cairnryan. In reasonable weather conditions it's a short crossing – just a little over two hours. On a day like this, with the wind touching Severe Gale 9 on the Beaufort scale, it takes considerably longer. The book he's reading is *The Peregrine*, by J.A. Baker. It's a cheap paperback edition whose cover design doctors a close-up black and white photo of the bird to suggest, via subtle added shading to the wings, a streamlined presence pictured mid-flight, its speed caught in this artful frozen blur. Holding *The Peregrine* as he tries to concentrate his terrified mind on reading, his left hand is warming the picture of the bird on the cover in the same way as the 757 reader's hand will warm the picture of the eiders. But the eider-covered book has not yet been written. This is the reader of the past. For the moment, he is unaware of the connections that will link him to my present and future readers. At this point, none are aware of the others' existence. Before they become so, many ferries will have plied their way across this patch of sea; many jets will have criss-crossed the sky above the Atlantic; many miles of word-path will have been laid down and followed by numerous writing-reading eyes.

My three readers provide a kind of lens, ground with the abrasive of their specificity, that allows us to look through them at the way reading's labyrinth snakes through the human psyche, laying down networks of live wires and nerves upon whose fret and jump minds jerk into thoughts, moods, climates they might not otherwise have met. The labyrinth can be accessed through countless doors. I want to go in via this threefold archway. My trio of readers offer a manageable vista on a topic whose massive totality can be seen looming beyond them like a distant, misty shore, its scale daunting even in the most shadowy outline.

III

"So little do we know of what goes on when we read," says George Craig in a chapter contributed to *Real Voices on Reading*, edited by Philip Davis. "What is the true size and real use of a book," asks the volume's editor, "What is its relation to the life outside that is itself the book's very subject-matter?" We are so used to books and reading, they are so accustomed a part of our world, that to suggest there's anything opaque or mysterious about them, that we need to inquire into what reading involves or what a book is for, can seem curiously misplaced – betokening some kind of ignorance or ineptitude; a contrived naivety about what's altogether plain. Are the answers to such questions not obvious?

Like much that's apparently straightforward, there's far more to books and reading than meets the eye. It's a tired metaphor, I know, almost melted by repetition beyond effective re-use, but despite its battered, hackneyed mien, it's something very like that old war horse, the tip-of-the-iceberg image that canters forcefully into mind when thinking about this. In our familiar lives of custom and routine, the quotidian moment-by-moment passage of time, we navigate our way amidst scores of objects, engage in all manner of activities, that seem small scale, bounded, ordinary. We are aware only of the fingertips of their presence. These lay upon us the light touch of the expected, the usual; leave prints we recognize as unexceptional. But just below the waterline of the familiar are enormous bodies, shadowy presences of complexity and complication. Push just a little harder on the barge pole of the ordinary – with which we normally stave off such perspectives – and the kraken wakes. Then the fingerprints pressed down upon us leave deep and disconcerting marks; their fuller weight brands questions into what we'd previously glossed as unproblematic. Reminding us of the depth and density of writing and reading, beneath the masks of familiarity they usually wear, Sven Birkerts (in *The Gutenberg Elegies*) points out that:

> Writing is the monumentally complex operation whereby experience, insight and imagination are distilled into language; reading is the equally complex operation that disperses these elements into another person's life.

Just as the heart's twinned motions – systole and diastole – are each essential for life to continue, so writing and reading are conjoined in their operation; neither can survive alone. But though we're as familiar with the pulse of reading-writing as we are with our own heartbeat, how far do we understand the impact of the complex distillations to which Birkerts draws attention?

Of course the pulse of reading varies; readers are as different as the books that draw them in. "Reading" covers an enormously diverse terrain. It would be foolish indeed to seek some single garment of illumination that might clad with equal fit a child's stuttering attempts to read a schoolbook; a professor delving into Joyce; the rapt attention given to a well-paced thriller; the furtive voyeurism engendered by some pornographic tract; how a devotee's consciousness is lit by the words of a sacred text (and vice versa); the impact of a tightly argued scientific monograph. We read for all kinds of reasons – distraction, entertainment, comfort, devotion, information, titillation, understanding. The reason that interests me is nicely identified by Philip Davis in his Introduction to *Real Voices on Reading* when he talks about people going to particular books because they offer them "an opening onto what seems the very life of life." Later, in the same volume, poet Les Murray talks about the way in which readers are attracted to writing that (whether in poetry or prose) sends out signals saying "here the secret world is present."

Though far from precise, "the secret world," "the very life of life" point accurately enough for us to see an important element in the motivation felt by many readers over the ages. It is, very largely, what has drawn my three readers towards their books. We might try to affix further identifying labels to this kind of motivation, which coils and flexes through the heartland of the psyche, a potent but elusive isobar of our inner weather, hard to pin down with any single name. It has to do with our thirst for meaning. It seeks to warm itself at the fires kindled by metaphor and symbol and to see things in the light offered by such flames. It's concerned with carrying us across the chasms that pit the fabric of our world, offering ways to cross over between self and other, past and present, known and unknown, even between life and death. This is the haunting tocsin of our search for the sustenance of sense beyond the obvious; it's strongly pigmented with feelings of alienation and belonging; a desire to bring the tribe's unsettling salt to some common pool at which we might quench our thirst, navigate a way through the mysterious transience of our existence. But as shorthand, "the very life of life" and "the secret world" suffice.

IV

It's certainly understandable why someone might turn to J.A. Baker for "the very life of life." *The Peregrine* stands out as a book that leads into "the secret world." It's one of the books that's left the strongest impression on me. In large measure this is due simply to the impact of Baker's prose; in part because I first read it at an impressionable age, when I was a few years younger than the long-haired student on the boat. The book condenses into the narrative of a single half-year its author's experience of watching these magnificent birds of prey over a ten year period. But this is no simple ornithological study. As Geoffrey Grigson put it in a perceptive *Sunday Times* review: "The book goes altogether outside the bird book into something less naïve, into literature, into a kind of universal rapport." Grigson's "universal rapport" is, I think, allied to "the very life of life." *The Peregrine* conjures a closer sense of living-in-the-(secret)-world; it fine-tunes the contours of experience so that the reader feels enwrapped in a tighter embrace and so is made more sensitive to each rise and fall of the gradients of perception. This is writing that binds us to life's jugular; its proximity to the pulse of being is sometimes startling, laced with a sense of naked immediacy.

Indeed, J.A. Baker's sentences hit the mark so often and so hard that a reader can come away reeling, as if they've been undergoing treatment at the hands of some wild acupuncturist of the spirit whose expert probing for exactly the right curative point on the meridian of expression is unerring and remorseless. His prose strikes through to what feels real. Sloughing off the loose skin of approximation, and incinerating cliché with phrases possessed of an incandescence born of their unexpectedness and beautiful exactitude, his writing seems at times almost to sear the reading eye. Baker's prose has an electrifying current I've not come across elsewhere set – and maintained – at so high a voltage. His words are fired with such confident velocity and verve, are so compellingly on target, that my image of an acupuncturist soon crumples, pushed aside by the deadlier figure of an archer, whose elegance and lethal grace seem a more apt point of comparison for writing of such potency. I won't give examples – the whole book is like a quotation illustrating what I've said. I regard it simply as a masterpiece.

*   *   *

An observation of Alberto Manguel's in *A History of Reading* helps to explain something of *The Peregrine's* impact and places it in a wider context. Manguel is recounting his visit to Iraq in 1989 to see the ruins of Babylon and the Tower of Babel which for him, as a Western reader, constitute "the starting-place of every book." He writes:

> Since the earliest vestiges of prehistoric civilization, human society had tried to overcome the obstacles of geography, the finality of death, the erosion of oblivion. With a single act – the incision of a figure on a clay tablet – the first anonymous writer suddenly succeeds in all these seemingly impossible feats.

George Steiner (in *Language and Silence*) also flags up the way in which writing addresses these "seemingly impossible feats." "All great writing," says Steiner, "springs from *le dur désir de durer*, the harsh contrivance of spirit against death, the hope to overreach time by force of creation." *The Peregrine* is no exception. Millennia removed from the moment of Mesopotamian genesis that Manguel points to, it is yet close kin to the same fundamental desires. At root, Baker is concerned to celebrate and lament the peregrines he watches with such passion, "to overreach time by force of creation" and leave his smouldering testimony to their existence – and what he saw as their imminent extinction (he was writing at a time when organo-chlorine pesticides were wreaking havoc on the birds). In the act of reading Baker's prose – however unique its point of particular focus may be – we are reconnected with this ancient Mesopotamian innovation and the thread that it has sutured into the human psyche, a nerve connecting us to readers of the past, present and future as they, like us, seek out that "force of creation" by which "the finality of death, the erosion of oblivion" may be faced.

V

For a long while Baker was relatively unknown; the clay tablets of his writing left mostly dormant, undisturbed by the necessary awakenings bestowed by readers' eyes. *The Peregrine's* style and subject didn't gear it to mass-market popularity; the author's self-effacement helped ensure a marginal status in the contested territory of contemporary literature. If anything, though, this rarity and marginality added to the appeal of book and author for those few readers who had discovered them. For a while, reading *The Peregrine* had a sense of secret complicity about it, as if it conferred membership of some esoteric sect wary of sharing its knowledge with the uninitiated, keeping discreetly hidden the whereabouts of this trove of glittering verbal gems.

Again, Alberto Manguel makes a point in *A History of Reading* that casts light on what it was like to read Baker before his current renown became established. Travelling on the Toronto subway, Manguel sees seated across from him "a woman reading Borges's *Labyrinths*." This makes him "want to call out to her, to wave a hand and signal that I too am of that faith." "She is closer to me," says Manguel, "by the mere act of holding that particular book in her hand, than many others I see daily." I can certainly recall similar feelings on those rare occasions when I saw *The Peregrine* on someone else's shelves. It sparked a sense of kinship, likely bonding – the fact that we had both walked Baker's word-paths, both felt the same lithe musculature of prose, had the ligature of descriptions stop our breath with the novelties of their precision. It brought a similar sense to unexpectedly meeting in a far-off foreign place someone who grew up on the same street as we did; a feeling of secret communion, of being co-religionists amongst unbelievers.

*   *   *

Beside me on the desk is a copy of *The Complete Works of J.A. Baker*, published in 2010. It's edited by John Fanshawe with an introduction by Mark Crocker. It contains *The Peregrine, The Hill of Summer* (Baker's only other book) and his unpublished diaries. This *Complete Works* is testimony to Baker's growing appeal. Far from being the unknown figure he was in the 1970s, he's now acknowledged, as Mark Crocker puts it, "as one of the most important British writers on nature in the twentieth century." A key milestone in this widening recognition was the republication of *The Peregrine* in 2005 in the New York Review Books Classics series, in an edition with an introduction by Robert Macfarlane, for whom the book "sets the imagination aloft, and keeps it there for months and years afterwards."

Though I've no doubt the student reader of *The Peregrine* would have echoed the assessment made by Macfarlane almost forty years after that stormy crossing, though he would have applauded Mark Crocker's view that "a case could be made for *The Peregrine's* greatness by the standards of any literary genre," his pleasure at seeing Baker's writing receiving the attention its quality warrants would also, I suspect, be tinged with an element of regret. This would be rooted in a concern that a book once possessed of rarity in every sense (even securing copies was, for a long while, difficult) might be rendered ordinary by becoming common knowledge. Just as there has often been a reluctance to put scriptures into written form lest this should compromise their sacredness (the Hindu Vedas are a striking case in point), so a similar sense might attend widespread dissemination of *The Peregrine*; the fear that making it popular risks making it less special. Although Annie Dillard, Reg Saner, Barry Lopez and others have elevated this genre with works of consummate artistry, putting *The Peregrine* into even the highest echelons of nature writing – its usual categorization now – leaves me uneasy. It belongs, rather, in a category of its own; it is sui generis, unique.

*   *   *

In *Orality and Literacy* Walter Ong claims that "more than any other invention writing has transformed human consciousness." It is a plausible, if unprovable claim with which I'm minded to agree, but tracing out in any detail the transformations caused by writing/reading (let us not forget the twin) would be formidably difficult. The external memory writing provides, the way in which its linear scaffolding supports and structures particular patterns of thought (and inhibits others), its ability to hold the mind's nuances intact and transport them over time and distance, between mind and mind, are impressive indeed – but beyond such general features, could we detail point by point the physiognomy of the transformation it has worked upon us? Who can say for sure how the word upon the page or screen ripples through our pools of inwardness, how writing/reading sculpts the intimate caverns of our psyche?

To try to assess what reading does, how it changes us, what difference its presence or absence might make, would be a gargantuan calculation. Its sheer difficulty apart, perhaps it's not yet time to attempt it. Despite writing/reading's origins some 5000 years ago, mass literacy – and the reading patterns it facilitates – is a much more recent phenomenon, dating largely from the nineteenth century. As such, it may simply be too recent to stand back from and attempt any kind of summation in which its impact on us is calculated as if it were complete. In *Beyond the Written Word*, William Graham stresses "the historical novelty of our modern relationship to words and books." For all our viewing it as commonplace, the act of private, silent reading – the individual hunched alone over a text – only came into prominence a few centuries ago. Reading's footprints on our sand of being are still quite fresh; who can say as yet what tracery they'll leave upon us?

What difference does a book make to the world? What impact does reading have upon us? Such questions would be impossible to answer without honing the blade of their interrogation to a sharper edge. The resulting particularity, though, the precision of a question recast so that it points to some single volume, is not necessarily any easier to answer. Who could accurately assess the continuing pulse of influence beating rhythms from the *Qur'an* or *Origin of Species* into the fabric of the human mind? Even computing the much littler sums of how *The Peregrine* affects us, or how the eider covered book has acted on its readers, would be a far from easy task.

VI

We've travelled some way beyond the three readers with whom I started. It's as if those eiders in a gale had been rudely jolted – like a telescope elbowed from its point of focus and aimed at a different, distant shore. Instead of present particularities, or those of the near-at-hand past or future, the lens provided by that blue-grey paperback's cover has been refocused on dimly perceived scenes where unknown Mesopotamian figures are birthing the twinned miracles of writing and reading – of which my readers are the grateful inheritors – and the view has edged towards the great cloud of reading that billows over the last few centuries of our existence, rather than on individual engagements with specific texts. It's time to swing the lens back again to less distant scenes. Let's return to that stormy sea passage, for the long-haired student reader can help in trying to compute the "much littler sums" just mentioned.

I know that J.A. Baker's book came to occupy a place of special prominence in his reading life. His battered paperback copy of *The Peregrine* crossed the Irish Sea so many times you could almost imagine its lines of print starting to undulate in sympathetic mimicry of the waves. He subsequently secured the grail of a hardback first edition, and bought other copies too. They seemed too precious just to leave abandoned on the shelves of second-hand bookshops, prey to neglect or the chance discovery by others. In buying them, it felt more like rescue, more an act of fealty, than anything as quotidian as purchase. The book eventually took on the nature of a kind of sacred object, such that having it to hand on rough sea crossings came to be desired not only for the distraction and inspiration that reading it provided, but because the book itself had become a talisman. Having it close, even if unread, seemed to afford a measure of comfort. Because of the "very life of life," the "secret world" offered up in such abundance in Baker's text, the physical form of the book acquired totemic status; it became a touchstone, a charm, an amulet, almost a guarantor of safe passage, not just a printed text to read.

I know, too, that *The Peregrine* helped reinforce and crystallize a growing sense of what might be termed "the numen of nature," acting to legitimate and strengthen a way of seeing birds and trees and landscapes as possessed of more significance than our bland, matter-of-fact descriptions of them suggest. Baker's incendiary writing lit the County Antrim acres that were the student's home territory, further electrifying the hawthorn hedges, and grey skies, the marshy fields, the bullfinches, rooks and sparrowhawks which had already grown gravid in his mind, laden with more measure of significance than they were ordinarily accorded. For many people, birds are just a blur of movement, a few stray notes of song, things that happen on the margins and are scarcely noticed. Our student read them more as harbingers of the secret world, the very life of life, a way into the heart of the labyrinth of being – and Baker's raw psalm of violent devotion, celebrating just that, emphasized his vision; gave it licence to develop.

*   *   *

One stratagem for mapping the ways in which reading may affect us is to try to imagine what its absence might entail. It's impossible, of course, to remove any reading once it has happened, or to follow in the wake of its impact as it percolates through our attention and settles in whatever silty bank of the psyche retains it, minutely charting every shift and turn of the influence it lays upon us. We are in the realm of introspection here, rather than on the kind of solid ground that can support the weight of universal truths. No doubt our long-haired student would have managed rough sea crossings without *The Peregrine*, perhaps finding in some other book the crutch he needed for his terror. No doubt he would still have been interested in natural history, still been touched by the beauty of birds, his sense of something numinous in Ulster's woods and fields would have continued – the way in which even the rough tussock grass and muddy ditches seemed sometimes transfigured into portals leading far beyond themselves. None of this was dependent on Baker's fiery benediction, however much it offered to articulate it. Yet, had he never stumbled on *The Peregrine*, never read and then re-read it, I'm haunted by the feeling that, however elusive its exact effect upon him, he would have been left poorer by its absence; that in an indefinable but important way his identity, his spirit, the person that he is, would somehow have been lessened. Taking away *The Peregrine* would have meant unravelling a vital thread of complication from the spool of his being; closing off a capillary and leaving a blind-spot on the retina of what we might even call his soul. I'm cautious of using what Sven Birkerts terms this "vast elusive word" – but I find (as Birkerts found in *The Gutenberg Elegies*) that it comes irrepressibly to mind when thinking about reading. Like Birkerts, I'm using it not in any religious sense, but "to stand for inwardness, for that awareness we carry of ourselves as mysterious creatures at large in the universe."

*   *   *

Thinking about the impact of reading makes me picture readers inhabiting a kind of perpetual autumn, bright with many colours. Its leaf-fall happens via words. They flutter down upon us, drop from the book-trees we look at, their gentle touch unfelt as they stipple the reading eye with their brief moments of impact. They lie like ghosts upon the psyche and are slowly compacted by the weight of those that come after them, layer after layer, word lying on word; sentence upon sentence. And so the pressure of reading slowly, imperceptibly, begins to build until it's enough to turn this burgeoning accumulation into a kind of verbal leaf-mould; a womb of wordy humus. As thoughts and feelings grow from it, who can identify for sure the precise constituents of this rich book-compost and how it feeds us?

As the student read *The Peregrine* on that stormy crossing, the blood-heat of his body transmitted its temperature through his left hand to the picture of the bird on the cover. I imagine another invisible pathway of conductivity, moving in the opposite direction – as the heat of Baker's prose flooded into him, sparking a sequence of unmappable transactions. Just as house timbers creak and groan at night, cooling after a day of summer sunshine so, if you were able to listen at the right wavelength, the noises of his psyche would perhaps be audible, gently shifting as *The Peregrine* laid and lifted its pressures. The student's left hand warms the book. His right hand will – I know because it's mine – go on to write the book with eiders on its cover. Would I have done so had the leaves of Baker's prose not fallen on me? Did the eider covered book draw at least some of its essential nutrients from the rich mould left by *The Peregrine*?

VII

Sometimes, beyond my own solitary reading and re-readings of *The Peregrine*, I imagine the full complement of all the readers who have read – will read – Baker's masterpiece. I think of all the copies of this book in existence, wonder where in the world they are located, what a globe would look like, what pattern would be traced out, if every copy was flagged with a brightly coloured light (flashing when the book was actually in the process of being read). Each physical copy of the book, even unopened, is the repository of a dense tangle of stories simply by virtue of the milieu in which it happens to be set, part of the lives of unmet others and their unvisited places, fitting into their narratives and histories in ways about which I can only speculate. What, I wonder, would the whole tribe of *Peregrine* readers from 1967 until now look like? How many of them would there be? How would each one have heard about the book, how received it into their consciousness? In what ways would each life-story have been affected supposing they had never met with Baker's prose?

A more radical thought-experiment than considering individual tribe members and the impact of the book upon them one by one, would be to picture the whole root nerve of Baker's book extracted, whipped away – all those coloured lights on the globe indicating each copy suddenly put out. What shape of absence on the reading psyche at large would be left by such a deletion? Would it matter that the book had been extinguished? Might its removal influence the life of other book-tribes populating the world of reading?

Prompted by such thoughts, and supported by the greater contact between writers and their readers that now exists, compared to the situation in Baker's day, I sometimes think about where copies of *Words of the Grey Wind* – my eider covered book – have ended up; what shelves they sit on, what rooms they inhabit, what conversations they witness as time unfolds around them; where they fit into reading lives amidst scores of other volumes. It's easy, given Michael Benington's "Eiders in a Gale", to picture copies of the book flying across the sea to far flung destinations, settling with unknown consequences on unseen lives. I know of readers in America and Canada, in Australia and New Zealand, Brazil, Denmark, France, Sweden, Africa, Japan – as well as in Ireland and the UK. Even for a book of limited appeal and modest print run – and no claim to possessing the kind of vision *The Peregrine* offers – it would yet be a complicated task to chart even the distribution of its copies. How much harder to assess the way in which the book's sentences have fallen on its readers, what word-compost they've left in the accumulated leaf-mould of their reading; what may grow from it that might not otherwise have flourished. And will this be a reading-tribe fated to rapid oblivion, or will it still boast members a hundred years from now?

*   *   *

Looking at the genesis of writing in Mesopotamia some 5000 years ago, Alberto Manguel characterizes the writer as "a maker of messages, the creator of signs." To give voice to the meaning of these signs "required a magus who would decipher them." It is, I think, important – perhaps particularly for writers – to recognize the magus nature of readers. There seems to be an almost magical element involved in reading – some kind of alchemy – in the conjuring of meaning's riches out of signs, the reawakening of sense from sentences in which it may have been entombed centuries ago, in another language, by a hand that was of different nationality, gender, creed and color to the reader's. "Magus" also carries hieratic connotations that seem appropriate, conferring on reading's awakening of sense the shadow of a sacral act. Magi are also, of course, bearers of unexpected gifts. I know that I've been enriched by the unexpected benison of reader-responses to *Words of the Grey Wind.*

When I think about readers' comments – realize how much I've learnt from what they've said – I'm reminded again of Philip Davis's question, "What is the true size and real use of a book?" Is it really something that can be confined to the neat rectangle of its printed form? Is it something fixed and finished, static over time? Or is it something altogether more mercurial and harder to contain, part of a continuing conversation that is itself enveloped in the susurration of the tribe; the hum and buzz of humanity talking to itself? Who's to say whether, in reading *Words of the Grey Wind*, readers are not met with spectral whispers from Baker, not to mention others whose books have dropped their leaves upon me over the years? Is it always clear whose voice speaks to us when we're reading; whose voice we speak in when we write? Writing allows a multitude of hidden emissaries to speak through us; reading allows promiscuities of the mind to take place in innocent, enriching abundance.

VIII

"The hardest thing of all to see is what is really there." This assertion of J.A. Baker's has rung its clear peal of insight through my life for years. His great book shows the folly of thinking that even something as apparently bounded and specific as a peregrine falcon surrenders to any single account of it. His writing provides a consummate set of variations on the theme of "peregrine," effortlessly demonstrating that what sparks the variations is, in the end, uncatchable; that the variations could be endlessly continued. What a peregrine is, what it means, remains a mystery – and so acts as a symbol for the mysteriousness of life in general. Is what is "really there" defined by the kind of description you might read on a museum caption beside a stuffed specimen of *Falco peregrinus*, or does it rather lie in the fracturing of such limited vision that Baker's prose so magnificently achieves?

Long after reading *The Peregrine*, I came across a stray comment of G.K. Chesterton's (from his *All I Survey*). Written in 1933, of course it wasn't aimed at Baker (who'd only have been seven at the time), but it fits him to perfection:

> He set out seriously to describe the indescribable. That is the whole business of literature and it is a hard row to hoe.

Surely the grail we seek in reading, what we're looking for in the very life of life/ the secret world, is something that's attuned to this "hard row;" something that attempts to describe what won't yield to our descriptions, no matter how many variations we weave around the haunting base note of its continuing theme.

*   *   *

In the room dominated by wood and glass, silence still prevails. The barefoot reader sits on her floor-cushion, *Words of the Grey Wind* open on her lap. The coffee cup is empty, cold now, its steam vanished. As she shifts position, turns a page, continues down the word-paths that I made, new life moves within her and she smiles gently to herself at this unseen announcement of its presence. We all start our reading here, not in Babylon or Babel, but in the womb's warm cocoon; our first text one of blood and nerve and muscle, a primal reading that leaves its patterns indelibly imprinted on us; all our later wordy readings are overlaid with its aboriginal gridiron.

It's often said that music can affect the unborn child; that Bach or Mozart calms the embryo, adds to nature's cradling the harmony of additional balance, a welcome beckoning from the world outside. Can reading claim any comparable effect? Can the pre-literate psyche, struggling to interpret its little capsule home, be influenced by the books a magus-mother reads? When the wash of words percolates through her, do they adjust to some degree the complex thermostat of influence her body brings to bear upon its precious cargo? "Saccade" refers to jerky movements of the eye – or to short rapid tugs on a horse's reins. As the barefoot reader's eyes move across the pages in the delicate saccades of reading, as her nerves feed impulses to the brain, as images are sparked by the complex synapses of connection that fuse between writers-readers-texts, are the umbilical reins tugged and pulled, the embryo's course minutely redirected? Supposing the child reads *Words of the Grey Wind* years later, will there be any echo then of recognition; a warming of the blood at this unconscious memory of word-paths already taken via the mother's reading eye?

J.A. Baker died in 1987, twenty years after *The Peregrine* was published. As a reader, I never thought much about the shadowy figure of the author. He would still have been alive – in his late forties or early fifties – when I made that stormy crossing of the North Channel, clutching my copy of his book. He was, as Mark Crocker puts it, "a deeply private person." Very little was known about him when I first joined the spectral community of *Peregrine* readers, that assemblage of minds invisibly touched by Baker's prose. More is known now, but – though I'm interested in the details – I can't help feeling some of it's an intrusion. Certainly the publication of the rough diaries of such a prose perfectionist has about it the air of unwarranted trespass, almost desecration.

Though I'm wary of authors who leap into the limelight so readily that their presence distracts from what they've written, I welcome the greater possibilities of dialogue that now exist between writers and their readers – through book signings, conferences, email, websites. The 757 reader was someone met at a book signing in Oxfordshire; the Nordic barefoot reader is based on a buyer of the book at a conference in Oulu, Finland in the high summer of 2010. Reading-writing has always been a transaction; always involved a network of relationships, a feeling of connection, as we endeavour to read life and share our visions of it, but I'm pleased to be engaged in it as an author at a point in history where the sense of community, of participation, is more evident. Writing and reading may both seem solitary acts, but in tying and untying the knotted cords of sentences we are surely engaged in something that close binds us to others; in something umbilical in the sustenance it offers.

As befits an image of the future, my barefoot reader and her unborn child pose more questions than they answer. We leave them in that quiet room, not knowing how their story will unfold, what word-paths, life-paths they will take, or what light one will cast upon the other. We can only hope that, obedient to the thirst for meaning so deep-salted in our veins, they – like us – will turn repeatedly to reading and find there a richly nourishing harvest and the warming traces of many kindred spirits.

Afterword
(Reading essays)

It's always hard to know in a collection of essays where – or whether – to talk about the form and to make plain what should be obvious: that readers are not being offered an unbroken linear progression that starts from the book's first sentence and continues to its last, but rather a series of largely independent pieces whose interconnections are more subtle than any straightforward A to Z can map. Essays follow no great sweeping autobahn that leads from premise to conclusion. Rather, they take paths that meander, entangle, turn back upon themselves and simply stop. They do not have beneath them the foundation of some supposedly unbroken thread of continuous progression. The only continuity they can boast is that supplied by the precarious rope bridge of the essayist's personality and literary style. Their progress is sporadic; they jump from one thing to another.

As an essayist, I'm naturally unapologetic about writing essays rather than continuous book-length manuscripts. But I'm also aware of the suspicion with which some readers (and many publishers) view essay collections – reserving for them a near hostility that's rarely applied to poetry or short fiction, both of which also shepherd between two covers what, in terms of composition and structure, is just as singular and seriatim as essays are. I'm not sure why essays have the dubious distinction of attracting this kind of literary discrimination.

According to Richard Chadbourne:

> The essay is a brief, highly polished piece of prose that is often poetic, often marked by an artful disorder in its composition, and that is both fragmentary and complete in itself, capable both of standing on its own and of forming a kind of 'higher organism' when assembled with other essays by its author.

I'd like to think that my essays are capable of standing on their own – but that *Reading Life* constitutes precisely the kind of "higher organism" that Chadbourne alludes to here, such that the individual pieces act in a kind of mutually enriching way and that, cumulatively, they convey more of what I want to say, in the tone of voice I wish to say it, than any one does on its own. Chabdourne goes on to say of the essay that:

> Like most poems or short stories it should be readable at a single sitting; readable but not entirely understandable the first or even second time, and re-readable more or less forever.

And he concludes: "the essay, in other words, belongs to imaginative literature." I'd agree wholeheartedly with that. It's what I aspire to – though whether I succeed is of course open to question.

"At the heart of the essay," says Graham Good, "is the voice of the individual." One voice sounding in the great halls of time, chambered with its countless aeons; one voice amidst the babble of billions; one voice alongside the tidal enormities of the oceans; one voice overshadowed by the roar of storms across miles of forest, tundra, desert; one voice interrupted by all the cacophony of the everyday, by the din of history; one voice soon snuffed out by the silent immensities of time and space and death. How can it have the temerity to speak, still less assume a hearing? The heart of an essay beats with something infinitesimal in its smallness. Aware of the odds against ever being heard and of the presumption of speaking, its pulse is yet intense and vigorous. Regardless of how dwarfed we are, no matter how ridiculous it may seem to send our utterances out into the overwhelming vastness of the universe, it is part of our nature to raise our voices thus, and to try to fix and focus their sound in print.

This centrality of individual voice flags up the essentially fragmentary nature of the genre. For what is an individual if not a fragment, an isolated node of sentience? However much we surround ourselves with others – family, friends, lovers – we are, in the end, alone: tiny fractions of life, shards of a single species, fragments of humanity; micro-moments of duration, our blinking on and off almost imperceptible in the enormous span of time in which it's set. We may foster illusions of continuity, sew our beaded days together into the semblance of something whole, but essentially we are creatures of incompletion, more akin to splinters than to any tree.

Theodor Adorno argues that the essay "thinks in fragments just as reality is fragmented." Georg Lukács suggests that the essay can "calmly and proudly" set its fragmentariness against what he terms "the petty completeness of scientific exactitude." R. Lane Kauffmann talks about "the historical conflict between fragmentary and totalizing modes of thought – between the essay and the system." Lydia Fakundiny notes how the essay "steers away from conventionally ordered sequences of elaboration," that it "obeys no compulsion to tie up what may look like loose ends" and "tolerates a fair amount of inconclusiveness and indeterminacy." The form's "tolerance for the fragmentary" is precisely one of the qualities that, according to Phillip Lopate, "make it uniquely appropriate to the present era." Walter Benjamin talks about the essay's "art of interruption" compared to the "chain of deduction" typical of other discourse. Although essays strive for completion within the boundaries they set themselves, make efforts to ensure an intrinsic integrity, apply the high polish of composition that's suggestive of something painstakingly crafted and finished, there's no disguising the fact that – as this chorus of expert opinion attests and as should be obvious from reading *Reading Life* – they are a fragmentary form. Essays deal in the shrapnel of being, turning over now one piece, now another, carefully running the fingers of their prose along the edges, testing for sharpness, looking for hints of connection, feeling for the cut-off remnants of joins, trying to reconstruct a sense of setting, context, contiguity, extrapolating from the minuscule moments and objects that create a life reminders of the massive milieu in which they and it are embedded.

Fragments are interesting precisely because of where they might fit in, for nothing exists independently in self-sufficient isolation, no matter how apart and alone it may appear. One thing always connects to another. It is the fact that they are so suggestive of connection that gives fragments their allure. For it is in connection that the grail we crave seems always to be hidden: that elusive sense of something that could bestow meaning on our fleeting lives. To a large extent, I think my essays are an inquiry into – and celebration of – connection and relationship. They are explorations of the mystery of discreteness and continuity, of the part and the whole, the one and the other – and how they fit together. Essays trace out how things are linked and conjoined in the maze of being. For what seems separate is in fact cradled in a dense nexus of intricate connection. My essays try to point to such cradling. They offer a kind of cartography of the apparently separate bits and pieces that fall upon my attention. They map the networks of relationship in which they are held, for if you look carefully you'll see the lines of connection's isobars crisscrossing the weather of each moment. The essays in *Reading Life* pose questions about how one thing relates to others, how the contours of connectedness can be plotted across unlikely terrain. They show how densely threads of relationship weave and cluster around the fractions of existence that happen to catch my interest, how the pieces of our fragmentary lives point far beyond themselves. For all that the voice of the individual seems to perform unaccompanied arias, singing of its singular, splintered nature, hymning and lamenting the fragment, just beneath the surface it's tuned to the key of connection.

Why do some things seem possessed of a stronger gravity of attraction than others? What is it that gives them their beckoning promise, that quality which speaks of a degree of significance beyond the simplifications of commonsense perception and diction? Often, there's no immediate sign that they are anything other than utterly quotidian. The essayist's particular circumstances – history, location, character – will naturally determine which aspects of the world catch his or her attention and which aspects pass them by. In my own case, an Irish perspective is evident in my outlook and interests, something forged by the fact that I was born in Belfast and grew up in Northern Ireland at a time when the Troubles were raging. I hope this particularity, overlaid by years of living elsewhere, merely gives a kind of vestigial regional accent to my voice, a splash of local color, rather than making it stridently partisan or narrowly parochial.

In his Introduction to *The Best American Essays 2008*, Adam Gopnik identifies three broad types of essay – the review essay, the memoir and the "odd-object" essay. It is this last mentioned form that stresses most obviously the fractional nature of the genre. According to Gopnik, this kind of essay

> takes a small, specific object, a bit of material minutia....and finds in it a path not just to a large point but also to an entirely different subject.

I think Gopnik is quite correct in identifying specific objects as an important idée fixe of the form, in seeing essays as fundamentally concerned with finding and following circuitous paths within, or suggested by, these objects, paths which can lead miles away and take us to unexpected destinations. This recurring theme is a characteristic that again stresses the fragmentariness of essays, their interest in single, apparently separable objects; a few items from the blizzard of shrapnel that falls upon a life. But it's not so much the "odd-object" that needs emphasized here, more the ordinary object (or event or creature) that, once examined, once read, once *essayed*, comes to seem odd. Essays that stress the strangeness of the ordinary are surely far more interesting than those that just flag up what's weird. Estranging the familiar, making plain that the everyday is extraordinary, is more what I'm attempting in my essays than offering a peep show into mere grotesquery.

The eighteenth-century haiku poet Kobayashi Issa exclaims in one of his best known verses:

> What a strange thing,
> To be thus alive
> Beneath the cherry blossoms!

It would be a yet stranger – and more pitiable – state of affairs not to see the essential strangeness of our situation, to walk past cherry blossoms – or footprints in the snow, or a whale's tooth, or fallen fuchsia flowers, or any of the other circumstances touched on in *Reading Life* – as if they were something ordinary and without interest.[7]

---

[7] Noel Coward once likened footnotes to the doorbell ringing when you're in bed with someone. Few people welcome such interruptions (though as Joseph Epstein wryly observes, it all depends who's in the bed and who's at the door). Essays tend to eschew footnotes, not just because they force a kind of coitus interruptus on readers, but because they're viewed as unnecessary encumbrances. Mostly, I share that view and so have minimized the notes in *Reading Life*. But it seems appropriate in an Afterword to ring the doorbell for rather longer in order to identify the voices I'm quoting. In order to minimize the interruption, I'm locating this note at a point in the book that should cause least distraction. Richard Chadbourne's comments are made in an excellent article, "A Puzzling Literary Genre: Comparative Views of the Essay," in *Comparative Literature Studies*, Vol.20 no.1 (1983), p.149/50). Graham Good's claim that "At heart, the essay is the voice of the individual" is made in his Preface to Tracy Chevalier (ed.),

---

Encyclopedia of the Essay, Fitzroy Dearborn, London: 1997, p.xxi, the key reference volume for the genre. Theodor Adorno's "The Essay as Form" can be found in *New German Critique* no.32 (1984), pp.151-171 (tr. Bob Hullot Kentor & Frederic Will). The first quotation is from p.164, the second from p.162. Adorno's reflections on the essay remain essential reading for anyone trying to pin down the nature of this notoriously mercurial type of writing. Some of his characterizations have the gnomic suggestiveness of literary graffiti. For example: "luck and play are essential to the essay" (152); "the essay does not strive for closed, deductive or inductive, construction" (158); "the essay shies away from the violence of dogma" (158). He suggests that the essay proceeds "methodically unmethodically" (161), that it is "always directed towards artifacts" (165); "verges on the logic of music" (169) and that "the law of the innermost form of the essay is heresy" (171). Such pithily puzzling apothegms repay careful reflection. Georg Lukács' remark can be found in his "On the Nature and Form of the Essay," in *Soul and Form*, tr Anna Bostock, MIT Press, Cambridge, MA: 1974, p.17. On the same page Lukács makes his famous claim that "were one to compare the forms of literature with sunlight reflected in a prism, the writing of the essayists would be the ultraviolet rays." Lane Kauffmann's "The Skewed Path: Essaying as Unmethodical Method" is included in what remains one of the most compelling collections of reflections on the nature of the genre, Alexander J. Butrym (ed.), *Essays on the Essay*, University of Georgia Press, Athens, GA: 1989. My quote is from p.232. Lydia Fakundiny's *The Art of the Essay*, Houghton Mifflin, Boston: 1991, contains what I regard as the best short introduction to the nature of the essay. The quote is taken from p.17. Phillip Lopate's comment in made on p.l (i.e. 50) of his preface to *The Art of the Personal Essay: An Anthology from the Classical Era to the Present*, Anchor/Doubleday, New York: 1994. Walter Benjamin's comment in quoted by G. Douglas Atkins in his *Estranging the Familiar: Towards a Revitalized Critical Writing*, University of Georgia Press, Athens, GA: 1994, p.54. For Adam Gopnik's ideas on the "odd object" essay see his Introduction to *The Best American Essays 2008*, Houghton Mifflin, Boston: 2009, especially p.xvii. Kobayashi Issa's haiku can be found in many of the standard works on this fascinating literary genre. Having committed it to memory years ago, I no longer remember the particular source in which I found it. The fact that I quote this haiku in "Describing a Thought-Path" and in "Memory Sticks," as well as in the book's Afterword, is an indication of the impact that it's had – and continues to have – on me.

Acknowledgments

According to Richard Chadbourne – his comment is quoted in full in the Afterword – an essay "is capable both of standing on its own and of forming a kind of 'higher organism' when assembled with other essays by its author." For allowing many of the constituent essays of *Reading Life* to stand on their own in individually published form, I'm grateful to the editors of *Canadian Notes and Queries*, the *Contemporary Review*, *Hotel Amerika*, *The Literary Review*, *Sewanee Review*, *Southern Humanities Review*, and the *Southwest Review*. In moving the essays from single pieces into the "higher organism" of a book, comments from the editors of these journals have often been a useful source of guidance. I'm particularly indebted to Willard Spiegelman at the *Southwest Review* for his sensitive handling and welcoming reception of what he calls the "Arthuriana" I send him. Thanks are also due to George Core at the *Sewanee Review* for his praise of the title essay (after he read an early version of it in the *Southwest Review*). The encouragement his words provided came at a critical time in the evolution of this book.

Two of the essays in *Reading Life* have been included in other books. "Footnotes" was first published in *The Voyage Out*, edited by Kirsty Gunn and Gail Low; "When the Time Comes to Leave Them" in *After Montaigne: Contemporary Essayists Cover the Essays*, edited by David Lazar and Patrick Madden. I'm grateful to these editors, the Voyage Out Press (Dundee), and the University of Georgia Press for allowing republication here.

The good humor with which my family continues to face the mixed blessing of having a writer in the house is greatly appreciated. Their love and forbearance creates an environment that's hospitable to the strange business of birthing essays and the books that contain them.

During much of the time when *Reading Life* was being written, I was privileged to hold a Fellowship with the Royal Literary Fund. Not only has this provided financial security in lean times, but the way in which the Royal Literary Fund treats its Fellows constitutes a potent counterweight to occasional feelings of literary malaise. Under the sound stewardship of Steve Cook and David Swinburne, the institution offers writers a wonderfully supportive milieu.

Without the flare, professionalism and goodwill of everyone at Negative Capability Press, *Reading Life* would never have seen the light of day. Editorial Director Sue Brannan Walker saw the potential of the book where others had failed to. I'm grateful to her for taking it on and for shepherding it so expertly from raw typescript into published book.

A special word of thanks goes to Mary Hood, who pointed me in the direction of Negative Capability Press, having first – via the gift of one of my previous books – introduced its Editorial Director to my writing. Without this inspired piece of bookish matchmaking, *Reading Life* might still be looking for a publisher.

I've been honored to count some of the world's foremost scholars on the essay among my correspondents and have learned a great deal from the emails and letters we've exchanged. Richard Chadbourne and Lydia Fakundiny have offered particularly incisive comment, both on the form in general and my own efforts to write in it. Their deaths, within a few months of each other in 2013, marked a significant loss to scholarship in this area. I still miss the communication I was privileged to enjoy with these two exceptional authorities on the genre and am grateful to them for helping me to better understand it.